The Internet, Politics, and Inequality in Contemporary Brazil

The Internet, Politics, and Inequality in Contemporary Brazil

Peripheral Media

Helton Levy

LEXINGTON BOOKS
Lanham • Boulder • New York • London

Published by Lexington Books
An imprint of The Rowman & Littlefield Publishing Group, Inc.
4501 Forbes Boulevard, Suite 200, Lanham, Maryland 20706
www.rowman.com

Unit A, Whitacre Mews, 26-34 Stannary Street, London SE11 4AB

British Library Cataloguing in Publication Information Available

Library of Congress Cataloging-in-Publication Data

ISBN 978-1-4985-8513-2 (cloth : alk. paper)
ISBN 978-1-4985-8514-9 (electronic)

∞™ The paper used in this publication meets the minimum requirements of American National Standard for Information Sciences—Permanence of Paper for Printed Library Materials, ANSI/NISO Z39.48-1992.

Printed in the United States of America

Contents

List of Figures

List of Tables

Acknowledgments

I want to thank all media producers who responded to my requests and made this study possible and complete. I express my gratitude to Prof. Eugene McLaughlin, then the City University's students' tutor, who was supportive in incredibly hard hours of this journey. I owe a great deal to my research supervisor Dr. Dan Mercea, who accepted supervising this research and believed in me when the project still had considerable gaps. Dan deserves all the credit for his kind, balanced, and well-informed feedback. I appreciate all support received from Lexington Books, editor Nicolette Amstutz, Jessica Thwaite, and Bryndee Ryan, alongside the anonymous reviewers. I thank my close friends for their time and patience, Joe, Renato, Claudia, and Sandra, and want to say a big thanks to Robert Levy, my father. I also owe a lot to my partner for enduring the absences, and levels of attention that this work demanded from me along the years. I dedicate this book to all peripheral media producers in Brazil working under hard conditions to shed light on realities that were, until recently, invisible.

Introduction

In June 2013, massive protests erupted on the streets of São Paulo. Those weeks were of continuous media coverage, especially on the political nature of these events, which remain unclear (Winters & Shapiro, 2014; Shahin et al., 2016). Some authors argued that it was a crisis of Brazil's welfare, political and economic system (Sweet, 2013; Holston, 2014), others saw it as a contestation of the public space (Vicino & Fahlberg, 2017; Vieira et al., 2018). As a journalist working in Brazil, I watched the news developing on both mainstream and alternative media, with the latter gaining unprecedented degrees of prominence. The *Mídia Ninja* group is a good example. The collective called itself a "decentralised network of independent media, and alternative to the traditional media,"[1] later becoming notorious[2] in national and international press[3] for its non-filtered and spontaneous coverage, which, the group said, powerful TV networks did not deliver (Peruzzo, 2013; Vieira, 2014).

Indeed, since the 1970s and 1980s, the alternative press in Brazil has given multiple contributions for democracy (Festa & Silva, 1986; Kucinski, 1991, Woitowicz, 2009, 2014), but it is in the early 2000s that new media formats, such as blogs and web forums, started to get more attention from media studies. Internet platforms have appeared as oppositional weapons (Adhirgini & Pereira, 2006; Christofoletti & Laux, 2006; Adhirgini, 2008; Garavello, 2009), others saw them as promoters of civic practices (Albernaz, 2002; Oliveira, 2011; Bailey, 2009; Barbosa, 2010), and reviving a tradition of independent investigative journalism (Targino, 2015; Ramos, 2015; Requejo-Alemán-Lugo-Ocando, 2014). In Brazil, these expectations included the overcoming of the country's many socioeconomic divides (Marques & Bailey, 2012) or the boosting of the "peripheral" identities (Martins, 2015).

This book invests in the "peripheral media" as a way to contribute for the understanding of the alternative media in Brazil by presenting a broader panorama. I proposed an exploration of both present and past contexts of the country's media environment, trying to organize what I saw as a media ecology made by fragmented roots and disperse practitioners, wrapping them in the deep-seated concept of the *periphery*. Hence, more than a set of actors that emerges from the protests and activism, like they did in 2013, or as a self-absorbed phenomenon of the past, or only as "alternative journalism," the look at the periphery is meant to discuss these events as part of a new dynamics involving the growing politicisation of the periphery, which is both geographical location and social construction. This study could hence unlock the binaries that have placed the periphery and mainstream society in radically opposite sides.

As the starting point, I find important to revisit the background of the alternative media in Brazil, which points to the timelessness of a social justice agenda. That discussion leads to the complex interplay between inequality and media that the historical notion of periphery encapsulates very well. I also approach the origins of Brazil's scene of small-scale media groups, connecting local and global debates on the alternative media to present examples of expansion and change.

THE LEGACY OF ALTERNATIVE MEDIA STUDIES

The lack of contextualised information on the development of Brazil's alternative media after the 1960s echoes impediments that are related to the country's turbulent military regime (1964–1984). It is known that alternative journalists of the time have produced evidence-rich, but fragmentary reports on "oppressed" characters, with portraits aimed at reversing the image of economic prosperity sold by the military junta (Kucinski, 1991; Woitowicz, 2009; Mazzetti, 2009; Klein, 2009; Vinelli, 2010). After the 1964 coup, the dictatorship that ruled Brazil for twenty years wrecked most of its institutions (Fox, 1988; Abreu, 2002). Despite the occasional repression, it is known that more than 150 alternative tabloids, pamphlets, and other small outlets circulated between 1960 and the 1980s. They formed what some call the *imprensa nanica*, or *nano* press, which conveyed a strong idea of social justice in opposition to the military state propaganda of progress and industrial development (Pereira Filho, 2004:63).

The historical importance of the *nano* press has been none the less minimized. It is often remembered because of its ability to evade repression or as a vehicle of "counter-information," but having a temporary and elusive presence (Mazzetti, 2009). Alternative press researchers, such as Bernardo Kucinski (1991:12), have argued that this period should appear in the future as much more rich and important than a resistance front—more complex than a simple opposition[4]:

> An alternative press came from the articulation of two equally committed elements: The wish of the left-wingers to start the transformations they sought, and the search, by journalists and intellectuals, of alternative spaces out of the big media and the university. It is at the same time the opposition to the system represented by the military regime and to the limitations of the intellectual-journalistic production under authoritarianism that this articulation between journalists, intellectuals and political activists is found.

After the re-democratization, this "articulation" among many actors would produce the *popular* press. Journalists, activists, and their supporters celebrated the return of democracy that was in progress and imagined a new model of citizenship based on a hybrid communion. Priests from the Catholic Church forged a dialogue with union leaders, who allied with feminist and black activist groups (Alves, 1986; Mainwaring, 1987, 1987b; Kucinski, 1991:21). The 1986's book, *Communicação Popular e Alternativa*, by Regina Festa and Carlos Eduardo Lima e Silva, presented this moment as an umbrella for multiple subjectivities, lined up by strong Marxist ties and resulting in a joint expression of citizenship. Silva, an active journalist in the mainstream press, argued that the popular press was filling a gap within the Brazilian cultural industry. Frei Betto, a popular friar with a strong relationship with the Catholic Church, saw it as a struggle from the Church as well (Ibid, 1986). Raimundo Pereira (1986), himself a former alternative journalist argued that the popular press was weakened due to the emergence of individual interests or to agendas that political parties and social movements would start to champion.

At the same time, the mainstream press broke sale records and affirmed its hegemony in the 1990s (Barbosa, 2007:221), while popular outlets had at best dispersed; at worst, adopted a sensationalist agenda. In fact, the popular press has become, then, a genre aimed at violence and graphic imagery or the chronicling of cheap newspapers, as happened with the newspaper *Notícias Populares* (Amaral, 2005). Media producers have blamed the massive investments in big media organizations, arguing that only mass distribution could have taken alternative and *popular* values to other heights (Rolnik & Guattari, 2008:164). Despite all this, no defeat of the popular press can be claimed, some defend, as its socially sensitive journalism values influence Brazilian journalism to date (Waisbord, 2000:174; Matos, 2008:246).

The bottom line is that the very notion of alternative media in Brazil had grown weak or too abstract for the broader public in the last decades. First, because the growth of the mainstream media has meant media moguls consolidating their alliances with politicians, who have got many TV concessions in return (Santoro, 1989; Aufderheide, 1993; Fox, 1988; Fox & Waisbord, 2002; Almeida, 2007; Porto, 2012). Secondly, the later-created leftist publications forged new outlets that encapsulated parts of that lost alternative press ideal, while others turned into strict partisanship (Pereira, 1986; Festa & Silva, 1986; Ferreira, 2009). The popular as a concept would prevail in mainstream culture, but as a sub-product of media organisations, turning out to become a much less of a powerful theory (Araujo, 2002; Stroud, 2013:61; Napolitano, 2001, 2002; Robinson et al., 2017). After the 2000s, it is not entirely clear where the popular press stands. Peruzzo (2008) likened the current popular media to community media for its continuous "autonomy and independence." Meanwhile, other authors have referred to popular communication as *folk's communication*, dismissing further complexity in their discourse (Marques de Melo, 1999; Trigueiro, 2005; Melo, 2008).

At international level, it is clear that the alternative media should be a subject of a separate theorization (Williams, 1962; Hamilton, 2000). Authors have attested to its endurance amid aggressive media commercialisation, and confirmed that political power can, in fact, spring from within marginalised communities and challenge dominant ideologies (Rodríguez, 2001; Atton, 2002; Downing, 2001, 2011; Jankowski, 2003), where one finds "united yet autonomous" media networks, as it was the case of *Indymedia* (Platon & Deuze, 2003; Pickard, 2006; Milioni, 2009). More recently, the advent of digital media inspired new concepts. Whether the topic is "alternative journalism" (Harcup, 2003; Forde, 2011) or "alternative internet" (Atton, 2013), scholars pointed to hybridization to understand the motivations behind the media of "non-privileged cultures," but which can seek to adopt the practices of a conventional news organization (McQuail, 2010:184). At the crossroads between multiple types of alternative media, the *activist* media defines the role of media producers as "community interpreters" (Waltz, 2005; Hackett & Carroll, 2006; Rauch, 2007; Lievrouw, 2011). An extensive production of case studies has globalized alternative media studies in different areas of interest, while keeping subtle variations according to different emphases on technology or ideology (Atton, 2015). In fact, early expectations that this hybridization of the alternative media could lead to an inversion in commercial media domination have not been met yet (Couldry & Curran, 2003; Couldry, 2000:154; Spitulnik, 2017). After 2010, the intense use of digital media in moments of political instability blurred the lines between alternative media and activism, as blogs, tweets, and fanzines appear as crucial spaces for dissent or dialogue (Gerbaudo, 2012; Zayani, 2014; Barassi, 2015; Fenton, 2016). If there was discomfort with how technologies had initially assumed the protagonist role in some alternative media studies (e.g. Bennett, 2003; Rheingold, 2003), there was also a call for placing "media producers at forefront" (Rodríguez et al., 2014). Although the alternative media continues as an under-researched and under-represented field, there has been multiple efforts to theorize it into types, routines, and values (Bailey et al., 2007; Fuchs, 2010). Moreover, as Atton (2002:7–8) argued, alternative media initiatives have long existed as political and cultural hybrids in their own sense and realm, so the emergence of new outlets have continuously challenged such typologies and classifications.

In the late 2010s, authors continued to stress new interpretations for the alternative media in a world taken by digital platforms. Downing (2015) argued about the "overuse" of some metaphors (e.g. rhizome), as he proposed thinking of alternative media more as a continuous flow of ideas and people, like the dynamics of social movements (Ibid, 2008). Hamilton (2015) defended a more historicised approach, recovering the legacy of social movements from the 1960s and 1970s. Rodríguez (Rodríguez et al., 2014:162) argued against research aiming to "reinvent the wheel." Dean (2010:29–31) saw bloggers as "displaced mediators" aspiring to publicity rather than content and ideology. If, in the past, the alternative media stood out as an environment apart (Williams, 1962; Comedia, 1984), scholarly research goes a long way towards situating its endurance in a scenario of explosive activist media, co-existing with national or transnational political participation (Earl & Kimport, 2011; Fenton & Barassi, 2011; Kidd, 2014; Barassi, 2015).

Amid the many directions that this debate has taken, there also lies a polarisation trend regarding the ideological nature of digital media to what concerns the alternative media. Curran (2002:109) had revisited the historical roots of this division, but where the "polarisation" in media research had led to binaries between Marxist and liberal views, it increasingly becomes the nature of digital platforms that sustain it. Fuchs (2016) reflected on the "positivist or utopian" character of the Internet and social media, in which the "positivist" position places digital media as a by-product of the Internet. Whereas the "utopian" position refers to a less net-deterministic, the more dependent approach heads towards technology. Curran et al. (2016) reinforced this stance on the different understandings of the Internet, which include that of "radical politics."

This book encompasses this latter angle, one that still envisions the Internet and the digital media action for the public good. Neither ignoring the binaries nor overcoming the need for a critical assessment, it is necessary to invest in scholarship that does not divert from *alternative media* as a movement of creating conscious citizens, and, as a result, harvesting political engagement and civic participation (Dahlgren, 2006; Lock & Baldissera, 2012). While scholars have gone through many other media divides, it is still important to focus on the most effective way to mediate society's issues, which is to center in its most *legitimate* option, that is, the extent to which this reality can be "covered" by marginalised groups, as their new media outlets and projects are increasingly influential.

With that clarified, I do not need to necessarily take part in this debate on the "utopias" of digital media. It is possible to skip this polarisation by tackling these non-technological hegemonies that still constrain a new understanding of Brazil's bottom-up discourses. In the country, the trajectory of democratic upheavals and discontinuities compromises a broader understanding of what the alternative media have published about, especially based on a perception of their discourses and frames. This knowledge is important to engage with other narratives that might escape hegemonic definitions that have prevailed over the decades. Instead of *one* monolithic media environment (as one notion of alternative media), this book discusses the periphery as a fluid part of the media ecology, but which is able to reverse an external perception that these individuals are lying in stillness and passivity to then *explode* in a few occasions, such as those seen in 2013 (Pinto, 2013; Peruzzo, 2013). In the next section, I insist that the concept of the periphery has not received the proper attention in the past, as little is known about the local terms of their narratives and their visions of a new society.

THE PERIPHERY AS A COMMUNICATIVE LANDSCAPE

In Brazil, the word *periphery* dates back to the Luso-Brazilian colonial tradition, which later became much associated with the precarious reality of vast urban outskirts (Russell-Wood, 1998). Brazil often appears as a "peripheral and unequal" society, where the mainstream media profits from the lack of pluralism and connection to the rest of the world (Amaral & Guimarães, 1994; Porto, 1998; Lima, 1996; Lima & Motter, 1996). The boundaries of the periphery in Brazil are those of the country's inequality. It is where opportunities are lacking, a place of poor public services (Marques & Bichir, 2001) and one of an unimplemented welfare state (Gohn, 1985, Fleury, 2014). The periphery is also a location of the discontent, as one of the signs of the 2013 nationwide demonstrations stated: "You woke up now, the periphery has never slept."

Since the early 20th century, the mainstream society in Brazil knows the periphery from the expeditions of writer Euclides da Cunha, who visited the "uncivilised" man at the poor village of Canudos, publishing *Os Sertões,* or "the hinterlands," as a book, in 1903 (Lima, 2000). Indeed, the periphery is still the hard-to-reach location and a destination where commuting is traditionally non-existent (Becker, 2009: 48–49). The population living in the periphery is more likely to suffer abuse and humiliation from government officials and the police (Abramovay, 1999:46). The periphery also illustrates Brazil's internal inequalities, with the impoverished north and northeast as historically peripheral to the rest (Navarro, 1994; Henriques, 2000; Pedrozo, 2013). In sum, the periphery can mean a geographical location, and yet it can discourse and an identity for the socioeconomic disadvantaged, from whom, reactions are met with "persecution" or "punishment" (Wacquant, 2003; Penglase, 2007).

The periphery is, even so, a vast universe of people within a vast country. In 2010, 11.4 million Brazilians lived in *favelas* or one in every five dwellers of the city of Rio de Janeiro.[5] Thus, the notion of *the periphery* is broader than that of the *favela,* it can be assumed that the "peripheral" cuts across social class, ethnicity, and culture. The "peripheral" status of an individual can be as mobile as the relationships between social classes (Perlman, 2010). The growing touristic interest of visitors to the margins of the city has helped to popularise precarious locations (Freire-Medeiros, 2013). The example of this mobility has existed in the short stories by Lima Barreto, for example, who wrote about the adventures of the *muambeiro,* the man who sells cheap clothes, who frequently went from the periphery to downtown. This image has become the epitome of class divisions to this date, as those created by marginal writer João do Rio (Veneu, 1990). Since then, the political aspirations of the periphery has grown to match its size and go beyond such limited representations. Politically, the movement to create a stronger peripheral representation has been happening in the *favelas.*[6]

It is important for this book's argument to revisit the historical negotiations between the periphery and the center that happened through the alternative press. Prominent in the 1970s, the *Movimento* magazine has blurred the lines between the center and the suburbs by narrating the life of a series of low-income professionals, whose reality also included crossing the city to work and consume, either in trucks, crowded buses, and bicycles. It was the universe of *bóias-frias,* sugar cane workers, maids, drivers, and beggars. At the time, alternative publications had already created an idea of a combative periphery, which included sexual minorities, black populations, and feminist agendas. It was also the case of the magazine *Lampião da Esquina*, published in 1979, which pushed for gay rights, and *Brasil Mulher*, a feminist title focused on black women from suburbs, covering issues such as abortion, single motherhood, and racism. I dwell on this connection between small-scale outlets as conveyors of news that refer to the specific challenges that come from the Brazilian periphery.

ALTERNATIVE MEDIA AND INEQUALITY

It is clear that what has underpinned the alternative media discourse in Brazil are issues that stem from the country's historical inequality. The periphery encases debates on the intrinsic relationship between poverty and how unequal Brazilian society has been on its foundations. The periphery is a "singular" location where one's sense of identity relates to such issues (Souza & Sinder, 2007). Inequality in Brazil has largely meant intersectional economic, racial, and ethnic participation asymmetries, where one assumes a certain status based on affordances and scarcities (White, 2014). And yet, it becomes a naturalized behavior that sees a second-class citizenship status, what could lead the elites into blaming the state for "such poverty" (Barros et al., 2001; Reis & Moore, 2005). Reis (2000:145) argued that, from the elite's perspective, inequality connects to key subjects, such as violence, the "worker's health," and the "uneducated mass." In an economic sense, the periphery may relate to "pockets" of poverty that resist across the country (Del Grossi et al., 2001), which does not differ much from the "contentious" issues that these debates on marginalization spark elsewhere (Tilly, 2001).

The degree to which the alternative media can reflect and expand on issues that stem from the everyday inequality is one fundamental question that this book seeks to address. Amid such visible divides—such as elite vs the poor, white vs black, how could the work of thousands of media producers possibly change how inequality translates into a politicized discourse. While not embracing a deep discussion of the racial or socioeconomic implications of inequality, it is necessary to align the media discourse with this complex notion of inequality, but also with a stronger sense of adjustment that springs from a variety of outlets. For that reason, inequality for this study needs to be much more than protesting "the uneven distribution of resources and opportunities" (Purdy, 2005:121). On the other hand, references to inequality found on blogs and websites are complex and inconclusive. Conceptually, it was necessary to follow Amartya Sen's (1999) call for studying the gaps that lie between inequality and poverty; investing in other "deprivations" that must also count as "inequalities."

Empirical indicators such as the *Gini* index may not be enough to cover all these perceptions of inequality and their demonstrations. As far as many of the stories of the periphery have been the object of detailed and structured studies on race, income inequality, and naturalization of inequality (Wood & Carvalho, 1988; Telles, 2004; Barros et al., 2001), there is a new awareness that comes along with new frames. Issues such as the non-existent public services due to discrimination against a certain community, or the criminality that affects only those who cannot afford to pay for private security, while "the rich" live behind big walls (Caldeira, 2000), can appear in another level of priority that may get another degree of prominence among other publics.

During parliamentary debates, for example, cases such as the *PEC Domésticas* (a law that granted wage equivalence for domestic employees), have illustrated how this contrasting, relational way to refer to inequality asks for a re-assessment of framing. Black women in white aprons have personified the role of *empregadas* (maids) in Globo TV's *telenovelas* for years (Souza & Dalberto, 2013), but the opposite to this is to approach these women as responsible for pioneering agendas, which small newspapers have been defending since the 1970s (Fonseca & Woitowicz, 2016). In order to focus on the effects of this law change for house cleaners, the mainstream media prioritised "questions and answers" sections to help bosses to skip legal exposure,[7] while the alternative media dedicated time to explaining the roots of such inequality in Brazilian slavery.[8]

The choice of *PEC Domésticas* is just a brief example and yet informs us that producers from the periphery can choose sides, and those are invariably more beneficial to the most affected community. The media have played a key part to unveil the entrenched inequality that still exists in Brazil (Mendonça, 2013). My argument, in that case, is that while the mainstream media go on producing language, image, and text that are indeed more suited to reach a large country via broadcasting[9] the digital alternative media can be more efficient in *politicising* such issues. In the maids' case, it happened when websites started to present interviews with former underpaid maids[10] or by producing content that favored workers rather than their bosses (arguably, the less-affected party). Thus, the peripheral media eventually pursued a more democratic perspective of this historic moment, even though to a small, but mobilized layer of spectators.[11] Even knowing that the largest news organisations have extensively clarified what this law bill in the wake of the vote, in a country with such high inequality, a more politicised outlook has an empowering effect than an otherwise objective approach.

This book has mapped these kinds of interventions shaped as *coverage,* discussing the new repertoires that demonstrate a purposeful politicization of inequality from the periphery. This analysis will read the hegemonic context in which the periphery—as a content producer actor—has used highly controversial episodes to approach other angles and possible meanings. Where the mainstream society failed to include the periphery in certain discussions, or when it does in insufficient manner, it is where the peripheral media can thrive by promoting its insights. This book' aim is one of harmonizing what are actually different and simultaneous interests in inequality from media outlets based across Brazil.

The periphery can dispute the discursive structures that have marginalized and criminalized its dwellers. My goal is to conceptualize this reverse media coverage from the periphery as a kind of *politicization* of inequality that resonates both geographically (received in the periphery) and symbolically (sends out the periphery to other audiences). Politicizing inequality here means to promote a different awareness that breaks from a well-known charitable discourse (Stacciarini, 2002; Gallego & Galindo, 2008) and, for instance, revisits the uncertain welfare state provisions, the unequal public assistance, or ongoing measures to re-establish security in communities (Costa, 2009; Fleury, 2012). Politicization appears as a path through which peripheral media producers can effectively publicize their agendas, even if they have to ignore the mainstream media as a bastion of social justice. Politicization of the periphery may also contradict pacifying myths of equality and diversity that has misled a more proper coverage of issues.

Remarkable cases have shown similar commitment to democracy from the alternative media on international level. In Rodríguez (2001:83), it occurred through the use of video-making during the wartime in Colombia or a popular TV channel in Barcelona. Downing (2001) described how many forms of radical media in South and Central America, as in Southern Europe, were key to narrating the aftermath of dictatorships. In common, these studies have visualised the alternative media as continuums instead of delimited and historicized projects, as seen previously (Hall, 1982; Hamilton, 2000:373). One sees how a set of communities have efficiently deployed links between issues related to inequality in the everyday of communities, crafting appropriate responses and telling stories about it.

In recent literature, powerful cases have discussed the mobilization, activism, and participatory politics that stem from disadvantaged communities, some of which focusing on Brazil's reality (Loader & Mercea, 2012; Davis, 2015; Baroni, 2015; Custódio, 2017). This study, on the other side, dislocated the attention from ethnography and participation to focus on discourses and frames, taking on the knowledge on the discourse of historically marginalized communities, in a way to integrate well-known geographies (e.g. *favelas,* hills), with others which are less-explored, such as poor communities of countryside Brazil, the country's northeastern, remote locations in the Amazon, the homeless, all part of this enormous periphery. Without necessarily framing all these practitioners as activists or journalists, I refer to these actors as "producers."

Whether to confirm stories of oppression and "punishment" (Waicquant, 2003; Penglase, 2007, de Souza, 2006) or to display subjectivities that do not necessarily fit in this frame (Souza & Barbosa, 2005; Perlman, 2010), the main research question was on the extent to which the politicization of the periphery through its discourse can achieve a new coverage of inequality in Brazil. To what extent has the growing online mediatization of the periphery reflected a new way of reporting reality? Could 21st-century Brazil recognize the right of the periphery to communicate, forge new media representations, and have their say, despite the ongoing inequality? On the other hand, to what extent could the periphery, meaningfully, join political debates that used to stay among the elites?

FROM ALTERNATIVE TO PERIPHERAL MEDIA: AN OVERVIEW OF THE BOOK

This book analyzes these questions by looking at politicisation based on the confrontational aspects of the peripheral media. Whether checking if producers were in line with the tradition of the alternative press aforementioned or if they are creating what I saw as a *new* repertoire. Likewise, if it is clear that the alternative media had thrived during situations of conflict, democratic hardship, or complete marginalization (as in Kucinski, 1991; Downing, 2001; Atton, 2002), or acted as tools for disruption, documentation, or memorialization of social struggles (Festa & Silva, 1986; Vinelli, 2010; Zayani, 2014; Barassi, 2015), this book looks into a period said to have represented social change in Brazil, with the reduction in levels of poverty and inequality (Neri, 2008). My focus was on "coverage" of events, but also of the regular circumstances of life as it appears through producers' outlets and publications. I observed how this content has unfolded over the period of three years (2013–2015).

Whereas the literature focuses on the connection to professional journalism (Atton & Hamilton, 2008; Harcup, 2005; Forde, 2011) or on its opposition to mainstream society and state ideologies (Rodríguez, 1994, 2001, 2001b, 2011; Rohlinger et al., 2012; Downing, 2001, 2008; Couldry & Curran, 2003; Atton, 2002, 2002b, 2013; Rauch, 2007; Fenton, 2016), a few others see it as a purely activist effort (Lievrouw, 2011; Barassi, 2015; Custodio, 2017). In common with all these debates, this study has looked for new ways to show dissent and social change via small-scale media outlets. Different from them, it seeks to contribute to the literature by looking beyond media formats or participation, besides reconnecting to a long alternative media in Brazil (Kucinski, 1991; Festa & Silva, 1986; Downing, 2001; Woitowicz, 2009).

In advance to the main discussion, this book has to acknowledge the insufficiency of *alternative media* as a defining term for all these distinct movements, as everything can be alternative to any paradigm we decide to adopt (Downing, 2001:ix). Although not fully in agreement with this term,

I acknowledge its usefulness to define a diverse media ecology, but much conscious of this term's limits. In fact, the country has a strong notion of "alternative press," as one of "alternative media." As a deeply subjective arena, the study of *alternative media* involves no clear limits between these fields, having hundreds of empirical case studies dedicated to each name (Rodríguez, 2001; Downing, 2001; Atton, 2002; Lievrouw, 2011; Gerbaudo, 2012; Barassi, 2015; Zayani, 2014). I contend that we do not need to theorize on top of terms such as *community* or *grassroots*, and that resorting to the generic term *alternative* media was useful when referring to non-mainstream outlets in general. Moreover, I have employed *peripheral* to mention the outlets studied here.

The same strategy guides the preference for the term *media* over the term *communication*, as the latter appears more commonly associated with non-structured formats or the process of communicating (Bailey, 2009). For alternative publications of any kind or format, I refer to them as "outlets" instead of *blogs* (as in Marques & Bailey, 2012) as a practical choice amid changing platforms. When mentioning the "alternative press in Brazil of the 1970s," I might also refer to initiatives that took place in the 1960s and 1990s (Kucinski, 1991), as it is a conscious decision to refer to the past alternative press when its production was booming.

By *media production*, I mean the set of procedures that leads an individual or group to publishing a named piece or outlet. Although the literature has also mentioned *rituals* as part of the reality of contemporary media production, such as in Deuze (2003), I skip naming the differences and similarities between blogging, journalism, or social media. Consequently, alternative media practitioners are mentioned as *media producers*, or *producers*, rather than *bloggers*, *writers*, *citizen journalists*, or *community speakers*, except if those roles need highlighting for some reason (for example, a *producer* who may have had experience working in mainstream journalism). I am inclined to also skip ideological or partisan expressions, such as *left wing*, *critical*, *neoliberal*, or *radical*. For example, the Marxist *radical* media as the alternative media, while the *mainstream* (at least in this conceptual package) is often not seen as radical. I do not mention these qualifiers unless the outlets in question have claimed them for themselves (e.g. in Kucinski, 1991).

Aware of the tensions that involve deliberations in the public sphere in a Habermasian sense (Habermas, 1991,1992), this book instead focuses on *coverage* as the most suitable concept to understand the media producers' self-assigned mission to inform an audience. Instead of "public sphere" or counter public sphere or its siblings (Downey & Fenton, 2003; Milioni, 2009), I prefer the term "periphery" to reflect both non-mainstream media (the center) and to discuss the suburbia where producers live and can create their projects in Brazil. Therefore, the *peripheral* media is the one that speaks for the outskirts of the large metropolises, but also on behalf of populations that are victims of the country's divides. Symbolically, the periphery thus relates to what is not part of the main agenda of society.

It is still important to state that this book's argument does not assume that the peripheral media is one to respond to the center, or to the mainstream media, neither do I suggest that all citizens can contribute to a unique form of *coverage*. In any case, this research has explored if a *new* form of alternative media coverage could emerge from what has seemed a scattered digital contention, not owing to producers' "technical" affordance or dependency on the smartphone or equivalent ICT, nor to their "activist" purpose. The idea is to capture their agency through the individual *intent* of covering aspects of their everyday life in a politicized way, whether sourced from the mainstream, via a transformed content, or original output. What has mattered for this enquiry was media producers' ability to show a critical standpoint from the periphery. This shift into politicization happens when a story on the ruthless treatment of low-income dwellers by the police goes from another crime news to producers making it resonate as "the unacceptable." Stories such as "black, poor youngsters cause panic in middle-class shopping malls" can switch into "peripheral dwellers are mistreated in shopping malls" due to the same intent, as I show in Chapter 3. Politicizing this content is to move on from the little emphasis on elements of class, race, and prejudice towards a vocal criticism that has yet to exist in the mainstream media level.

The research on the peripheral media discourse also allows a new avenue in methods. I did refrain from mapping if producers were "exceeding" or "transforming" what the mainstream media did, because this vision has carried much of an idealism (Harcup, 2011), as the realities of both realms are hardly comparable (Atton, 2002:15). Otherwise, each producer's intrinsic relationship with the historical, cultural or socioeconomic realities of the periphery may suffice to unveil and discuss politicized frames, which could disclose unknown details of their story, or reveal their refusal of present narratives. Past research has found many ways to assess forms of "Internet contention," but that scholarship does not analyze alternative coverage in such detail of their discourse. For instance, Castells (2007) assessed what he saw as effects from "mass self-communication," which leads to a sort of "counter-power" of the web. This "counter-power" is limited to the "capacity by social actors to challenge and eventually change the power relations institutionalized by society" (Ibid, 248). Little is explored on this "counter-power" as power of recreating the current discourse.

Closer to this book's proposed discourse exploration, Couldry (2002:23–26) summarizes the many existing debates on the problem of "space" and "place" in media studies, as "media representations of space take precedence over the feature of space itself." While in Castells (2007, 2013) "counter-power" exists as a product of emerging networked social movements from the Internet to the offline world, in Couldry (2002), we find *framing* as a socially conscious decision of media producers of "charting their media territory." From both authors, I take this notion of *intent* to antagonize a shared notion of secluded space and create a parallel interpretation of it by seizing the notion of *periphery*. My preoccupation was one of measuring how the periphery has developed into counterhegemonic frames, placing their coverage as politicized statements from this new position producers carve out for themselves.

Politicizing through frames is a notion that much derives from the perspective of social movement research (e.g. Tarrow, 1992:287), which ties up frames to 'strategies' of organisations that convey different meanings. In this book, both conceptual tools, *coverage* and *frame* have enriched our understanding in two moments. First, when producers appear assembling multiple coverages and episodes into frames (their coverage is about workers, but it is also about slavery, progressive agendas). Secondly, from these ideas, I analyze in each chapter the framing opportunities that the periphery has explored in different occasions on a day-to-day basis. I believe this book's approach differs from only seeing the extent to which peripheral communities can rehabilitate their representation in a mainstream media perspective, through soap operas and films (Perlman, 2010; Jaguaribe, 2014), and it does not stay limited to the media producer as *activist* realm, which is another discussion, although drawing on a similar universe of media practitioners (Atton, 2015; Custódio, 2017).

To examine all these questions, in Chapter 1 I review a series of media constructions of the periphery as it appears in modern Brazilian history. The periphery is a part of the city, like the *favelas* and, at the same time, it is mainstream media creation. Yet, it is an actor that the state needs to assist. As part of the urban fabric, the periphery is where necessary guarantees are missing (e.g. security, healthcare, education); it goes beyond the central representation of poverty and exclusion. As a mainstream media stereotype, feature films and soap operas have seen it as a violent and drug-dealing place. For the authorities, the periphery is where dwellers are ultra-dependent on the state benefits, becoming a stage for populist politicians. This book's framework then dwells on the possibility of a new politicization based on these set of practices and discourses, to the extent that producers could popularize new media images from the periphery, in which, the strength of their insertion could play a (democratic) role in the whole media environment.

In Chapter 2, I start to introduce portraits related to inequality in Brazil's big cities. I show that producers have politicized interclass encounters that take place in public or semi-public spaces. They also look at homelessness, racial intersections of poverty, and issues that compromise the free access of the poor to the city. In Chapter 3, I focus on the *favelas* of Rio de Janeiro, São Paulo, and Recife to debate initiatives from these communities. Fighting against preconceived images of a troublemaker, producers reimagine the *favelado* as the "2.0" citizen. By deliberately designing their media appearances, they open their conditions of underprivileged, but investing in new mediatized subjectivities. The flip side of this personalisation lies in the struggle against police brutality, as sole victims are now named, and their lives' stories exposed.

Chapter 4 explores in detail the many experiences in which producers have tried to reclaim from the mainstream media what they see as portraits of inequality and themselves. First, I revisit the decades-old notion of *educomunicação* but only in contrasting with recent formative programs developed by media organizations. Overall, rather than disputing what they see as "bad" portraits, producers have positioned their coverage in such a way as to boost their content by creating a model of watchdog journalism and well-sourced reports. They criticize the mainstream media's lack of transparency regarding its productions and question its commitment with the periphery. In Chapter 5, on challenging the state, I begin by analyzing narratives of government distrust among producers, but I prefer exploring how producers who have received grants from the state or attended government-sponsored training still can follow counterhegemonic frames. I end this chapter by discussing evidence that points to the unmaking of the *assistencialismo* narrative, as I question producers on partisanship and political affinities to the extent that it overshadows producers' engagement with a politicized coverage.

The final chapter outlines the contributions of this book. Both discourse and frame analyses confirmed the prevalence of the adjustment of representation, feedback to power, and multiplication of frames. There are three main consequences of this new politicization of the periphery. I first argue that the transformation of the discourse coming from the Brazilian periphery amounts to marginalized citizens framing the news according to native expressions and demanding more accountability in public affairs. Secondly, producers of different backgrounds converge into similar strategies and intentions, distinct from the past of silence. Third, I argue that this assemblage of frames from the periphery disrupts a flawed consensus on inequality in Brazil, reaching a future avenue through which society will be able to see the socially-constructed periphery as part of a less unequal landscape. In the next chapter, I start by discussing the longstanding notion of periphery in its different levels of debate.

NOTES

1. According to its website http://ninja.oximity.com Accessed 18 January 2017.

2. "Brazil's ninja reporters spread stories from the streets"—The Guardian, available at http://www.theguardian.com/world/2013/aug/29/brazil-ninja-reporters-stories-streets access 08 February 2015.

3. "Brazil protests prompts shifts in the media landscape." Wall Street Journal. Available at http://www.wsj.com/articles/SB10001424127887323873904578570244226440374. Accessed 23 December 2015.

4. This is my translation as it is also the case of other studies repeated here, and which are available only in Portuguese.

5. According to the IBGE, Brazilian's agency statistics agency. Data available in the following article at https://agenciadenoticias.ibge.gov.br/2012-agencia-de-noticias/noticias/15700-dados-do-censo-2010-mostram-11-4-milhoes-de-pessoas-vivendo-em-favelas.html. Accessed 15 April 2018.

6. As reported in the Extra newspaper: https://extra.globo.com/noticias/brasil/grupo-se-articula-para-criacao-de-um-partido-da-favela-19441859.html. Accessed 12 January 2017.

7. Many mainstream stories have featured Q&A on the changes of the new law. The point here is the prevalence of an angle favoring house cleaners' employers rather than an explanation of the issue's historical backgrounds and the country's need to provide income justice for these professionals. An example is this extensive report by Globo's website G1as they offer a Q&A entitled "PEC Domésticas, read questions and answers and solve your doubts." Available at http://g1.globo.com/economia/seu-dinheiro/noticia/2015/05/pec-das-domesticas-leia-perguntas-e-respostas-e-tire-suas-duvidas-2015.html.

8. "The long transition from slave to house cleaner." Outras Palavras. Available at http://outraspalavras.net/outrasmidias/destaque-outras-midias/a-longa-transicao-entre-escrava-e-empregada-domestica/. Accessed 08 May 2016.

9. The campaign "postcards from the periphery," led by "*Mídia Periférica*" blog appears as an example of this publicity to peripheral zones, banned from mainstream representations. http://midiaperiferica.blogspot.co.uk/2014/03/participe-da-campanha-postais-das.html. Accessed 08 May 2016.

10 In this post, blog Geledés, publishes an interview with a former maid, in which she tells of the many abuses she suffered as result of the lack of such a law of equating wages and conditions with 'ordinary' workers and domestic workers. Available at http://www.geledes.org.br/creuza-maria-oliveira-se-a-pec-das-domesticas-existisse-nao-teria-sofrido-tanto/ Access 04 July 2016.

11. The editor of blog "Mídia Periférica" from Bahia has reportedly received death threats after publishing about police violence in peripheral communities, especially against black youth. As reported by the website Bahia Notícias at http://www.bahianoticias.com.br/noticia/167895-editor-do-039-midia-periferica-039-relata-ameacas-apos-criticas-a-pm-e-sai-de-salvador.html Access 08 May 2016.

Chapter One

The Periphery in the Context of Brazil

Having reflected in the introduction on the scattered trajectory of the alternative media in Brazil, whose power of contention has emerged during weeks of massive protests in 2013, the previous chapter revisited the scholarship on the alternative media. By applying the notion of *frame* to *coverage*, I defended that one way of improving our grasp of the alternative media is by looking at its discourse. In this chapter, I refine ideas of Brazil's periphery. As I propose the concept of *peripheral media*, I look at a wider number of outlets and media producers as a sample, with which I could engage by following a different approach than that seen in literature. For example, as I analyze *how* the peripheral media discourse is, I consider the traditional notion of alternative press talking about inequality (e.g. newspapers, magazine) as Brazilian scholarship (Kucinski, 1991; Woitowicz, 2009), but I also look at NGOs and civil organisations, as well as at the work of activists, scholars, celebrities, sportspeople, politicians, and other actors converging into the same agency of fighting inequality via the alternative media.

By theorising the *periphery* and *discourse* of such varied category of outlets, this approach could enlighten on the essence of the periphery in Brazil according to new media outlets. I depart from a vision that sees discourse as a game changer for the power relations in the media (van Dijk, 1996), whereas my attention has attention to the repetition and framing potential for resonance that could mirror that of past movement (Benford & Snow, 2000). On the other hand, there is an opportunity to get close to a layer of Brazilian society that much entails resistance, but on which very little is known except for the absences one finds in it. Souza & Sinder (2005:24), for instance, have singled out "precarious" and "non-Europeanized sectors" of the population, and "because of their abandonment," they tend to "a growing and permanent marginalisation."

At the global level, the periphery is an idea that unites other common struggles in world cities, such as gentrification, expulsion of the poor from central locations (Harvey, 2012; Sassen, 2008). What is the response found among these populations? This book's approach inquires into other angles through which one might look at the periphery. With particular respect to the fact that the poor are "punished," the "black" are punished (Mitchell & Wood, 1999), the extent to which they can fight the state or the media discourse that discriminate them (Montoro, 2002; Waicquant, 2008, Penglase, 2014) should not be minimized. Despite not being able to provide in-depth analyses of these phenomena at length or to formulate further descriptions of the periphery, this book's exploration narrows it down to capture debates that happen in the periphery through what I call the peripheral media.

To what concerns the history of the non-mainstream media initiatives in the country, the word *periphery* may still recover Brazil's own sense of "radical" or "popular," which are concepts of fundamental importance to past case studies on the alternative media (Downing, 2001; Peruzzo, 2013), but which may arguably not find a comprehensive illustration in the increasingly urban reality. On the other hand, from a past of voluntarism and spectacle of inequality in the mainstream media (Leu, 2004; Gomes, 2008), the peripheral media could address a series of new locations and reveal different interlocutors who might not act in consonance to each other, but they can repeat the same messages and form a single discourse. To show the strength of this periphery is to discuss how this entity is far more complex than in the charitable campaigns that have displayed poverty in communities for decades, such as the Globo TV's *Criança Esperança,* which has offered little in political power to them (Stacciarini, 2007). Therefore, while the periphery could geographically point to clear spots, such as on the outskirts of big cities, or the *favelas*, this book's approach can talk through the periphery as more than one single location, focusing on the mobile settings of this discourse, as the idea of *popular* once was, and which could be reproducible on the "mainstream media" or outside the well-known parts of Brazil.

I start this chapter by stressing the meaning of the term *periphery* as it appears in samples extracted from the literature. These ideas have been helpful to detach from a general (and often vague) understanding of *alternative* media to then focus on a meaning that is essentially responsive to these different constructions of the periphery. I conceptualize each of these ideas of the periphery, but the idea is to verify each one of them, how they appear in the outlets I looked at, through a separate, but interdependent analysis that will base each of this book's chapters. These cases eventually are aimed at a single interpretation of how the peripheral media politicizes inequality in reference to a past context of stereotyping and downplaying, and how it is meaningful for believing in a new power of self-representation. Hence, the change from the charity discourse will be regarded here as a sign of unprecedented politicization. Next, I review why the periphery in its direct relationship with the city's outskirts, which has appeared through the profiling of some city's characters.

THE PERIPHERY AS PART OF THE CITY

One of the strongest examples of how Brazilian society have reduced and marginalized the periphery as the surrounding areas of the country's largest cities appears in the 1970s' alternative press. I am talking about newspapers and magazines that, even under heavy repression from a dictatorship, envisioned unexpected ways of bringing up the issues that affect such populations. Mostly poverty, but also taking into account intersectional inequalities, such as feminism and blackness. On a remarkable cover of the *Brasil Mulher* newspaper,[1] writers would employ deprecating language, such as "third-class passengers" captioning the image of a black woman playing with a child. Even if this title made use of sarcasm to denounce extreme poverty, this cover showed in a very straightforward manner how the populations that live on the margins of big cities could have their faces on the cover of a magazine. In this case, one of a black woman playing with her child. Her portrait reinforces that every narrative from periphery must follow a perspective of getting rights fulfilled, a discourse that has historically tied rights with concepts like citizenship and democracy (Aldé, 2004). This discourse has mixed issues of poor urbanization with the deliberated condescendence from mainstream society, which many studies have reflected as if demonstrating the shortfalls of the poorest (Gohn, 1985; Marques & Bichir, 2001).

As mentioned, the periphery in the context of the city is where one wants to leave from, but where the exploited can live. In the 1970s, we find the case of the *bóias-frias* or sugar-cane plantation workers. They are named after "cold meals" and, although their case relates to rural inequality and tied to the type of "oppressed" worker, it is in the outskirts of medium-sized cities where they live or where they are from (D'Incao & Melo, 1976). For these reporters, they do not give in to their "oppression"; they accept work in the middle of the Brazilian countryside and face their reality with dignity (Kucinski, 1991:5). One of the covers of an alternative newspaper, *Movimento*, depicts a group on the top of a truck, which is their daily precarious commute; this is a feature on a 1976 edition. The case of the *bóias-frias* helped to personalize the tragic conditions of the low-paid agrarian work in Brazil (D'Incao e Mello, 1976) in so as far as this sense of social calamity and exclusion "appears" for the first time to a broader public (Reis 1999; Telles, 2004; Spink & Spink, 2006; Silva, 2011).

This sense of forging a "presence" for the periphery, as an entity, in the sense of showing that it is closer to the city than urban dwellers might think, has configured the only narrative in that respect. That imagery of suffering could explain why such representation still resonates to this day when one talks about the periphery. Martín-Barbero (1998) argued that the action of such producers in the cities has offered this counterhegemonic possibility, one of unification of the people in search of their lost power. The counterhegemonic resistance incorporates other cultural practices and a total immersion in the disadvantaged culture. Instead of normalising the population in the everyday life of difficulties, the alternative press stressed this hardship as a counterhegemonic possibility. In other words, journalists went on to personalize Brazil's vast periphery and its difficulties to the extent that it could capture the ordinary citizens' opinions, their legitimacy, and perhaps generate any sort of pressure, a democratic pressure against politicians.

Thus, the city is a critical platform for the notion of periphery because it gives the disadvantaged citizens one of their rare chances to be visible to middle-class citizens. Increasingly aware of that, alternative journalists of the time aimed to invest in discovering the poor's traits, routines, and subjectivities. The *Movimento* newspaper, for example, once featured a story of two boys who worked selling candies at a traffic light in the city of Porto Alegre, as they reported (the italics are mine):

> The main concern of these *little executives* is about the [city hall] guards. Celso and one of his friends explain that it is important not leaving the money in their boxes, because otherwise 'they take everything out and the damage is bigger.' 'Once, one of us has brought some food for dinner. When they came in, we had no time to take the food away. We came back and there was nothing. It makes no sense. What they [government] really want is seeing us pickpocketing instead.' (*Movimento*, 01/09/1975. Carlos Mossmann column)

By exchanging the name of the boys with "little executives," the above report also promotes a personalized portrait that gives a narrative for the presence of these children. As Kucinski (1991) puts it, the ethics in the 1970s' alternative press is a prominent element that goes along with the will to *cover* social issues. Much of this ethics stems from a vision in which the oppressed had to be rescued off, but which has not necessarily meant implementing practical solutions at the public policy level. Instead, "removing factors of oppression" seemed to be the ideal solution. I found an intrinsic link with what Boal, whose theater was very influential then, says:

> To understand this poetics of the oppressed one must keep in mind its main aim: to change the people—"spectators," passive beings in the theatrical phenomenon—into subjects, into actors, transformers of the dramatic action. (Boal, 2000:122)

Only after the 2000s, this relationship of visibility and invisibility of the periphery in heart of Brazil's cities started to change. Boal's urge for "eliminating spectators" and creating actors remained as an impulse for contemporary narratives on the periphery. In the 2010s, the idea of a "creative periphery" as a dedicated *hub* for creative work in distant corners crowned the development of what seemed a nascent grassroots industry. These "cultural factories" would put an end to the uselessness of the periphery, giving a job to the people. This branch in scholarly research has grown in consonance with the economic "boom" of that decade, allowing the peripheral youth to develop their "potential" (Bentes, 2009; Freitas, 2010; Nascimento, 2012). Sprawling urban outskirts in megacities such as São Paulo could host thriving film production areas (Martins, 2015), as well as in non-metropolitan areas (Freitas, 2007). An innovation is to see how much the social networks could generate images directly from distant neighborhoods (Freitas & Espírito Santo, 2015). These images will be the opposite to the suffering individual that the *bóias-frias* had embodied for many years. Local youngsters would not need to cross the city in trucks, or neither did them resemble the oppressed proletarians of before, as literature has documented it in many opportunities (Mattelart & Piemme, 1980; Festa & Silva, 1986). Whether all these promising ideas have materialised or not, the expectation of seeing an urban and thriving periphery would continue, none the less, without much access to institutions such as the Brazilian Congress, the public universities, and government administration (Shahin et al., 2016).

One of the recent gains for the periphery after the 2000s is that the Internet has made unreachable locations somehow present in daily mass media programs. As Becker (2009:50) pointed out, if the TV had, in the past, the possibility of broadcasting "the routine of big cities" into the houses of the Brazilian periphery, the online media can—in its terms—reverse this logic by broadcasting the suburbs to a wider audience. Initiatives such as *Voz da Baixada* or *Rio on Watch* are innovative due to their unique transversality from the periphery to the city. Digital media producers have the chance to differ from the popular depiction of *favela* characters in *telenovelas* as they transcend into another recognizable image of entrepreneurial and political individuals. If the *poor* dwellers are necessarily charismatic and sweet (Gomes & Nascimento, 1998), the digital narrators of the periphery can show further complexity.

I approach in the next section the specific challenges posed to the citizens living in *favelas*. As far as these communities are part of the broader scheme of media representations of the periphery as a component of the city, there are distinct elements that place *favelas* in a form of representation of their own. This differential also stems from these communities' native pamphlets and magazines. More recently, some communities, especially in Rio de Janeiro, have gained world prominence beyond their well-known existence by the population of Brazil's largest cities. Despite their detachment and isolation, manage to appear internationally, ultimately embodying attributes that have been generalized as that of Brazil as a country.

THE PERIPHERY AS THE *FAVELA*

The history of the periphery is not complete if I do not approach the publications coming out of Brazil's *favelas*. The oldest one dates back to at least 1925, when the *Voz do Morro* came out. This pamphlet appears as the first so-called "newspaper" written from a *favela* (Souza & Barbosa, 2005:40). On a monthly basis, the *Voz do Morro* publicly displayed the *morro* (hill) culture, featuring poetry, and *samba*. Although these outlets have conveyed what is like living under many levels of socioeconomic constraint, it is not possible to underestimate their ability to report social issues and, at the same time, evoke lyricism and music. Both kinds of elements turned out to communicate well both with the public image of inequality and spontaneity, which are characteristics that were especially evoking to outsiders (Fischer, 2008). These soft narratives would later help to consolidate, if not part of, a sentiment of cultural citizenship in Brazil, which has come as a common denominator for the disenfranchised (Dagnino, 1998, 2004).

None the less, this way of looking at the constitution of the *favela* has not been unanimously agreed upon among scholars. *Favela* researcher Licia Valladares (2005) argued on the "invention of the *favela*," where she believed that a more integrated approach—i.e. seeing the *favelas*' issues as part of a broader urban setting—would favor a less prejudicial outlook towards these communities. She argued against the reductionism of seeing multiple and diverse communities through one frame. Before accepting that there is the *favela* media, Brazilian scholar Marilena Chauí (1993) considered popular culture as an instrument to flirt with social issues but from which stemmed a kind of "conformism," while producers and hill-dwellers discussed "resistance" only at the cultural level. A similar argument on "softening the resistance" existed in relation to the use of popular rhythms such as *brega* by the military regime (Araújo, 2002).

To Chauí's point, this tradition of spokespeople acting on behalf of these communities and feeding informal communication outlets goes back to the 1970s and can be stronger than that of the locally-tailored outlets. In many other examples, in which no outlet is known, the Catholic Church fulfilled that part of communicating the daring conditions of the community through regular visits from bishops and priests. In brief, the Church was often the only voice available to broker a dialogue with mainstream society. In the figure below, one sees the late bishop Dom Helder Câmara, who was the so-called "bishop of the *favela.*" He paid frequent visits to these communities and introduced himself as an interlocutor (Serbin, 2002; Valladares, 2005:85). Only in the following decades, in the 1990s, the presence of social movements and NGOs, such as the influential NGO *Viva Rio*, has added up to this set of the *favela*'s spokespersons, but it would not necessarily help dwellers to reclaim their mediated voices or form through it any kind of native leaderships (Ibid, 2005:168).

In the 1980s, the *favelado,* or *favela* dweller, settled in the public imagination as a stereotype that mirrored an engendered inferiority. The strength of this image was big enough to stick with individuals who were no longer inhabiting a *favela.* Their blackness, brownness, or simply, social standing, could be enough to be called a *favelado* (Gondim, 1981). The generation that grew up under this stigma, people who are in the late 2010s in their thirties, are those who aim to reflect more about it, as did rapper *Eduardo Taddeo,*

Figure 1.1. Bishop D. Hélder Câmara during visit to a community in his diocese, Recife, 1970. (Archives Ciric)

who published a music video in 2012 that he branded as *"The Undeclared War According to a Favelado."*[2] In another take, historian Marcelo Belfort, himself a *favela* dweller,[3] offered his personal experience of questioning this image:

> I've had a poor childhood at [favela] *Nova Holanda*, and this has made difficult for me to have my basic needs fulfilled, such as feeding. But I have good remembrances of the people with whom I lived, and of my child's plays, such as playing marble. [. . .] For me, despite everything, being a 'favelado' was something very good because I could experiment [with] freedom and creativity, which later, has constituted fundamental values for my life. (Belfort, 2013)

Apart from this legacy of social relationships based on stereotype, things can change, even if subtly. With an increasing number of *favela* dwellers having access to the Internet, in 2015 it was 50% of the *favela* population,[4] and this number growing even more if we consider access via mobile, it became easier for them to challenge this historical stereotype, or at least try to spread patterns that lead to other identities. There are far more serious concerns that relate to perpetuation of stereotypes, such as looking like a *favelado* and then being screened on the streets and stopped at checkpoints (Beaton & Washington, 2015). Though these implications are enormous, there also lies a counterhegemonic opportunity for the *favelado*, not necessarily in denying what it has suggested from an individual, but in reaffirming its derogatory meanings for the sake of protest and triggering political or politicized discussions.

As an acronym for who lives in poverty, the *favelado* is a reminder of society's burdens and the overall failure to promote social justice for all. The *favelado*'s presence has put to test a range of mixed feelings regarding the periphery, as only the image of poor dwellings in precarious constructions can do (Souza & Barbosa, 2005). As the *favelas* grew nationwide and dwellers started to fearlessly circulate through the center, especially after the 2000s, claims of being "natural" police targets have increased. Wacquant (2003) credits this "criminalisation of poverty" to a U.S.-based style of persecution, as well as the perception that people with such background are "invaders" of the public space grew as a common frame in the media (Penglase, 2007). These perceptions problematize the limits of the periphery and pose communicative challenges, whether to engage with these mainstream discourses or how to react against it to 'buy' the necessary support from society.

Digital media could, in this sense, help the *favelado* to at least increase the perception that there are movements in and out of the center that are happening. It is a specific target of the peripheral media to deal with these implications, rejuvenate this stock of images, and push this and other stereotypes out of ordinariness, normality, and towards a sustainable quest of citizenship and at what speed. By problematizing their projections outside communities, can the *favelas* put their populations in even more exposure and voyeurism from outsiders? Otherwise, by investing in a settled identity of the *favelado*, could the *favela* dweller choose not being a *favelado* if he or she does not want to? To what extent is reproducing a derogatory stereotype an improvement of their own position as narrators of their reality? These are questions that I will address in Chapter 4. Next, I emphasise now the origin of many of these terms have been part of a universe that inherits images from mainstream media constructions.

THE PERIPHERY AND THE MAINSTREAM MEDIA

Apart from the notion of authorship and self-empowerment that have the periphery defined *from* the periphery, I also find it important to contextualize a background of other media representations *on* the periphery. I see these dialogues happening on two levels of engagement. First, the consciousness that the periphery is the *poor* and it is *precarious,* which stems from the pamphlets and from scholarship (Souza & Barbosa, 2005; Souza & Sinder, 2005:24). Secondly, that this marginalized universe is, above all, underrepresented or misrepresented in the media, which is not new. I will dedicate here to the second way of seeing it: the constain in the right to representation of disadvantaged groups, especially due to its size and dominance (Amaral, 2002; Paiva et al., 2015). It is possible to find the prevalence of stereotypes that sought to depict the harsh everyday of millions in a rather softer or positive way, often funny and exaggerated, in exchange of audience (La Pastina et al., 2014). Recently, the successful *Avenida Brasil* was an example of such aesthetics taken to the mainstream (Fischer & Nascimento, 2016). I do not discuss much of these assumptions in depth, but I must dwell on the extent to which this variety on how the periphery looks like have helped to solidify a misguided view and, as we shall see, will stir reactions from the periphery in the late 2010s.

I must ponder on the centrality of Globo TV in Brazil's media environment and its implications. It is not the only player to represent what is the "mainstream media" in Brazil, but I have chosen it for this book due to its hegemony, which has triggered understandable criticism from many sectors of society (Sinclair, 2002; Paiva et al., 2015). To what concerns the coverage of inequality that I sought to investigate, the frequent complaint is that Globo TV does not read it in much democratic way, in the sense of allowing participation and access (Aldé, 2004; Porto, 2012). However, the degree to which Globo or other mainstream media players have influenced, partnered, or restrained alternative producers from disadvantaged backgrounds has appeared more recently in a few studies (e.g. Baroni, 2015). In the case of the Globo organizations, the vast literature[5] has focused less on this latter part than it has on regulatory issues, particularly as a result of the clientelism in the Congress and the distribution of broadcasting licenses across the country (see Azevedo, 2006).

This deadlock made by a series of issues relating to concentrated ownership, homogeneity, and the centralized control of the media environment leads to frequent tensions that affect all media ecologies, which the alternative media case studies have catalogued well (Atton, 2002; Harcup, 2003; Forde, 2010). To put it short, these tensions are summed up by the expectation that the alternative media producers *have* to be against the mainstream media (Hamilton, 2000). This book focuses on a vision that, beyond fighting "monopoly," the periphery might have other interests that mingle with this agenda, but which contemplates items that can only refer to the universe of the disadvantaged, some of which dwell on other levels of debate. The gap in this literature lies in engaging insufficiently or inappropriately with these points and representations from the periphery. It is rather about having a limited repertoire outside the media law turmoil. In short, the focus on the commercial media does not help a deep exploration of what the peripheral producers have accomplished by themselves, under such circumstances. As I defend in chapter 5, to look too much at the mainstream media is to lose sight of all media initiatives that happen on the margins.

For that reason, I have to consider that in the category "mainstream media," beyond current scholarship that privileges TV and mass communication, as also finds other organisations such as NGOs that have had some influence over the public. Certainly, there is much more to understand in the broader role of NGOs for development in Brazil's marginalized communities (Mercer, 2002; Sanglard, 2006), but in this book I look at how those organizations have blended in with key mainstream media organizations, such as Globo over the last decades. Together, they have created a set of media representations that depicted extreme poverty and hunger, but, arguably, they did it so by showing the periphery as the needy partner and the inferior character in the national landscape.

Primeira e Última was a short-lived newspaper released in 1992 that aimed at denouncing not only hunger, but also inequality and racial exclusion from Rio's *favelas* (Giumbelli, 1994). It later merged with the *Jornal da Cidadania*, a newsletter commissioned by the Institute of Social Analysis (Ibase) (Fico, 1999; Kingstone & Power, 2000:167; Stacciarini, 2002:160–79). Published in a 1995 edition of the institution's newspaper one finds a cartoon, there is a much straightforward situation depicted, where a hungry child begs on the streets of Rio de Janeiro to a woman's dismay, it reads: *"Mr Guard, this chit has his stomach growling at me"* (Stacciarini, 2002).

The emergence of this layer in the midst of the vast NGO sector, in partnership with the mainstream media, has bridged realities into content, often doing it through competent journalism pieces. These publications have had much boost once *Ibase* started to collaborate with Globo TV, in the 1990s. The charismatic sociologist *Betinho* was head of the *Ibase* at the time (Gusmão, 2000). The 1990s also saw telecharity[6] initiatives with prominent campaigns, such as the *Teletón* that have influenced Latin America in a variety of ways (Stacciarini, 2002; Gallego & Galindo, 2008; Ivanova & Marcondes, 2014). Without deepening in the complexity of this event, it is a classic example of NGO-mainstream media partnership, achieving such an influence on the public awareness on hunger and poverty, but politically neutral with regards to the inclusion of the periphery in parliaments, for example. By focusing on the urgent hunger issue (Didoné & Menezes, 1995; Cabral, 1996). Otherwise, solidarity campaigns have gotten full acceptance from politicians and society alike. For some, it has resembled an "ideology," with reduced impact to the "empowerment" of communities (Gusmão, 2000).

Were these NGO-like images good or bad for the representation of the periphery? Have they improved society's perceptions on the latter's issues, as opposed to reducing a broader context into existing prejudices on hungry, impoverished places? The answer is that whether or not these partnerships between NGOs and Globo TV,[7] or with other broadcasters, have produced programs that unprecedently set a standard to TV charity, this sort of narrative has continued to this date. In fact, they went on to produce well-watched programs that employ popular rhythms as a backdrop (such as the traditional samba to show the *favela*), and a discourse that overall was aimed at showing the "reality" of the suburbs (Moreira, 2009; Rocha, 2013). Appropriately, McQuail (2010:47) warned that charitable media campaigns were subject to "socially approved goals" and "filter conditions." Perhaps, *Globo* TV and its competitors, such as the *SBT* network, have served the cause of extreme poverty, but the extent to which it has helped to integrate the periphery as a counterpart in this struggle is arguable.

Likewise, the early 2000s marked the success of feature films such as *City of God.* In the following decade, the entertainment media have actualized such narratives of poverty but adding to it the co-optation element in the *favelas,* mainly by drug-dealing and criminals (Penglase, 2007; Jaguaribe, 2004; Jaguaribe & Hetherington, 2004; Perlman, 2010; Jaguaribe, 2014; Amparo-Alves, 2014; Larkins, 2015). While no longer taking on the over-dependent poor, the mainstream media have moved from solidarity and hunger to the military police front. To be fair, evidence also points to the representation of the so-called "culture of the periphery." It has improved in recent years, much due to the allowance of a forgotten aesthetics of the suburbs that now comes up on TV (Grijo, 2014). The risk then is one of reproducing what might sound as sanitized versions of realities and discourses.

To what concerns this book, both developments, the NGO media and the recent feature film representation, are crucial for understanding the periphery's sense of "adjustment" that I visit in the next chapters. These media frames will respond to decades of such incomplete media representations, in which producers move towards an idea of ownership of their images. It is possible that ideas of "good" or "bad" representations are useful for the sake of a common alignment around what the mass media have produced. Yet, when looking at pieces that the "periphery," considering its representatives, author, there is overall positive change, even though producers might repeat some of these ideas historically received by the mass media. What this book aims to do is to capture new variations of these reproduced discourses (on the *favela,* on the *favelado,* for instance), noting improvements on the self-awareness and *politicization* of communities.

These authored representations, especially on the level of the *favela,* must receive a special look also because of their overall contribution for democracy. Keane (1991:178) argued that a democratic media system has to attend to many sets of tastes and opinions and constantly revised to check what is missing. Young (2011:245) pondered the importance of promoting an *adjustment* so that territorial, cultural, and social differences do not augment impressions of domination and oppression. In both senses, to look at the *favela* as part of the periphery advances to the extent it equals fairness and adjustment from this previous scenario, which is central to consider another stage of media development from the margins. In the next section, I discuss how much of this mediatized periphery that have existed on the mainstream media has existed thanks to narratives that have their origin in political communication.

THE PERIPHERY AND THE STATE

The relationship of the periphery with the state dates back to colonial times and, in early Republican Brazil, includes accounts of writers such as Euclides da Cunha with his book "Os Sertões" (*The Hinterlands*). In the following decades, discourses that link both state and inequality started to involve more direct references to what concerns the media and the politicians. Fischer (2008:91) argued that by naming himself as "the father of the poor," Vargas stood for a mix of "propaganda, rhetoric, legislative deed, and orchestrated charity." Vargas's governments were the ones to "like the poor," a term that, in itself, carries an amalgam of needs (including hunger, unemployment and education) and was ultimately a cliché of the cross-class relationships in the country (Wolfe, 1994; Levine, 1998). These are the underlying statements of *assistencialismo* (roughly, *welfarism*). This last term encapsulates the extreme dependence of the poor on the state, historically tapping into populist aims (Barbosa, 2007:171).

The extent to which discourses like Vargas' *assistencialismo* have reduced the importance of the periphery in the media is what interests this book. There are clear examples in the form of imagery of how politicians have used poor, distant, hilly neighborhoods as place to exercise such image of caring fathers. Vargas, for instance, was keen to appear interacting with the under-class. However, despite this flirting with populism from Vargas and beyond, it is during his terms as dictator and President that "popular" newspapers started to feature poverty and inequality as issues that were harmful to society. As far as these issues could fit in as "social tragedy" in the mainstream media, studies on this period have also suggested that this discourse have the state *owning* these issues, and indirectly getting to an idea that the financial support needed to tackle them was not everyone's responsibility (Sodré, 1998;

Figure 1.2. Ex-president and ex-dictator Getúlio Vargas (in white) talks to a disabled man on the streets. (Fundação Getúlio Vargas–Archive)

Dantas, 2014). This constant tie to *assistencialismo* in the political discourse, which is at the same time detached from society, but aimed at society, may have contributed to the archetype of behaviour that has taken inequality less seriously, on which authors have later associated to a thesis that for the people it is a "problem of the state" (e.g. Reis, 1999). Had this accommodation by "pushing back" the responsibility helped to consolidate the media stereotypes regarding poverty (Mendonça, 2015)?

This pattern of having the state or the government dictating the urgency of poverty, and yet, the same entity downplaying inequality, went on to reach modern times. In the late 2010s, the Brazilian media, quoting research institutes such as the *Fundação Getúlio Vargas* (FGV), tended to reclassify dwellers of the periphery as "emerging" socially, becoming the *Class C* (Neri, 2008). As discussed earlier on, this portrait stemmed from the economic boom, a time during which class mobility was sold as possible and as a direct consequence from the popular poverty alleviation programs (Neri, 2008). While focusing on class transitions,[8] even if it is still an arguable phenomenon (Mauro, 2014; see O'Dougherty, 1998 for comparison), has meant no longer treating poverty and inequality as the same thing. On the other hand, that change did not mean having topics such as gender, and violence as elements as properly addressed, whereas these constraints continued affecting the periphery, and the "improvement" factor being restricted to the financial side (Soihet, 1997; Penglase, 2007).

It is noteworthy that Brazil left the 2014 UN Hunger Map, an event that crowned more than a decade of poverty reduction and a sharp fall on inequality indexes. "Brazil without Misery" would be President Dilma Rousseff's government motto (2010–2014). However, partisan appropriations of the issue of hunger from both sides of the political spectrum[9] still continued to exist as media representations. Therefore, one might ask if the *Fome Zero* scheme (*Zero Hunger scheme*), the first of the Workers' Party hunger-reduction policies, has also meant a return to the narrative of hunger that is managed by the state, with officials as its main sponsors and mediators, on which other examples exist (Ferreira, 2006; Hall, 2006). If contrasting it with Vargas's "father of the poor" discourse (Fischer, 2008) and with the voluntarism that set the agenda of the 1990s and the 2000s, this period was still largely leaning towards the former than the latter. If government leadership was to, ideally, appear as a necessary enforcer of a new vision, it has not given a satisfactory version of what class-transcendence looks like on the political sense without giving it to people's worst fears. It configured a blur that has prevented a sharper look at inequality, as other studies have debated (Scalon & Salata, 2012; Salata, 2016).

In sum, the media reporting on the surge of *Class C* has indeed clarified the *transition* of Brazil's lowest classes into an expectation of them turning into wealthier ones, but it hardly contributed to shed light on the complex dynamics of inequality. It could be said that by removing full attention from poverty as a scarcity of goods, the Brazilian society could finally concede to a broader understanding of other racial and gender aspects that are part of the economic inequality debate[10] since long ago (De Francisco, 1997; Osório, 2013). While that case clarifies what in this book I mention about the need to update the representation, it fails by engaging with the roots of the issue, as defined elsewhere (Grohmann, 2014). The reason I chose to problematize these angles is that the role of the state in Brazil, as seen, is not only one of forging society's interest and buy-in to social issues, but one of finding in the periphery whatever social justice case politicians have needed, which have drawn on graphic images and easy solutions. This is a short background of the mainstream media and the state producing images of the periphery, but it is enough to confirm this book's argument for the urgency of understanding another kind of inequality discourse in Brazil that might stem from the periphery. In the following section I present further opportunities that are at the heart of the peripheral media.

UNDERSTANDING THE PERIPHERAL MEDIA: TOWARDS A NEW POLITICIZATION

To call it the "peripheral media" is to draw on the potential of the digital media producers spread across all these diverse landscapes aforementioned, as opposed to pointing to any formal establishment of media producers. Ideally, they will contest the failed antagonism of the past and successfully challenge the image of the passive, silent, and idealised periphery and along the way unprecedented political ground. This politicization of demands and images derives from tackling *hegemony* in a Gramscian way. I refer to a Gramsci (2011) when I see a link between national consensus and mainstream media apparatus. While past research had worked with concepts such as *antagonism* and *apparatus* to capture how major media organizations frame poor communities to fit in their media formats (Amaral & Guimarães, 1994), as seen, there is a chance to transfer this discussion into the arena of the discourse of the periphery. Certainly, Globo TV comes up as key example of an organization that concentrates the power of narrative. Recent studies have mapped its centrality for the life in black communities (Soares, 2016) and it remains omnipresent; apart from the *telenovelas,* it also concentrates the production of a vast amount of national films (Champagnatte, 2015).

On the other hand, we should not look at hegemony as an organizational, liberal problem of market leadership that one could expect from small media producers. It is, rather, about more subtle ways in which such groups can, at their best, tackle existing limitations of the media discourse, especially to what concerns the understanding of inequality. Jaguaribe (2014:201) concluded that, after years of lack of mediation of the *favelas*, forms of authorship could count as an empowering element:

> Forms of authorship are empowering because they give voice and visibility to the periphery and the favela through self-representation, but they can also be limiting to the extent that authorship becomes conditioned by cultural traits, territorial belonging, and symbolic identities.

In this way, I conceptualize as *hegemony* as this gaze to the periphery in a way to reaffirm it as an inferior landscape and a dependent territory. As far as the extent to which "voice" can exist on different levels and complexities (Couldry, 2010), I settle this notion of *authorship* by looking at the peripheral media based on the variations of producers' discourse, either because they are creating a new language and vocabulary, and more importantly, they are putting out new frames. It is about how the periphery could build on trivialized images (e.g. in *soap operas*) (Rêgo, 2014; La Pastina, 2014), or tackle the elitism and the filters imposed that are naturalized amid mainstream society (Reis, 2000; Moreira, 1999). Producers can do it by embedding the periphery in other discourses, or by expanding its borders into other publics (Holmes, 2016). In Gramsci (2011), *hegemony* stems from an *apparatus*, and historically, it is for the lack of infra-structure and distribution routines that the alternative media have fallen victim to a problematic turmoil involving media, commodity, and capitalism (e.g. Hermann & McChesney, 2001).

What I consider to be counter-hegemony relates to the tradition of alternative media studies of trespassing the issue of apparatus through the radical discourse. For example, authors have explored this 'radical' aspect as a helpful specificity of the alternative media (e.g. Ford & Gil, 2001; Downing, 2001:44), in which it "expands the range of information, reflection, and exchange from the often-narrow hegemonic limits of mainstream media." In Rodríguez (2001:19), this is about "citizens who participate actively with their own identities, the identities of others, and their social environments, they produce power." The extent that this radicality can be successful lies in the ability to contour Gramsci's notion of hegemony, whether playing it against notions of *antagonism* or overturning the *apparatus,* or even disrupting *consensus.* Inasmuch as the "public opinion" might also act to debilitate the "antagonist," there is a place and discourse of this antagonist, where many authors have named it as a context of "contentious politics" (Tilly & Tarrow, 2007). I skipped the complexity of being "contentious" to focus, instead, on new and creative meanings that could sound politicized and counter-hegemonic.

Therefore, my expectation is to analyze Brazil's case based on this backdrop of consensus on the potential for social change that stems from the alternative media internationally. In this book, I will particularly look at the growing politicization of the discourse within a broader panorama of Brazil. That is, the way in which producers have envisaged a critical visibility for inequality issues as opposed to perpetuating stereotypes linked with inequality, in which they can shatter such myths through the elaboration of old issues into new frames. In the past, there have been many examples of how politicized their media interactions can be, based on contentious issues that echoed thanks to the powerful alternative press. The profiling the victims of an enslaving labour system (the *bóia-fria*) or the reproduction of old categories of exclusion (such as that of *favelado*) were positive examples, while shocking, because of their potential to detach the dwellers of the periphery from these vague categories, bringing them into an idea of autonomy and control.

As I shall discuss in the next chapters, the improvement of socioeconomic and political conditions that happened in the last decades has inspired a new generation of media producers to change the country's perceptions of itself. They have aimed at the replacement of hegemonic discourses of charity, cohesion, and enforced unity, to then focus on *indignant* discourses that demand another type of coverage for their communities. This politicization abandons the peaceful settings in search of more authoritative instances. Inasmuch as Downing (2001:3–5) also saw in the *radical* media a reaction against hegemonic discourses and Martín-Barbero (2008) saw "mediations" between culture, communication, and hegemony as the reality in "Latin" America. This book's look for fresh confrontation episodes could sharpen these views to capture smaller issues but which pose greater relevance, once these past limitations appear as a constant pattern over the decades.

After the rise of the left-wing Workers' Party to power, Brazil seemed to champion an idea of the *Class C* as a positive, prosperous renovation for how ordinary citizens faced the disadvantaged classes. But it is not sufficient to engage with its underlining argument of class transition, while disregarding the historical permanence of the periphery as such powerless agent in Brazilian history (e.g. Souza & Sinder, 2005). As depicted below, if one looks at a brief log of democratic disruptions, the "alternative" media have surged during decisive moments of the power struggle, whether during Vargas' *Estado Novo,* his dictatorial regime, or in the dictatorship of the 1960s. As seen in Sodré (1998), the idea of the *radical* press might not have consolidated in Brazil, but that of the periphery appears to have retained its strength and vitality due to its visible aspect, whether in the hills and the suburbs, or whether the "peripheral" has appeared in the center.

Figure 1.3. Brazil's democratic ruptures and alternative media surge. (Sodré, 1998)

These aspects inform this book on the urgency of capturing the contemporary periphery. From the viewpoint of a favorable political conjecture that had set in after 2003, which might have given the periphery dwellers basic socioeconomic conditions for their empowerment, but also from the subsequent crisis, which might have changed the fortunes in contemporary Brazil. In both ways, the periphery is a participant of this political trajectory, but its responses and inputs are not entirely understood. For example, in past crises, authors have dwelt on the divisive role of the mainstream media during contentious political episodes, such as president Collor's impeachment in 1992 (Amaral, 1994; Waisbord, 1997; Abers, 2000:52; Porto, 2012:81). However, a more serious constraint is not having considered the same in-depth analysis on the positions of the periphery during these episodes. Especially after more than a decade of the Workers' Party in power, a party whose political power has recently emerged from the "urban" lower middle classes (Baiocchi, 2003). How could this huge amalgam of citizens living in poverty possibly have weighed to another orientation of the political scene? To what extent does the public know of their thoughts and versions if their media outlets are not part of *Brazil's* media ecology?

Apart from this pressing historical and political backgrounds of Brazil, other questions on politicization and counter-hegemony stem from elsewhere, while studies approach other issues (Robinson et al., 2017). Harvey (2012:163) reviewed cases in which citizens mobilize against corporate-coordinate enterprises, which make life in the city hostage to private developments and neoliberal organisations. Sassen (2008:338) saw digital networks replacing the concept of *state authority*. The former destabilizes the latter thanks to intense digital contention, as in Brazil, which could happen to connect the poor periphery and the influential center. This same kind of urban politicization is still consonant with movements against the militarization of the city in Graham (2011), and with what Young (2001) argued on the necessity for bolder instruments of inclusion in contemporary democracies, where "formal deliberation is not enough."

Therefore, authorship can also transcend the issue of "territory" if the legitimacy of the lived experience can make itself present in other media ecologies. What I call "politicization" of the periphery in this book has much of a "historical repair" that media producers have sought with their content. As opposed to that, I would see the permanence of the charitable discourses as leading to an otherwise limited perception of the periphery. Whereas the dwellers have been limited to appear as beneficiaries of donations and aid, they can recover their agency. It is not to state that forms of charity cannot be political (as in Paulo Freire, for instance). It means to reverse a trend that has led disadvantaged citizens to avoid confrontation (i.e. apart from the temporary settings of protests, activism). I do not mean to suggest that concepts such as *deliberation* are at odds with that of *protest, activism,* or *contention,* neither do I use them as synonyms (see Mendonça & Ercan, 2013). By using politicization, instead, my intention is to unite these different forms of coverage to defend the end of a "silence" that supposedly surrounds the periphery. Otherwise, these different notions of how one adds up to democracy can be articulated as to find autonomy and confrontation as the ultimate resource to establish a new record of political action.

In summary, I have organized these opportunities to the "peripheral media" around key challenges posed to the periphery. Either from history, from the state, or from the mainstream media. Politicization can mean the improvement in *community organisation* (Festa & Silva, 1986; Martín-Barbero, 2008; Woitowicz, 2009), a better *feedback to political institutions and the state* (Abreu, 2006; Porto, 2012), and new *adjustments of representation* (Young, 2011). Also, I saw the improvement as *civic practices* (Sassen, 2008; Harvey, 2012, 15; Holston, 2014; Maricato et al., 2015), and as pursuing the *diversity of frames* (Amaral, 1994; Porto, 2007) as alternative scenarios that result from further politicization. This book concentrates on the *adjustments of representations, the diversity of frames and the feedback to political organisations* as forms of politicization with which I could better engage by looking at the discourse of the periphery. Furthermore, a contribution to this literature would be to observe how these aspects appeared in non-disruptive fashion, that is, apart from protest upheaval, to find in a real and sustainable discourse, perhaps continuous, structured, and reproducible enough to forge a long-term dialogue, if not influence, with the media, the state, and the mainstream of Brazilian society.

Therefore, this book seeks to understand the peripheral media as this mix of socially committed, innovative, and authored action based on the Internet to produce a long-standing agenda against inequality, shared among the periphery and addressed to the power holders mentioned herein. Based on this framework, the next chapters observe frames that follow this pattern of politicization, to the extent that it is possible to contrast them with this past of charitable discourses about the periphery, which has become the dominant reading of communities. The extent to which the periphery can now raise their stakes and politicize the debate on inequality in Brazil enables another perception of its contribution to the broader media environment.

CONCLUSION

In this chapter, I have presented a theoretical framework that grounds this book's interest in understanding the peripheral media. I offered a critical overview of the "periphery" as a concept that not only underpins poverty, but also features deep references to inequality in the country. I also discussed how the periphery appears as a concept articulated in different locations and by different interlocutors. The first one is inclined to present the periphery as a less important part of the city, which is covered in prejudice and a lack of public services. The second one has the periphery represented by *favela* communities, which have also been featured in a set of media representations. Third, the periphery appears as a mainstream media creation, whether to promote charitable initiatives or to idealize the life in the *favelas* through feature films. Fourth, the periphery is known because its dwellers depend on the state and are a stage for populist politicians.

In all these scenarios, I contend that there are some opportunities to reverse these perceptions into more confrontational discourses, which I define as *politicization.* I discussed some of the scenarios in which the peripheral media could weigh in to change the discourse on inequality and increase the participation of the peripheral media producers as political actors. I discuss the feedback to political institutions, the diversity of frames, the adjustment of representation as some of these ways to dismantle the hegemonic consensus around inequality, as these three topics can also advance the understanding of the peripheral media as a realm apart. The idea was to contrast this politicization with softer instances that still place the periphery as a passive agent. In the next chapter, I start this book's exploration by looking at the urban constitution of the periphery.

NOTES

1. This is Brazil Mulher's first cover. In the *Cartografia dos Direitos Humanos*, or the "Human Rights Cartography," a project sponsored by the University of São Paulo, Brasil Mulher appears as the first feminist newspaper ever published in the country, as one also finds interviews with some of the participants. More about this initiative and this newspaper can be found in the following website at http://www.cartografiadh.iea.usp.br/jornal-brasil-mulher/. Accessed 02 February 2018.

2. In Portuguese, "A Não Declarada Guerra na Visão de um Favelado."

3. Article initially published in NGO outlet *Redes da Maré*: "Favelado: What's this?" available at http://redesdamare.org.br/blog/noticias/artigo-favelado-afinal-o-que-e-isso/. Accessed 10 July 2016.

4. The Internet access in favelas can vary according to some studies. Neri (2012) saw favelas with access indices of 90% of Internet access from 24% previously reported. As this study from Brazil's FGV confirms at http://www.cps.fgv.br/cps/bd/mid2012/MID_texto_principal.pdf. Accessed 10 March 2016.

5. Based on the following literature: Straubhaar (1984, 1991); Amaral & Guimarães (1994); Sinclair (2002) Fox & Waisbord (2002); Porto (1998, 2007); Matos (2008); Thussu (2008) (Paiva et al., 2015).

6. See Ivanova & Mardones (2014) for more on the concept of 'telecharity,' as applied in the Chilean reality.

7. Globo TV has consistently developed programs with the intent of gathering more language and aesthetics of the Brazilian urban periphery. One of these examples comes with the "Central da Periferia," presented by host Regina Casé, who has developed a frequent narrative of interacting with the lower classes, using their discourse and trying to mirror their interests.

8. Looking at Brazil's mainstream press, one senses different approaches for classes, for instance, many stories reporting on new habits, and new environments that now receive the "new middle class" some of which may sound as ordinary as the access of this part of population to airports or shopping malls. Yet, as a barometer for the reduction of inequality, it may have sensed a break from the old order, as a deep social inequality has banned certain populations from such spaces. An example is at this story published by newspaper Folha de S. Paulo at http://www1.folha.uol.com.br/fsp/mercado/me1909201002.htm. Accessed 06 July 2016.

9. For example, I considered the appropriation of the hunger issue during the 2014 presidential election, which saw, the Workers' Party using the image of a family around a table looking at empty dishes. As still seen on Youtube at https://www.youtube.com/watch?v=UiNabwXjbd0. Accessed 12 December 2016.

10. Because race, gender, and poverty intersect in many of Brazil demographic studies, therefore improving economic class may improve the visibility of such groups, as narrated by Telles (2015) also in Reis & Schwartzman (2012).

Chapter Two

In the City

In this chapter, I start by debating evidence that shows how patterns of discourse explained earlier can change in the peripheral media. For instance, contemporary media producers reacting to the old prejudices against the poor, but in nuanced ways. By reassessing the urban settings of inequality in Brazil, I do not intend to question or analyze complex issues such as gentrification or the dynamics of street-level protest, but I aim for highlighting that these topics have made producers' coverage to the extent that they assume bolder politicization of such visible and invisible urban divides. They stretch or dismantle old sayings that involve the so-called "elite's perceptions," touching upon sensitive topics such as the "invasion of the poor," and other racial-economic stereotypes that many studies have debated at length (Reis, 1999, 2000; Nascimento et al., 2008). It is true that the idea of "citizen journalism" has likened one's ability to "witnessing" and reporting as a form of journalism or "collective" reporting that have become clearer in the "digital age" (Couldry, 2000; Baroni, 2012; Allan, 2013). Here, I follow this same meaning but focusing on the degree to which this act of witnessing becomes or is meant as "escalating" stories and issues based on new terms or the reframing of old ones, such as *segregation.* As far as this book does not invest any further in the complexity embedded in such taxonomy, this chapter can discuss the uses and appropriations as other purposes of a broader politicization.

Besides this "citizen journalism" framework, I must acknowledge the effort of past empirical research, especially in Kucinski (1991) and in Woitowicz (2009), where we find other purposes of Brazil's alternative journalists. For example, that of contrasting the life of the poor against the life of the rich, in the sense of comparing, relating, which has appeared as a recurrent discursive strategy that also base other studies (Tilly, 2001). In fact, much of

Brazil's discussion on inequality emerges from this notion of *contrast* with what the "rich" has, but which stretches up to what is forbidden to the poor. What one sees in recent peripheral media is a continuation of this contrast, found in verbiage that privileges encounter and relationships more than the contrast of one category against the other. There are descriptions that range from the slavery time (*senzala*, *quilombo*), from which vocabulary is often "recycled" to illustrate conditions faced in the present. Other languages meet terms that are already in the public knowledge, which satisfy an intent to describe housing issues and precariousness (*barraco,* or shack) or to exaggerate the places where the rich live to suggest its inaccessibility (*mansão*, *VIP*). To explore how producers have departed from these rustic, spontaneous ways to bridge an otherwise sophisticated knowledge of the city and to link them using statistical grounds, I deepen in this duality between past verbiage versus its contemporary, online usage.

Later in this chapter, I also flesh out other variations of this discussion, based on the result of the frame analysis. An urban *encounter* has become a counterhegemonic act to the extent that the marginalized citizen can use their own physical presence to test the effects of attending te so-called middle-class spaces. Producers have published pieces that effectively show mainstream prejudices "live," making use of new sources of content (CCTV footage is one of them) to stress the occurrence of such episodes which used to be much more subjective and hard to probe. This situation happens, for instance, during the *rolezinho* row, that is, the censorship about the presence of young, black/brown students in middle-class shopping malls. I take on contemporary theoreticians of the city, in Brazil and elsewhere (Sasken, 2008; Harvey, 2012; Maricato et al., 2015), to discover how latent symptoms of these divides can be transformed into real stories of inequality. I start by reflecting on the issue of access to the city as a major topic for producers.

DISCUSSING THE LACK OF ACCESS TO THE CITY

The first paradigm to appear at stake in the peripheral media lies in the city's accessibility for the disadvantaged. Producers have advocated for the right to be part of the mainstream city and against the conception of restricted space (*centro*, *bairro de rico*, expressions meaning the "neighbourhood of the rich"). Producers have developed a series of content to show how concerned some peripheral dwellers are, to the extent of walking in their neighborhood without being a police target. Another aspect lies in their understanding of how unequal is the permanent "occupation" of the city. Particularly, they questioned the profile of each neighborhood's households and how this directly relates to what they call the "expulsion" of the marginalized or of the poor from the center due to gentrification. Third, producers then aimed to raise the awareness on the increasing loss of public spaces, wherein the disadvantaged could express themselves. They have drawn on the importance of skate or hip-hop practitioners as key components for the peripheral expression, a fact that complements past studies on this practice (Weller, 2000; Pereira, 2005).[1] I explore these three aspects in the following sections.

Segregation, Gentrification, and Marginal Expression

During the interviews, I have questioned producers on the value of the city for their coverage and on the origins of their interest to what happens "downtown." These answers could shed light on the degree to which their discourse reflects the overall "politicization" of the city, or otherwise, an entity from which they expect solidarity and harmonious relations. The fact that they showed complete awareness of the bureaucratic dynamic behind the city development shows that they are well positioned to publish data as their raw material. Moreover, they have confirmed that much of this knowledge stems from a longstanding interest in covering urbanization issues—not only because the "poor tend to live in hills, distant neighbourhoods," but also in the name of those who live in the center, whom the unequal real estate market affects at most, resulting in the eviction of low-income families from the city's center. Producers were especially keen to approach the situation involving beachfront quarters and areas with good public transportation links, in which eviction is happening more quickly. The italics are mine:

> The city is built and rebuilt during all times. Whether by the hands of politicians, by the hand of real estate developers, or by builders, one rebuilds the city all the time. The people in these [peripheral] environments also go rebuilding things. They come down from the *hill*; they live in the *baixada*;[2] they want to have their space; they want to show they are there. They do it in many ways, they do it in tattoos, skate, and these are urban elements, and this is what is pulling us to them. There are a lot of things going on, a lot of urban activity, and we think they have to have a space for this, for registering this. (Media producer 22)

As seen above, the way in which expressions such as the *hill* or *morro* defined both poverty and marginality reveals a common intent to rehabilitate terms and expressions that do not find space at the mainstream media level. Producers have said to consciously turn to this vocabulary because they aim at having a positive aspect of suburbia. When questioned on the reasons for such discourse, they argued that they had no other way of improving the perception of peripheral communities amid mainstream interlocutors if they do not employ such terms. At the same time, they mentioned that this issue of vocabulary that is flagrantly "peripheral" is also problematic, as it might lead to their "classification" as of the periphery and cause other image issues where the job market is concerned. This producer has discussed these aspects of the coverage:

> One of the most interesting things in our coverage and in our involvement over the years is to understand why many of them [inhabitants of the periphery] are out of [the] job market, totally out. Why? Because the fact they live where they do makes it unfeasible for someone to trust in them. Therefore, they are not only marginalised, but at the margins of the job market, and of any possibility of emerging to a job that is dignifying and not an *enslaver* one. (Media producer 42)

This rediscovery of new terms was just the beginning for a wider development of materials that vowed to put the periphery at the forefront. Their goal was *visibility* in a way that could lay bare the *real* relationships between the "disadvantaged" and the mainstream society. The notion of visibility has had a role since the 1980s' cultural expression, with much of cultural groups also embodying many kinds of political expression in Latin America, whether we see them as cultural collectives and artistic manifestations or as media outlets and journalists (Dagnino, 2004; Lugo-Ocando, 2008). What becomes clearer from this evidence is the extent to which the issue of visibility gets more organized and data-anchored as opposed to the use of affective vocabulary, a key resource in the past.

The *Rio on Watch* website, for example, created the *Map of Racial Segregation* of Rio de Janeiro as to put up numbers that, for them, was the ultimate way of showing inequality. High-income neighborhoods have become the target of denouncements that involved intersectional inequality, an issue that some producers have seen as a problem of wealthier neighborhoods, where they point to multiple cases of class-based racism. Due to the highly contrasting number of dwellers in upper-class areas who were white with a residual number of those who are non-white, this outlet found that framing this divide as *segregation* could help to call more attention to the issue, even though this term has literally another meaning.[3] They defended this term as conveying the sentiment existing amid the majority black or brown population: that they were banned from such places.

In a similar stance, producers saw that this frame allowed a broader movement of calling for affordable homes. For them, contrasting different areas, mapping them, their whiteness, and using the 'who lives where' frame were opportunities to ensure that public resources could do more than meet private interests. The access of the disadvantaged who want to live in the city center is a right in its own, they argue, and therefore, it is a central thing for their reporting. This producer justified the many stories of gentrification they covered in the period:

> You see families, you see elder people, you see children, it's different. The central issue in an unequal society is the housing issue. The city is thought [about] according to the real estate interests, by gentrifying areas, and we see the struggle for housing as a central thing. (Media producer 12)

Far from deepening in the gentrification issue, which is far more complex than these opinions can demonstrate, my intention is to show that "gentrification" has become part of a *politicized* perspective. More than the full concept of "gentrifying," what I aim to show here is that, even though not a fully perceived phenomenon in Brazil,[4] and hardly a popular agenda, it is key for producers have defined what is up to their coverage or not. This producer gave a definition of gentrification tied to unequal real estate development and to the state of inequality in general:

> The city hall had a project for a certain area. It was a gentrifying project because it wanted to raise the [land] value. After realising that they could come to face eviction, we started recording [a film]. When we got this 'edital' [public funds], we realised we had a lot of material to talk about the beachfront [homeless] people, but those were things that we did with no need of people giving us money to, and this kind of idea was crossing a lot with other things. (Media producer 12)

Many producers with whom I spoke mentioned the *Ocupe Estelita* as one of the most successful activist events in the late 2010s. This movement has involved not only the right to inhabit, but the right "to see" the city. Its struggle specifically fought for "public space" in a broader perspective. The protest started when a group of real estate developers had received authorization to demolish a group of historic warehouses in Recife's historical center. The Heritage Department has granted the permit, which would allow companies to raise a new set of skyscrapers that would destroy the city's century-old vistas. The project came as a demonstration of the power of developers over the local government. Some producers have credited themselves as the ones to make this issue visible in the national media, pointing to the silence of the southeast-based media on the issue:

> The best example of this, which for me was shocking, was the *Ocupe Estelita*. That was a fantastic experience. We had national-level artists, in a more comprehensive way than the 'independent' media [from São Paulo]. Of course, they would not have a representative in Recife, or someone who would produce

quality material over there. That is a clear limit. That's why, overall, I thought their participation very small during the *Ocupe Estelita*. (Media producer 13)

Less visible than the *Ocupe Estelita*, but an older struggle, was the struggle for the city as a site of cultural production. As I mentioned earlier, the cultural side of politics in Brazil demands a much deeper approach due to the long heritage of social media movements as culture promoters (Dagnino, 1994; Vinelli, 2010). From what I discussed with producers, their focus comes down as innovative because it can not only reconnect with this trajectory of "popular shows," "popular concerts" that have served as instruments for solidarity, as it systematizes current issues around their organizations (collectives, fan groups), "covering" their experiences based on their occupation of the city and the extent to which their artistic expression has to be respected in the law. Producers touch upon a tradition of "streets that speak," i.e. graffiti, skate, and hip-hop at forefront. Many appreciate these artistic expressions and the location where they take place as an immaterial good (Pardue, 2004; Souza, 2007; Oliven, 2013). Therefore, producers refer with surprise to the fact that such heavy bureaucratics can surround and constrain this world of free expression, as this producer told:

> Our intention is to give a space for these people and we see that their effort is huge. For example, we cover an activity called 'Graffiti collective'; therefore, we choose a community to cover and then we only talk about that specific community, just that periphery [. . .] The fact [that] we can give them a voice and take them from obscurity and this contact with the periphery is what motivates us most. Our outlet is mainly turned to the hip-hop culture and if we are not down there with them, there is no sense of having this space, if it is not to give voice to these people. (Media producer 21)

On the other hand, this supportive coverage of cultural collectives protesting gentrification had also a side role in stopping associations of this youth with crime. Movements against gentrification tend to be the same ones which battle other prohibitions. City hall administrations have, many times, revoked authorizations on the grounds of the danger offered by these cultural practices. Peripheral media producers showed further interest in exposing these prohibitions, especially when directed at groups associated with marginal practices, or because the mainstream society links personal attitudes and wardrobes with those of criminals. We find an example of this coverage when the city hall decided to forbid the so-called *Duel of MCs*:

> BELO HORIZONTE MUNICIPALITY CHARGES 33 THOUSAND REALS PER YEAR FOR HOSTING THE MCS' DUEL, EVEN [WHEN] IT [IS] TAKING PLACE IN PUBLIC SPACE: An arbitrary development comes boycotting

> important events for urban culture and hip-hop in Belo Horizonte. Since 2007, the Família de Rua collective was 'de boa' [in good will] promoting its beautiful weekly gatherings, the MCs' duel and the Família de Rua of Skate, under the Santa Tereza Viaduct, with no trouble or damage [to] the city. (*Mídia Periférica*, 30/03/2014)

Thus, favoring this cultural *marginality* implies covering artistic demonstrations that are not unanimously accepted among mainstream society, such as graffiti, but here producers have taken a step beyond by looking at these practices by asserting their importance. While Brazilians encourage most artistic interventions on walls and in public spaces (Caldeira, 2000, 2012)—and street art paintings, if authorized—another form of graffiti consists of *tagging* buildings, façades, and monuments called *pichação*.[5] As a contentious practice, tagging is punishable by law in Brazil, although anthropologists see it as a cultural manifestation that holds legitimate grounds (Pereira, 2005). Producers argued that their take on *tagging* aims to bring back the debate on what is art, seeking to distance it from what society perceives as *vandalism* of public monuments and buildings.

Reports found on the website *Viva Favela* tried to frame *graffiti* as a family-orientated, artistic intervention on public walls, with photos of children practising it and an overall peaceful environment surrounding the artists. For producers, the purpose is to bring practices such as *graffiti* closer to a common narrative, making it look less as *pichação* or *tagging* and more as trivial, urban artistic practice. This counter-representation of such practices so one could dismantle the association with crime was also to include *hip-hop*, *skate*, and other music genres from the periphery, such as the *funk*. Their discourse has appeared to follow the anti-capitalist culture of the alternative media in Brazil (Becker, 2009b), as producers were keen on "non-corporate" urban culture. Here, to promote social justice is to develop a mutually understandable language that reaches the poorest string of the population:

> We are concerned with marginalised stories, both in the mainstream media and in society. We see social movements, the marginalised culture, or the housing issue. We seek to portray issues that are not visible in the mainstream media. Our true need is for a narrative. The one used [in the mainstream] is not the one with which we can feel represented. We think that these people are agents and they have no voice in the mainstream media. (Media producer 07)

If not only about the mainstream and the alternative or the center versus the periphery, the three aspects visited here—namely, segregation, gentrification, and the marginalization of disadvantaged culture—I reviewed *encounters* that put to test a few myths of extreme scarcity or wealth, such as *mansão*, the VIP mansion where the rich lived. On the other hand, important agendas, such as racial prejudice, gentrification and cultural policy, have continued on producers' repertoire in a more sophisticated way; this time, it documented the concentrated wealth and its inherited relationship with whiteness in some neighborhoods, and backed by data and studies. I move now from discussing how this process of re-framing takes into account collective causes and practices (*tagging, gentrification*) to seeing how they turn to the case of sole disadvantaged individuals that live on the margins.

From Collective to Individual Marginalization

Apart from the "big issues" visited in the last section, most producers have worked with other agendas. They firmly believed in the freedom of citizens to stand on their own in squares, parks and public locations, for example, as individuals should not suffer from the (other) consequences of being poor or marginalized. This producer illustrated the discrimination that those who do not take "proper" jobs face (in the sense of respectful, fairly paid). These are the profiles that one sees too much of in any Brazilian city, but which society refuses to accept:

> What would the world be if everybody could have the right of recognition? What are you going to publicise? 'I am the guy who sells water in the streets. I am the traffic light performer, this is what I want to be and to show off.' (Media producer 41)

Based on other passages in which similar issues are discussed, this "right of recognition" translates as not having to give "the voice" these individuals need regarding several issues, such as capitalism, neoliberalism, and "oppression" (as in Couldry, 2010), as the *format* of this voice has appeared as a pressing condition. To "promote voice" is to escape the "aseptic" tone of professional journalism, which appears for them as ignoring such professions or individuals that do not conform to the acceptable. Debates on the nature of professional journalism have addressed the many constraints one finds (Aldridge & Evetts, 2003). However, it is more productive to focus on the extent of this tension that stems from complying with such code. For instance, Rodríguez (2001) saw the Peruvian indigenous elaborating their presence on TV by changing their wardrobe while reading "the news" in *their* language on live TV. In short, there has been an issue regarding the standard in which the alternative media producers will be producing their content.

At the same time, while not deepening in the professional vs amateur dilemma (Platon & Deuze, 2003; Deuze, 2003), I could see that the image of an "amateur" or otherwise has not been embedded in producers' self-description. Moreover, it does not relate, as an identity, to any point in specific in relation to this context of politicization discussed here. I am also aware that the topic of "identity" can be much complex and tied to a number of other ways in the Brazilian context, particularly when concerning the demonstration of citizenship (Cogo, 2004). On the other hand, no relationship is found between producers' language with the contemporary, global sense of *identity* politics, especially in a "redistributive" sense, i.e. giving each one a role or a time to speak (e.g. as in Fraser, 2009).

What I found was a general orientation to identity in respect to one's position amid inequality. How disadvantaged or privileged one could be—that being the identity mentioned on websites and social media. One producer said that their purpose is not tied to any particular "culture," neither did they claim it was this individual in the city that was part of a culture of "theirs." Their purpose lay in naming populations by their "marginal status." There are "personal attributes" that link these individuals to the context of the city they inhabit, and their focus was on connecting these individuals' names and "civil" identities, i.e. name, date of birth, to images of streets, bridges and squares. Eventually, producers re-state that individual's place of origin. In sum, that *is* the place where one dwells. This relationship refers much to the case of the numerous homeless population of São Paulo and to the violent repression of these individuals' presence in the urban fabric; in a scenario where a mass of rambling crack drug smokers, homelessness is only one of the issues affecting this population (Brandão & Conceição, 2017).

To another extent, this sort of coverage is ambiguous because it aims to prioritize the completeness of individuals for who they *are* in their supposedly "natural" state, but one cannot ignore their incompleteness due to the lack of essential aid from the state. This ambiguity is present in the work by *SP Invisível*, which started as a *Tumblr* blog. The page features deeply personalized profiles of the São Paulo homeless population, telling the life stories of these individuals and illustrating them through fine photographic essays. *SP Invisível*, which translates as "Invisible São Paulo," has also set up an *Instagram* account that boasted more than 40,000 followers. On the home page, one reads: "My name is Julio, I am forty years old." One reads details of the life of these individuals, in which they appear with their meals, caring for their stray dogs, and pulling their trolleys, most of them filled with recyclable materials collected in the streets and later sold to cooperatives.[6]

Such proximity with the homeless population intrigues and, before one could see voyeurism, one can also consider the detailed descriptions and *care* from producers for what they see. It includes calling hawkers and beggars by their names and *personalizing* their appearance in the streets by creating customized maps with the name of these individuals (e.g. this is John's street, because that individual lives there), in a way that the population could recognize them as human beings as well as their locations. To wrap up this case, this outlet tied-up the precarious life of many with their locations in the city in a way that is easily identifiable by many who read these outlet's social media profiles and websites.

This personalization of the homeless has also led to other consequences, such as the appropriation of the topic by mainstream entertainment productions,[7] but producers argued that their kind of media boost works as a beneficial thing for these individuals. At one level, it stands out from mainstream coverage because the usual professional reporting does not give homeless people the "correct kind of publicity," which is much more focused on those who can afford to "give interviews, pick up the phone, write emails, have pictures of oneself, in brief, those who "have a story." At another level, the "correct" kind of publicity would be one that engages with the latter purpose of "removing any degree of incommunicability," as these producers have confirmed:

> What we look forward to in this reporting is [to share] what we usually talk among other independent communication outlets. If we are discussing groups of historically oppressed people, the so-called 'minorities,' it is not worth going to them, writing a story, then offering a written analysis by me or by another producer, and then describing their issues. We understand we are there to listen, to give voice; the video has no off narration, it is all about people speaking, interviews, so we search for it. (Media producer 49)

> We used to say we don't want to be the guitar, we want to be the amplifier; it is something like this. (Media producer 07)

This discourse becomes similar to that of the alternative press of the 1970s in the way of displaying a similar intention of revealing street-based inequality in the most honest, relatable form. While not entirely engaged with the same ethics of the oppressed reviewed in the introductory chapters, I can still assert that part of the peripheral media producers with whom I talked had mostly cited leftist magazines as their foremost references:

> When we were journalism students and had some involvement with the leftist militancy, this was very straightforward. We ended up having contact with magazines such as *Caros Amigos*, *Carta Capital*, and *Le Monde* in Brazil, which are critical outlets. And, after getting to know a lot of people in São Paulo who experienced that [dictatorship], I started to understand what the militant media in Brazil are, as a way of saying, also [I got to know] the background of dictatorship, the fight against being clandestine, and all hardship [. . .]. (Media producer 15)

Whereas the evidence says that little influence from the alternative press exists, producers' contemporary concern with the "individual marginal" appears in more thoughtful and well-designed format than in the past. These are stories that also break into new agendas and new understandings of a diverse periphery. This report revealed a protest on the *Baixada Fluminense*, a low-income region of Greater Rio de Janeiro, calling for no homophobia in the community:

> Baixada reacts to homophobia with a kiss-in
>
> Around 500 people, among them straight and homosexual couples, group of friends, 'traditional' families were at the Skate square, in Nova Iguaçu, on Friday (16/1) to participate in the Solidary Kiss-in Against Homophobia. The intention of this 'kiss-in' event was to protest against an episode of intolerance in the beginning of the month, when a homosexual young man was attacked. (*Viva Favela*, 19/01/2015)

In the above example, a single case of homophobia led the community to unite for a "kiss-in" protest. In fact, as many producers have argued, "being poor" or as staying "on the margins" are no longer the only angle available for them, while richer, more complex pictures are possible if one looks at the wider landscape of the peripheral media. Precisely, it was about having skate-riders and gays congregating in the same area where the mainstream media have just framed as that of low-incomers. Likewise, there is no such frame like that of the "victims from the system," which was much used in the 1970s (Kucinski, 1991). Rather, producers tended to frame themselves through morale-boosting slangs (e.g. *o cara,* or *the one*), where the greater interest for the individual habits reaches other aspects of one's life (being gay, being homeless, being 'whoever you want,' live the way they want) as long as they are able to do it *in* the city. Even though no membership is refused, whether into social movements, unions, clubs, collectives—one must forge a place for such subjectivities to grow more visible than before.

In this section, I explored the enrichment of the dialogue on urban inequality in Brazil. I focus next on the content published on the websites and their frames that point to the same direction. The frame analysis revealed other angles of these struggles, as I explain the notion of *urban encounters* in which producers have narrated issues, but whenever they go away from friendly dialogue, they end up touching on events of far serious consequences. Parallel to this section's discussion on the different modes in which disadvantaged populations appear in the city (collective vs individual, oppressed vs new subjectivities), I clarify the extent to which these periphery-center dialogues can be framed to offer new proofs of persecution in semi-public areas. As producers try to communicate with mainstream society, they also debate issues the latter's refuse to accept them on their own grounds. That negotiation occurs when reporting "squatting" (or "occupations"), for instance. To what extent do such politicized frames convince the mainstream that there is class prejudice and what could be the political gains of such coverage or what are the drawbacks central to this book's argument.

TRANSFORMING URBAN ENCOUNTERS INTO CLASS DISCUSSIONS

In the peripheral media, contentious episodes in the city have arisen in two distinct kinds of narratives. On the one hand, tensions appear from clashes between the middle class and peripheral dwellers, even though both share the same habits and cross with each other at locations that might be considered for the rich, but where the poor also started to go. On the other hand, a minor part of the coverage turns to reconciliation and calls for community union. This book does not focus on crime and the deep implications for Brazilian reality as well as the ties with inequality, and yet the evidence has led to show how pro-active producers were regarding disappearances and assassinations, some of which end up finding no justice mostly due to inequality. I have gathered two examples of headlines that point to that direction in their coverage:

> Rio de Janeiro: The map of disappearances (*Agência Pública*, 07/03/2014)

> Those who should provide security and ensure the law are those to break the law in favour of an elitist society. (*Mídia Periférica*, 17/04/2015)

While I do not argue that urban encounters only exist through the perspective of violence, producers saw in it a way to *politicize* that speaks to a broader public. Such stories have triggered enormous mainstream media attention, as producers have built on this to stretch, recreate and prolong repercussions that have stemmed from any "viral" scene of inequality. On one side, communities appear as getting together to achieve common goals and overcome the issues or when *favelas* receive visitors and where tourists are welcome amid insecurity. On the other side, other *urban encounters* include class divides and cases of intolerance against the poorest. I highlight a story that mixes a positive view of the Olympics with a demonstration of the community's long-standing self-esteem:

> The favela is hand on with the paint: Since Rio de Janeiro has been announced as the host of the 2016 Olympic Games, the concern in housekeeping to receive

> athletes, journalists, and tourists has taken place. Favelas, as a part of the city in need to look prettier, safe, and organised, is receiving special care from the public administrators and private sponsors, and even from international sponsors. For specialists, one needs to take care so [that] the Olympic legacy be real and effective, as all cariocas deserve. (*Viva Favela*, 04/01/2015)

In fact, considering that the Olympics was such a polarizing event in Brazil at that time, there was also a substantial effort in pacifying and promoting understanding in a moment when inequality was on display to the whole world. I mean lavish stadia that co-existed with precarious dwellings a few meters away. Only for a brief moment that producers downplayed the real degree of interactions or impeded relationships between the marginalized and the wealthier parts of society in exchange of less confrontation. However, most coverage in this period was still related to *tensions* that emerged between the privileged and the underprivileged, on which I should extend this discussion.

Different from the mainstream media, these outlets were attentive to sensitizing on the urban inequality that manifested in the everyday. Producers have shown the intrinsic tension between an elite's event versus a banned majority, who could not afford to attend the world-class stadia and other events. The next sections expose the perspective of this challenger citizen in a broader way, with protests and traffic disruption as part of a routine that also involve the police acting against dissenters. In a second part, and in more peaceful settings, it is the portrait of groups of underprivileged youth making it through their difficulties to ensure they can walk or *hang* around in monitored spaces. These cases have been motivated by the creation of a specific vocabulary, which also denote fear, clashes and persecution.

Protests, Vandals, and Arrastões

Earlier, I highlighted the strong words that echoed from producers' repertoire while others got another meaning, such as *segregation*. In this section, I expand this vocabulary to analyze how the words *extermínio* (extermination), *massacre*, and *ditadura* (dictatorship) were applied interchangeably to episodes of police responses to protests and their extreme use of armed force against disadvantaged individuals. In 2013, the collective *Nigeria* covered a series of protests staged in the city of Fortaleza, creating a short-length video about the action of the police in these demonstrations. The group's interpretation dwells on who provokes whom: if the rubber bullets shot at the demonstrators or the presence of dissenters on the streets. The camera close-up is on the face of activists, some of them appear scared or wounded, while the policemen look at them from a distance. Ultra-radical groups, the *Black*

Blocks are punk-like individuals dressed in black, who used to wreck bank branches and shops. These groups are not important for their narrative, as *Nigeria*'s main point connects distinguishing their action from those of peaceful protestors. The police, though, choose not to do so, according to their narrative.

By titling this video reportage *Vandalismo* or vandalism, the group has re-incorporated the language of society to accuse it of pushing for more violence. Most protests covered by this media group fought for an improvement of precarious public services, showed anger at the state of corruption, and shouted against the unnecessary 2014 World Cup. The group insisted that if it was the overall economic crisis that was generating more poverty and inequality, the authorities should be "punished," not the protesters. The same kind of dialogue with violence and the roots of violence happens in *Defensorxs,* a long-length film (Figure 2.1). In this production, *Nigeria* sets out to explore Brazil's immense countryside in the perspective of public prosecutors. They interview some of these civil servants, as some of whom have fought the law system and armed land owners to guarantee the right of populations under risk in remote cities in the Amazon and elsewhere.

However, what interests me in *Vandalismo* is the degree to which their frames also relate to the access to the city by the marginalized, while in *Defensorxs* there is the opposite, the issue is the small possibility of the state reaching out to remote corners. Comparing these scenes to recent international protests that had also claimed to speak on behalf of a marginalized majority, such as the Occupy Wall Street (Gitlin, 2013; Kidd, 2014), there is some similarity on the way producers have been united to claim a major overturn of the rules that have allowed the perpetuation of a disinterested, monopolizer, and unfair establishment. This is especially true with regards to the politicization of the everyday disruption, the presence of protestors/media producers amid the temporary chaos staged on the streets.

Figure 2.1. Footage of Defensorxs by Nigeria (2016).

Some ambiguity lies in what concerns the aims of both actors. First, producers have not totally engaged with "activism," but with profiling, filming, staying in the locations they portray. Secondly, instead of the impossibility of peaceful encounters between state agents and demonstrators, producers' discourses pointed to the belief in an efficient state that is still to come. In the sense of investing in challenging the repressive state, which is understood as intolerant to *their* presence, producers focused on what are actually "poor people occupying the streets." Alas, the language of *vandals* has itself official roots, as it is the way in which the authorities have usually referred to demonstrators in the past (Conde & Jazeel, 2013). In any case, as seen in the first section, the *intent* of showing persecution, fear and the overall concerns of peripheral dwellers is what drives the dwellers' appropriation of this language to express their wishes to be seen at the heart of the city.

This similar mingling of protests, violence and the reversal of vocabulary also happened during the coverage of the policies aimed at preventing the *arrastões*. This word is a slang for petty crimes committed on Rio de Janeiro's beaches, when a band of robbers act simultaneously to take sunbathers' belongings. According to the general population, this series of crimes are associated with young black *favelados* or the "typical" *favela* dweller. Still in 2013, in an attempt to stop *arrastões*, Rio's police authorities introduced checkpoints aimed at preventing poor and young *favela* dwellers, the "traditional" suspects, from reaching the beach. This deliberately racist policy, which employed the violence argument to justify banning the *favela* population from Rio's most popular and accessible leisure activity, received contrasting coverages from the portal *Rio on Watch*'s report and from Rio's biggest daily, *O Globo,* which here comes as an example:

> Anger in the north zone at the security response to the *arrastões*. [. . .] Educator and community photographer Léo Lima, from Jacarezinho, wrote on Facebook after sharing the story: 'This news is unbelievable! Its name is racism, for those who think this [issue] is over. This is called a divided city, the public space becoming elitist.' (*Rio on Watch*, 30/11/2013)

> Buses heading towards the south zone beaches will be stopped by the police." (*O Globo*, 22/11/2013)

As far as these measures have clear classist connotations, they resonate in the media and among the population. Authors approach it as a sort of military "punishment" historically applied to this population (Penglase, 2007; Wacquant, 2013). I would like to highlight that the peripheral media coverage has unprecedently set the ground for denouncing them in real time. While *Rio on Watch*'s coverage valued the reactions to this controversial measure, gathering community commentators, scientists, and data to argue against it, the *O Globo* newspaper developed its coverage on the grounds of traditional journalism. That means that, quoting Rio's Secretary of Security at the top of the story and offering the potential discriminatory implications as a secondary element. The newspaper has missed questioning the police on the racial implications of the checkpoints and mapping their impact on the marginalized. For media producers, that police procedure was unacceptable regardless of the existing background of robbery, as it would inevitably link to each citizen's skin and their *favela* address.

Both coverages of *arrastões* and the *vandalism* politicized these events by using a vast range of new implications. While not offering a plea for peace, producers prioritized state violence above confronting the violence started by citizens. In other words, disrupting protests should not serve as justification to maintain poor dwellers' unequal status in public areas such as the beaches. Without proper remediation of the risk of increasing inequality, there would be no legitimacy for the so-called preventive "measures." Slowly, peripheral outlets were redefining the violence perpetrated by the police as another major *crime*, as this story published by *Coletivo Papo Reto* attests to:

> Case Eduardo de Jesus, we from *Coletivo Papo Reto*:
>
> We consider this as a criminal murder, the verdict that appoints 'legitimate defence' as the response for the cruel and brutal extermination of the young Eduardo de Jesus, 10 years old, murdered on the 2nd of April, at his home's door, with a shot at his nape and at his back, at the *Complexo do Alemão*. (29/11/2016)

Another example is found at *Brasil 247*, which employed irony and metaphors to headline the developments: "Poor, and *favelado*? Not on my beach."[8] Below this title, one could spot images of the police operation, with the focus on young boys lined up in front of a bus, making it into a dramatic angle, not seen at the mainstream media level. Even if this outlet follows a certain tradition of radical framing of its headlines, as in British tabloids, it is not possible to assume its images of violence take on an exaggerated tone. Brazilian broad TV programs have daily broadcasted violence any time, occasionally using sensationalism and displaying graphic images (Montoro, 2002). The absence of such elements can arguably make this imagery much more powerful and serious to the average spectator. Instead of "order," official violence is deemed as deliberate murder.

The differential that I saw in these weeks of coverage in the peripheral media does not stem from responding to "sensationalist violence" with more sensationalism. It is, rather, the engagement with the negative narrative portrayal of the media but as a way to appeal for the re-birth of its critical consciousness. First, because producers refused to limit the violence coverage to a range of "appropriate" times, whereas such coverage appears compressed in a few minutes of television coverage. Instead, producers have channelled these images continuously in social media feeds, without the control of the spectator (e.g. whether of language or escalation). Producers have perceived that if they hijacked this apparently uncontrolled stream of violence, there could emerge an opportunity to appropriate this ubiquitous imagery, but giving the spectators such unrestricted dose, as to raise another form of awareness towards the saturation and then awakening for such tragic facts happening every day.

Secondly, the peripheral media do respond to mainstream banalization by returning to the discourse of *oppression*—much like the alternative press of the 1970s. Yet, in the latter's sense, one finds that violence was meant to sound like a consequence of capitalism (Sodré, 1998). Here, the unsettling content aims at showing that an otherwise *peaceful* population is corrupted and destroyed by consented violence. According to this framing strategy, some citizens (poor, black, from the periphery) are targeted to suffer persecution, where others try to live up to normality and the status quo. This politicization by contrasting, drawn between groups that live so close to each other, does not stop at Rio de Janeiro or Fortaleza, but is an overall tactic seen in a similar case in São Paulo.

The Case of the Rolezinhos

The so-called *rolezinhos* or *hangouts* caused much controversy in 2013 and 2014. This happened when a group of *black* or *pardo* (brown) male youngsters decided to hang out together in shopping malls. It is a spontaneous kind of meeting that has happened in other cities around Brazil,[9] but the sudden presence of groups formed by ten to fifteen young boys in a São Paulo shopping mall led administrators to call the police, fearing lootings and obstruction of public circulation. The dispute ended up in court,[10] as shopping mall representatives argued that the presence of this youth compromised security and affected its customers. Further episodes led to violence, as the police made use of rubber bullets to push these youngsters out.[11] Human rights advocates argued the racial and class roots of the controversy, as shop owners were acting based on prejudice against the youth's imagined "dangerous" behavior.[12] While these facts were in debate across alternative and mainstream media, the repressive actions taken against these groups became *viral* through blogs as CCTV footage emerged. It showed security guards employing violence to break up group encounters. Nevertheless, these meetings continued to pop up on social networks.

There could exist an inclination to liken these shopping malls and common areas to "spaces of citizenship," in which young people may talk rights and accessibility. Especially in the *favelas,* the exercise of these informal episodes of conversation amidst disadvantaged youth can be dangerous and targeted by the police (Holston, 2009). However, I would not associate the access to shopping malls to young people necessarily trying to exercise citizenship, the essential point here continues to be the access to public spaces and how producers aim to politicize this issue. Indeed, producers explored the fact that quality public spaces are non-existent in the periphery, as the center offers limited spaces for the public gatherings of young people with far-reaching consequences for their development (Caldeira, 2000; Pinheiro-Machado & Scalco, 2014). But participant youngsters, rather, recorded the *rolezinhos* to a broader purpose that did not appear to connect with any civic reason or socially-committed enough to sound as *politicized.*

On the other hand, producers seemed aware *how* popular these meetings were appearing nationally, partly thanks to mainstream publicity, as far as they were sharpening their frames after the news circulated. Broadcasted *rolezinhos* via social media seized the national agenda once mainstream society reacted against it through a judicial dispute. Newspaper *Brasil 247* headlined "Veto over the *rolezinho* consecrates the Brazilian apartheid" and illustrated the story with an image of police officers escorting brown young men up to the exit of a shopping mall. As seen earlier in the case of the *arrastões*, in which the use of strong vocabulary such as *extermination* became widespread, here, the use of *apartheid* sought a powerful frame for the persecution against the *rolezinhos*. Having accepted the apparently consumerist, leisure and inoffensive purposes of the *rolezinhos*, the peripheral media concluded that the inequality was the real factor, as the fear from the middle class for the group of brown or black young men hanging out together had demonstrated. Publications asserted this in multiple headlines:

> Rolezinhos raise questions about inequality in Brazil. (*Brasil 247*, 18/10/2014)
>
> Brazil's rolezinhos: Shopping as a social inclusion agent. (*Rio on Watch*, 16/10/2014)

The period of coverage also revealed other divides, that of supporting mall-goers versus criticizing them for their "superficial" behavior. To the contrasting tone of both mass media coverage and alternative media coverage, data have indicated a permanent dispute of meaning, from peaceful to disruptive and vice-versa (Gonçalves, 2014). This research's data allows us to get even closer to perceive a shift from cautious to supportive tone. The mainstream media have somehow accepted what the youth was doing on the shopping malls, but in this sample, it is also possible to see producers strategizing the *rolezinhos* by presenting them as "planned protests" and no longer a spontaneous and uneventful ritual. Meanwhile, mainstream media headlines became more careful about reporting further disturbances, although not exactly supporting the youth in their assumedly leisure intent. The mainstream journalists' discourse legitimized the shop owners' fears, an aspect with motivations that were continuously underlined:

> Youth book meeting through the Internet and wreak havoc in São Paulo shopping mall. (*Folha de S.Paulo*, 08/12/2013)[13]

> Despite recent fights involving the *rolezinhos* in São Paulo, new youth meetings will happen in squares, shopping malls and parks in the next few weeks. (G1, 17/01/2014)[14]

While this is not enough to prove that the mainstream media was against or in favor of the *rolezinhos*, or if it had an *opinion* at all, professional journalism language was clearly not enough to report what was really at stake during the *rolezinhos*. At best, *rolezinhos* were for these reports an ordinary disturbance to "wreak havoc," a hypothesis that ran uncontested in the mainstream media. This initial way of reporting could have led society to support the exaggerated police repression; it is also possible to claim that the versions that spanned from the periphery have softened the public opinion on the repression, moving the episode to the grounds of irony and the right to leisure. As I wrap up both sections next, I discuss the extent to which this episode, along with others in this series of interspersed encounters and tensions, would not have appeared as direct products of the country's inequality if they had happened ten, twenty years ago. I analyzed producers' repertoire to what concerned new ideas about the issue of class prejudice, and contributions for the coverage of urban boundaries, racism, and the alienation of marginalized citizens at the heart of the metropolises.

COVERING CONFLICTS, DE-NORMALIZING CLASS PREJUDICE

During this book's research, Brazil's mainstream society has debated its fear of violence based on real experiences of *arrastões*,[15] the gang robbery on the beach. Since the 2013 protests, the radical actions of the *black blocs* have also provoked fear of vandals,[16] as these groups contributed to a sensation of panic and destruction in many cities across Brazil. It is in this context that the peripheral media producers have worked their frames to reverse what were only the repetition of images involving violence and disturbance, frequently dismissed as part of the routine, to leverage this coverage so it could read as issues of class, race, in sum, of inequality. Importantly for this book, it is to question how new were these challenging stories, particularly to escape binary terms and search for new frames—the good "worker" that lives in the periphery and the "brown or black boy" who is a threat were now basing complex stories.

At the same time, producers ended up introducing other binaries that could change the first ones—e.g. the white "middle class" against the marginalized "black" youth. This repetitive effort gets close to what in social movement framing is called "line of action" (Benford & Snow, 2000), that is, the spreading of terms to reach a further meaning, as we saw in the repetition of terms such as *segregation* and *precariousness* to the point of becoming a common marker to contest the middle-class fears of poverty. In that sense, the studied outlets also differed from past alternative media because the latter vowed to sensitize audiences in a less confrontational way, as many documented examples show, also because the agendas are different (Woitowicz, 2009).

Why does that happen? In Benford and Snow (2000), we find that American movements of the 1970s and 1980s have worked for the "enlargement" of markers and identities: e.g. instead of "black" individuals, you have "black power" as a group. Here, producers have worked similarly to put all stereotypes that directly relate to inequality at the forefront of their publications, i.e. being from the periphery, being a vandal, or personalizing one's homelessness status. Media headlines from the periphery raised the profile of those characters, who were used to be obfuscated in society due to commiseration or prejudice, giving them a new agency—e.g. the peripheral youth that is poor, but who also want to engage in mainstream habits such as going to a shopping center; the vandals who want media recognition; the homeless people who pose for a professional photographic essay. Otherwise, the *rolezinhos* could admittedly represent the conjunction of this performative sociality among boys that, according to them, were not used to go downtown. It is new black youth generation standing up for their rights, based on a new self-confidence, perhaps brought by the affirmative policies of recent governments (Vargas, 2014). In any case, I argue that this counterhegemonic stance is broader than that to the extent that producers have shown an ability to aggregate other agendas along the way (which could involve key issues or not). In any case, what I saw was a number of producers politicized meaning and, consequently, the resonance of these factors.

Their availability to such permanent politicization also informs correlated contexts. For example, in the aftermath of the 2013 protests, expressions such as "voice of the streets" proved to be a common point among scholars that summed up the "crisis of representation," amid a greater discontentment with political parties and institutions (Vieira et al., 2018). On the other hand, this and other jargons came to symbolize that alternative media, activism, and the social justice that stems from the streets were closely tied (Peruzzo, 2013; Holston, 2014; Bastos et al., 2014). Here, I argue that more than taking the "streets," which still sounds like a generic statement, evidences go further than this to reject the idea of *equality* as *availability* that have been assumed in these movements. In other words, to say anything related to the "street" would entail the abolishment of the deep hierarchies that govern the public space in Brazil and to suggest a continuous presence of the population on these debates.

These ideas demand a more complex sense of accountability and adjustment in the longterm. To what concerns this book, the "politicization" found in this evidence is far more detailed and aware of minimum variations in the official discourse. For example, producers have figured out that not all protests and disturbances are treated in the same way, then they demanded that black or brown protesters that were road cutting could be received with the same tolerance that happens when white demonstrators do it. In connection to this point on the nature of claims in Brazilian public exercises of citizenship, Brazil's historian José Murilo de Carvalho (1999:227) has indeed foreseen that a Brazilian model of citizenship could emerge in the future, but only if people's reactions and alignments could fix these different power realities in the detail, and not necessarily by the nature of the conservative state forces or by the arrival of an entire new ideology.

Producers' narration of events has also contributed to reverse what used to be "total normality." They talked "segregation" (or other similarly exaggerated terms such as *genocide*), wrestling with this concept to explain class and race in contemporary Brazil. This takes us to the North American tradition of *racializing* the debate on inequality, the "race coding" issue of the press, as Gilens (1996) argued. Gilens found that reportages on welfare and poverty were inevitably tied to black groups. In this book, producers have approximated from rejecting the depiction of reality if the portrait is always the same. By showing areas in which the poor or blacks could not afford to live, producers changed the objective narrative (non-affordance was no longer the accepted diagnostics of reality) to then call it *segregation*. This use of *segregation* does not refer to any state-sponsored racial policy, as it happened in the United States or South Africa, but is useful to particularize the issue so it makes sense for the broader society.

This departure from the objective reality, taking a generic agenda into a more assertive struggle also involves the reporting of crime and poverty in cities like Rio de Janeiro. The "convenient" criminalization of the poor, the automatic labelling of the *favela* dweller as a criminal by appearance (Valadares, 2005) are now turned to the mainstream society as gestures considered as authoritarian. Even though police might be responding to the damage of commercial facilities (as seen in *Vandalismo*), producers articulate their discourse to demonstrate that this is society's price to pay for their complicity in preventing poor and young beachgoers from reaching the beach (as in the *arrastões*). The fears of persecution felt by the poor and the fear of violence by the middle class are to a greater extent embedded in the same double standards of prejudice that govern Brazilian society.

Framing processes are those to "situate or place relevant sets of actors in time and space and by attributing characteristics to them that suggest specifiable relationships and lines of actions" (Benford & Snow, 2000:632). Following this, producers have, in sum, attempted to *re-organize* the city according to their perceptions of what collective and individual rights are historically neglected. This reorganization is then set to unveil society's racist bias by situating it as backward and Brazil as a delayed society. As seen earlier, the maps of "segregation" reads highly desirable areas as zones of exclusion, and ultimately, of disinterest. In another way, the increasing number of "invasions" or *squatting* in abandoned estates in central, often expensive, neighborhoods come up as a "necessary" routine so as to forge a debate on proper housing. Whether legally or not, producers do not see squatting as "disproportionate," but for them, the "greatest" violence is to deny constitutionally-enshrined rights, as it has been for decades (De Souza, 2006).

As said, while this book does not wish to reflect on the causes of such urban phenomena, it is not possible to ignore that this series of mediated clashes connects with other studies that put housing issues as a contemporary priority (e.g. in Harvey, 2012:75 on real estate development). So, it is not a surprise that the peripheral media have included them in their "feedback to political institutions," by having their say against the Mayor's decisions about real estate. The most innovative aspect, nonetheless, is one on forging creativity amidst the impossible living conditions of the cities. Producers have skipped discussing the reasons that may have led someone to be homeless, but they delved into something beyond, such as one's past of rejection due to sexual orientation, or into the economic factor that will generate homelessness. This investigation reaches a point of intersection between both collective and individual dimensions, as producers do make sense of it through culture. They were convinced that the more marginalized is the culture (black, indigenous or mixed-race), the lesser is their ability to express themselves, to see the city as a safe location, be it because of the lack of official recognition or because resources are not allocated for that purpose.

On the other hand, this attachment to what we call "marginal," as to cultural practice owes to what Dagnino (1994, 1998) saw as a permanent link between culture and the sentiments of citizenships. For her, this "culture as citizenship" movement came along with the "expansion" of citizenship in 1980's South America. Martín-Barbero (2006) discussed the "appropriation of topics" in Latin America. He saw it as a context in which multiple, often chaotic intersections do not structure their narrative priority, otherwise they happen simultaneously (e.g. events that do not need date and time and simply "happen"). Here, producers have shown interest in *rap* or *hip-hop* songs, as in many other cultural collectives, reporting attempts to stage concerts and events at the city's *center*. Behind these attempts, it is a struggle to craft arguments that could resonate more technically, by arguing, for example, that the center was the obvious location because it would cause less "chaos" as attendees could arrive by bus coming from distant peripheries. These are cultural arguments dressed in technical justifications, so they can get any possible alignment with decision-makers.

As Martín-Barbero (2006) still sees it, *mediations* among young people are typical of those discovering the city and, alongside, finding its limitations and problems. Here, it is not only a mediation but an *escalation* of such images by using vocabularies, or simply by reproducing the language of the streets in certain moments, which takes on other kinds of tensions that were previously informal and thought to be *resolved* on the street level. Not only were they not resolved, but such interactions would not have happened due to the lack of this exchange among populations that can meet at previously class-demarked zones or "territories" (Sasken, 2008). Where their underrepresentation in these places becomes *segregation* and evictions are *gentrification*, they open the possibility that other disadvantaged individuals reframe social phenomena at their peril. In sum, they were not meant to necessarily *inform* citizens, but to make them interested in the current struggles.

A final way of seeing this framing strategy stems from what Gitlin (1980) mentioned as the "conditions" met by "producers of meaning" to reach a stage where they could frame reality in their own way. Atton and Hamilton (2008:22–41) reasoned this in the alternative media by citing the higher "expectations" that base this practice. According to them, "To the degree that these derive from bourgeois journalism," there are new angles that are worth exploring. As seen, the "conditions" for reporting both cases confront the real existence of these disturbances to the extent that society has demonstrably shown indifference to their repeal. This assimilation of violence to deal with "deviant" youth would be one of these conditions. A second one happens as mainstream journalism subordinates the violence to the officials' versions of events, thus diminishing the relevance or impact of the victims' claims. For producers, without such tough language, no commitment exists to reform these issues, nor enough attention is paid (via media coverage or discussions sponsored by the establishment) to the underlining issue of inequality.

To summarize this discussion, politicizing what otherwise would be "frictionless and non-disruptive" in the city gets to actualize the perspectives about how the urban encounters of an unequal Brazil really take place. Is this growing tension a symbol of an overall improvement in the access and use of so-called "middle-class," semi-public facilities? Is the role of the peripheral media to lay out class tensions a way of broadening the discussion towards a stronger inequality agenda? One thing has become clear, that the politicization of urban disputes, have not necessarily repeated old radical jargons. Instead, producers sought to keep the discourse of the "oppressed" at minimum, otherwise giving new colors to the generic media jargon "the voice of the streets." There is a fresh start for narratives that publicly shame a repressive state, result of an interplay with the entrenched prejudices of mainstream society. By reapplying prejudicial terms against the society that created them, producers claim to incorporate new assessments of the experience of the periphery when attempting to cross the border towards the "other" city.

CONCLUSION

In this chapter, I started by discussing the peripheral media coverage through its effort to engage and describe urban inequality. Either by drawing on cultural events such as hip-hop or stories of homelessness or by returning their focus to activism and its relation to vandalism, producers explored a wide range of situations: those living far from the center; the youth prevented from going to the beach or the shopping mall due to their poverty and skin color; or those who get to live in the heart of the urban center and who are still criminalized, evicted or made invisible. Frame analysis revealed an attention to collective and individual identities that relate to parts of the city, where it applies to the mainstream society's indifference to inequality. In their repertoire, producers used terms such as *segregation* or *apartheid* to politicize their arguments and enhance their claims. In the next chapter, I continue to discuss similar dilemmas of access and acceptance in the city as they appear in Brazilian *favelas*. We learn how producers have also politicized their demands by challenging old caricatures, unmaking stereotypes and criminal associations that have jeopardized their existence in multiple levels.

NOTES

1. As these practices are growing popular in Brazil, research has developed in the role of street hobbies such as skate to marginalized culture. Weller (2000), for instance, tied Brazil's street culture to German-Turkish rappers in Berlin, as both seem to develop new identities based on their exclusion from mainstream society.

2. Translated literally as "lowlands" from the Portuguese, but which in Brazil has a meaning of *poor suburbia.*

3. I see the use of "segregation" as much influenced by the American scholarship (e.g. Telles, 1992), which have often referred to rules created or enforced by the state to separate populations by racial criteria. Although the periphery has a high majority of black or *pardo* populations, state enforcement of this condition has not been directly enforced, thus "segregation" gets more of a meaning of separation, divide.

4. Gentrification has triggered much analyses in scholarship applied to cities in advance capitalism (Harvey, 2013, for instance), but its existence in Brazil is much controversial. During the years of economic boom, *favelas* were seen as quickly gentrifying largely due to the increase at housing price, displacing part of the old dwellers (Cummings, 2015).

5. Although *pichação* is also seen by ethnographers as a kind of expression and protest against class divisions in its cryptic typos (Souza, 2007), it is a contentious topic in Brazil. In early 2017, the recently elected Mayor of São Paulo, João Dória, has declared the end of tolerance with *pichação* as tagging, but on the other hand, vowing to protect the graffiti as an artistic practice. The borders between both concepts are ambiguous. Further context in this New York Times report. Available at http://www.nytimes.com/2012/01/29/world/americas/at-war-with-sao-paulos-establishment-black-paint-in-hand.html. Accessed 20 January 2015.

6. There are thousands of informal recycling workers who make a living from collecting disposed packages, and other recyclable items from the streets, delivering it to deposits. In 2010, ex-President Lula lobbied to transform the *catadores* in a formal profession. More context in http://ultimosegundo.ig.com.br/politica/voces-me-ensinaram-a-governar-diz-lula-a-catadores-de-papel/n1237893099937.html. Access ed 12 December 2014.

7. One case of personalization of homelessness with the purpose of entertainment was seen in the case of the *mendigato,* which translates as 'the sexy beggar.' Once photographed amid reports of police drug raids or at any other circumstances, the media transformed the image of a white homeless man, Rafael Nunes, possibly crack cocaine user, into the image of a sex symbol. The media would then credit the "Internet" for transforming these individuals in sexual symbols (with hashtags, social media profiles) as reports continuously showed these individuals getting married and leaving the life of the streets. See Brandão & Conceição (2017).

8. "Poor and favelado, not on my beach." Brasil 247. Available at http://www.brasil247.com/pt/247/favela247/197966/"Pobre-e-favelado-Na-minha-praia-não!."htm. Accessed on 30 October 2015.

9. According to mainstream news coverage verified in this book (mostly G1 and Folha), rolezinhos happened first in Minas Gerais in 2013, in the city of Contagem, and in 2014 at the Metro Itaquera shopping mall.

10. "Luxurious shopping mall gets clearance to stop rolezinho." Terra. Available at http://noticias.terra.com.br/brasil/cidades/sp-shopping-de-luxo-obtem-liminar-para-barrar-rolezinho,50be08e1b138341 0VgnVCM10000098cceb0aRCRD.html. Accessed 10 May 2014.

11. As widely reported on key occurrences, especially in São Paulo. "Police use teargas and rubber bullets in action against rolezinho." G1. http://g1.globo.com/sao-paulo/noticia/2014/01/policia-usa-bombas-de-gas-e-balas-de-borracha-em-acao-contra-rolezinho.html. Accessed 03 December 2015.

12. Their concern was based on previous episodes of robbery and looting, as reported at http://www.em.com.br/app/noticia/gerais/2013/08/18/interna_gerais,436663/seguranca-e-reforcada-em-shopping-da-capital-apos-tumulto.shtml. Accessed 03 December 2015.

13. "Shopping in São Paulo suffers arrastão after 6000 youngsters have invaded the place" at http://www1.folha.uol.com.br/cotidiano/2013/12/1382637-shopping-em-sp-sofre-arrastao-apos-6000-jovens-invadirem-o-local.shtml. Accessed 05 December 2015.

14. "During rolezinho, we only steal the girls' attention." G1. Available at http://g1.globo.com/sao-paulo/noticia/2014/01/rolezinho-so-tem-roubo-da-atencao-das-gatas-diz-participante-em-post.html. Accessed on 05 December 2015.

15. "Arrastões and robbery raise fear among dwellers and tourists in Rio de Janeiro" at http://g1.globo.com/hora1/noticia/2015/09/arrastoes-e-assaltos-assustam-moradores-e-turistas-no-rj.html. Accessed 20 December 2015.

16. Brazil's black blocs have also attracted the attention of the international press for their destructive action on the streets of cities like São Paulo as this report on CNN portrays. "Brazil Blocs" http://edition.cnn.com/2014/06/02/sport/football/football-brazil-black-blocs/. Accessed on 20 December 2015.

Chapter Three

In the *Favelas*

In the last chapter, I listed many episodes of urban clashes and the coverage that they received in the peripheral media, revealing a set of discursive strategies that producers used to transform the meaning of existing inequalities. There were old tensions which producers escalated by including race issues, disruptive protests, and homelessness. I dedicate this chapter to a similar kind of exploration. I consider the amount of issues and findings that address the distinctiveness of life in the *favelas,* a big periphery in itself. I study outlets reporting directly from these communities.

Digital media outlets have surged in the *favelas* after the 2000s, thanks to their young ICT-user population, as many studies have brought up (Bugs, 2014; Nemer, 2015). In the past chapter I worked with the notion of *encounters* to look at the trajectory of class conflicts in Brazil, here this concept is less emphasized due to the isolation of the *favelas,* which do not feature that many number of *encounters.* At the same time, other details of the everyday life in these communities emerge, to the extent that dwellers use their personal, social or economic constraints to tell stories and get allies. There are a few case studies on the partnerships established between the *favela* and external actors (Davis, 2015; Baroni, 2012, 2015; Custódio, 2016). Yet, it is still possible to investigate native forms of politicization through the media that has involved responses to issues that mostly affect *favela* dwellers, such as crime threats, and rights violations (Penglase, 2007; Leu, 2004).

To ease the understanding of these specific challenges, I opted to call by "*favela* media" the sub-type of the peripheral media that lists all these issues. The fact that there are taxonomies and responses that refer to the topography of the *favela* justifies an entire chapter that could give proper space to frames and discussions that do not exist or apply elsewhere. A first section is dedicated to the reconstruction of a new *favela*, an idea that stems from the unmaking of the stereotype of "troublemaker" that still burdens the younger dwellers. I found producers seeking contributors who would help them to fight against decades of marginalization and association with crime, as known (Pires, 2004). The second section discusses the use of terms such as *apartheid,* a feature also seen in the last chapter. Such politicized frames have added personal features to victims of inequality and opened their perceptions, in which they inform this book regarding the current advances, as well as the longstanding opportunities for the *favela* media producer.

DEFINING A NEW AGENDA FOR THE *FAVELA* IN THE MEDIA

I have sought to position the interviews with the *favela* media producers in a way to offer a view on what they have done to respond to the media-driven conceptions of themselves. This forging of a new agenda for inequality in these communities, which include aspects that take on their own personality, matters to what I call "politicized" frames. It is important to say that the category *favela* citizen still appeared as elusive and simplistic as earlier argued (Valladares, 2000). Distinct in profile, educational background and age, producers have presented a repertoire that could be divided into different categories and interests. I selected two patterns that naturally spring from their agenda. First, it corresponds to their behavior as journalists, writers, photographers or dwellers; secondly, it derives from their collaborations with the mainstream media and the latter's influence. I look at how these actors end up guiding them and the public through topics and discussions that mirror the contemporary *favela.*

This duality in and out of the community is because most producers have to respond to both universes, the *favela* and the rest of society. Long-standing eyewitnesses of conflicts, drug dealing and urbanization issues, the media producers, as dwellers themselves, have taken on their affiliations, education profiles, or engagements with NGOs or other organizations to produce content that can sensitize, but also entertain, educate, unite. Some mention "*o morro,*" or *the hill*, as well as the *favela*. Others prefer to refer to it as the *comunidade* (community). Based on these general references, I explore these two stages of the communicative *favela*. I first analyze how facts from long ago still matter to build new discourses—e.g. evictions, demolitions, or scarcity of water or food, in sum, agendas seen before (Valladares, 1978). On the second step, I analyze the extent to which a younger generation negotiates with external partners their credentials to the outer world, from troublemakers or unemployed into a new *favelado*, a dominant term that may sound derogatory, but which increasingly gets a new resonance.

Taking Back Control of the Facts

Most *favela* producers with whom I spoke have indeed prioritized the precarious state of public services. For that reason, covering the lack of running water, the infrequent litter collection, or the everyday electricity outage were issues that were at the top. At the same time, there is a degree of ambiguity in those who acknowledged these issues: They did know and spread the issues, but they also did prioritize the "positive, growing" *favela*, as they said they did not want to appear as second-class citizens. Although they were skeptical about short-term changes in the reproduction of their images as dependents on the state, they struggle in skipping these issues in their publications. In any case, producers encompassed a sentiment that their role is to make sure the community does not fall into political populism anymore. Politicians have, for decades, used the urbanization of the *favelas* for empty promises, as we find examples in different periods (Pino, 1997; Fischer, 2008), therefore it is crucial that quality of life remains in the agenda, even though there is pressure to involve with broader subjects belonging to the Brazilian political realm.

While this book does not focus on production, producers have pointed to their aim to decentralize their sources for stories and, from that, to create a joint discourse of micro and macro politics. Editors said they are guided by the inputs from dwellers, yet the formers are the ones to make the final cut and frame issues according to current debates:

> We have contributors who write articles, who are often ordinary dwellers, teachers, and agents from our community who want to write about anything. Then we open the space for these people, so that they can send us [articles]; this also allows the newspaper to have different views. (Media producer 36)

> The person who proposes the stories for the newspaper is the same person who writes the story. For example, when we have more stories than space on paper, we check similar stories, the people who proposed it and try to make the people work together. In meetings, we always have a cut. [If one needs to] speak about public service and we [have] already approached the [topic of] transportation, the issue of sewage, the issue of education [. . .] These meetings are interesting because each one has a viewpoint and each one [is in a different] territory, each one with a difference and they gather together in this project. (Media producer 35)

There lies a sentiment of *solidarity*, whether in relation to the indifference from the mainstream or to the need to generate new success stories. In that sense, to *politicize* the *favela* is to take all kinds of demands to the "outer world," like this producer/dweller argued for a collective effort:

> If you talk to anyone in the *favela*, you will see this ideology in their mouth. 'Everyone has to rise up together; I like my community; I don't want to leave my community; I want my community growing less unequal.' (Media producer 41)

I interpret the "I don't want to leave my community" as part of an ongoing recognition of the limits that divide the *favela* from the *asfalto*, the urbanized city center. These limits are, for instance, those to stop dwellers from seeing themselves as "marginalised," as they want the *favela* to look good because "people now know where it is." They feel uneasy if "outer" people, in mainstream society, see them as receivers of government benefits, as proper recognition would mean seeing them not because they live in the *favela*. Having said this, their need to politicize inequality to a public level of recognition meets other types of socio-cultural necessities. Producers are eager to change the image that defines their place, because they want the people to know that their community is more than a "dangerous" place, as these testimonials show:

> We are concerned with *the marginalised* stories in the mainstream media, as they [the media] are in mainstream society—that means, in social movements, the issue of *marginalised* culture, the occupations for housing issues. We try to portray these issues that have no visibility in the mainstream media. We do not relate to this often-used narrative. And we think that the people are agents *who have no voice* in the mainstream media. (Media producer 49)

> In *Baixada Fluminense*, for example, we have many cultural movements, many *saraus* [*public readings*] which happen in public squares. I think it would be very nice for the [mainstream] media to broadcast it *for everybody*, so that when they have the chance of being in Rio de Janeiro, they could visit the *Baixada Fluminense* with another sort of view. Otherwise, the media states 'Do not go there, it's *dangerous*.' (Media producer 47)

In other words, more than politicizing the basic needs of healthcare or education, some producers have also sought to gather support for receiving new visitors, which would help to normalize the *favela*. Knowing how "indifferent" mainstream society can be towards *them*, a broader consciousness could come from external recognition. In fact, there is a slight detachment from a tradition of internal mobilization that amounts to the 1970s' alternative press. While the "alternative media" has had links with social movements and "proletarian" associations (Jameson, 1988), and with both they developed very straightforward wills (Kucinski, 1991), interviewed *favela* dwellers their mission as a broader one; they do not subordinate their action to that of the organizations working close to them. While seeing oneself as an individual, they preferred to call this level of collaboration with aid agencies and similar bodies as *partnership*, as this producer argued:

> Educators, teachers, unions. These are the points that have a broader reach to their classes, as far as they also reach students, schools, and libraries. Thus, we thought that these are important ones to receive our content. They can spread more didactically, each one in its own way, what we want to share. For example, regarding social movements, we aim to get close to its base. On social movements, we become aware because of these exchanges between them and us—i.e. the student unions and the regular unions. (Media producer 36)

Understanding how the *favela* media producers form their audience and "crowdsource" their content is important because it informs on collaboration and on discourse. Achieving strong politicization, for them, depends on what kind of content resonates better among their audience, and the way they can reach these partners and prominent actors involved in this struggle. Producers want to be at a strategic position, so they can inform prominent journalists, commentators, and influencers with fresh angles of the local disputes and forward to their emails unseen images of conflicts. I shall develop more later on this "insider" role for their politicization, but to what concerns their views, they saw themselves as interacting with a broad range of audiences, from students to social movements, from communities to individuals, all of whom are not necessarily media consumers, but can engage with their content. By doing so, these groups scape the typical poverty stereotype, especially because they do not subscribe into the representation that has been common of their isolation and stillness (Cardoso, 1978; Rosas-Moreno & Straubhaar, 2015).

Therefore, the reversal of stereotypical representations is not necessarily one of "appearing" good on TV or in the media. Most of producers seemed more comfortable about sharing news and content from the backstage than at forefront of reports. Selecting trustworthy partners seems more important than promoting themselves indiscriminately. Framing critical issues (such as crime episodes, insecurity, and economic constraints) must thus carefully acknowledge the people's material deprivation and fragility, but also make sure that this reporting does not constrain further relationships with "external partners," and as a result, provoke more prejudice against the community or frustrate the former to the point of indifference. The way in which producers seemed to execute this delicate approach to the content of their own was to focus more on conquering "rights":

> In the communities we visit, the idea of wealth is arguable. I think the people want to access several rights. This is what they deny us on a constant basis. It is the right to own a house, the right of being black, of being a woman and not being raped, of being a worker. (Media producer 42)

I approached *where* these external contacts are from to find out that many of them are tourists, visitors or foreigners. A few producers then admitted that they target mainstream commentators by sending emails to their publications. They argued that they differ from most Brazilians, as the latter group does "carry an inherited degree of prejudice." The growth of tourism in *favelas,* a phenomenon better noticed after the 2000s, as well as its "gentrification" (Freire-Medeiros, 2014; Jaguaribe, 2014; Cummings, 2015), has boosted the relationship with foreigners and direct reporting to international NGOs. As Freire-Medeiros (2011) asserted, there are concerns that tourism might create *urban safaris*, but this advent could also help on improving their visibility and overcoming the issue of "prejudice," which seems a keyword in producers' repertoire. On the other hand, would the presence of "outsiders," be that tourists or visitors, constrain producers' liberty to be radical and hinder their counterhegemonic intent? I italicize some hints on what it is like to be *inside* and *outside* the *favela*:

> A lot of people from overseas come into the *favela*. I think that there is a little bit of that idea [of exotic]. Though we never speak about it, people from the *outside* do surround the *favela*. And these people come to set up new relations and this is not that idea of predatory tourism, but it is a relation in which one wants to get to know who lives there, what they do, how they dance—this *exoticised* thing. (Media producer 41)

> We were called to join [other media initiatives that advertise the *favela*] at the City of God *favela*. So, many meetings happened, but our idea is to focus on our community, our territory. (Media producer 36)

In sum, the definition of *outside* or *inside* depends on who has offered strong support to the *favela*. It is against those who are *outside* that they are more likely to rebel against: the case of politicians and members of mainstream society that look at them from afar. A good coverage is the one to tackle this broader level of indifference, either stemming from the locals or foreigners, but one that challenges the image that the *favela* is a place "hard to reach." Although "the rich" may also live close to *favelas*, the perception from producers is that their prejudice is more challenging due to historical reasons. Yet, foreigners (assumedly) would turn up less influenced by the national media and its racial or social prejudices.

When asked on *how* to recreate and change people's "assimilated" image through a new self-representation, the producers said to diversify their news agenda so they ensured a coverage that could sensitize both those *inside* and the *outside* communities:

> We don't need to preach for them [favela dwellers], but I think it is interesting because each individual comes from a different tradition in our group. The hybridism is an interesting thing. That producer has developed a perspective on the state, as he is studying law. To this other producer, who is from the *hip-hop* [culture], he is much more the 'individual,' the rage. For that other one, because she has a university degree, she understands more about social justice. This exchange is positive. (Media producer 42)

This discussion sets the ground for my later incursion into the intent of other forms of politicized coverage, including the one involving crime episodes. I aim to show how producers express some caveats, as much of collective knowledge that exists in *favelas* stems from so-called "assimilated" prejudices of society. The sources for their strategies, some of whom are also their audience (universities, social movements, journalists), will include responses to these real or imagined prejudices as part of their discourse, which resonates a great deal, especially among mainstream actors, tourists, and foreigners alike. These factors are helpful to understand the *politicization* from the *favela* media as this amalgamating effort to place historical demands at the forefront, such as sewage and better public services, but also which turns to partners so producers can reimagine the *favela* together with them, shaping new media representations. In the next section, I invest in this new, normalized portrait of the average *favela* dweller, which, especially, suits the purposes of the youth.

Projecting a New Favelado

When analyzing interview data, I noticed how many young producers have questioned the historical significance of the *favelado* both in the positive and negative senses of the term. They generally vowed to overcome or change that image into a transcendent form of self-representation. I tried to engage with them to understand why this reference seemed so significant. First, it became clear that authors or editors of the digital media outlets were, on average, 20 to 30 years old. Although the age factor was not the basis of this book's framework, it did offer a clue to know why the majority spoke of "inheriting" a stereotype, which seemed otherwise inescapable, perhaps not even a matter of reflection in the past.

This brief retrospect on the *favelado* as a negative stereotype may be commonly recognizable but it never was fully accepted. I found that the younger generation, those in their twenties, have offered another take on the *favelado*, one that springs from its reinvention and had little to do with its hateful origins. They mixed this background of inequality and misrepresentation with their technological fluency to frame a new *favelado* on the grounds of their creative capabilities, as these producers illustrate:

> *Cadu* is one of the colleagues in the group; he's *b-boy*, graffiti artist, DJ—he sings and composes rap songs. I think this expression was already there. Adriano was less [fluent]; he was [performing] dance, that was one part. The part of [teaching them] the media, this was up to us [in terms of] investing in these boys. (Media producer 41)

> Our web-radio happens in São Paulo through collaborators, Junior and Augusto. We hire [some] of the contributors through the Internet, and others through in-person activities. The 'gang' joins in, likes it, wants to join in again and, somehow, who comes together and whoever comes is very welcome. (Media producer 45)

As producers have confirmed in the above testimonials, the way in which *favela* dwellers collaborate to media outlets is a fluid and open process to those who want to join. I do not invest in understanding it as a "subjectivity," neither I draw on this concept further than this. It is known, however, that much of the media images can translate into behavior and vocabulary among the *favela* residents (Felix, 2009). It is to this kind of repetition and appropriation that I refer to in this book. This is how I interpreted the "adventures" of this new *favelado* and how producers have coupled it with other identities of the participants, whether that of media practitioners, bloggers, photographers, or communicators, but also playing with that of builders, plumbers, drivers and so on. In other words, no matter their occupation in the *favela,* producers have spoken about themselves and neighbors or friends as *favelados*. Producers showed that, through charisma, they can overcome old stereotypes, but they do not abandon that a critical appropriation has to be the goal to escape trivialization.

In the newspaper *Voz das Comunidades*, for example, accounts of the *favelado* include their role of insiders during armed conflicts happening at their doorstep. Then, this duality of a "good" *favelado*, the one to inform mainstream media organizations,[1] and the old image of unreliable and marginal have competed in some degree. The young *Rene Silva*, who was born and raised in Alemão Favela, in Rio de Janeiro, embodies this duality. Silva has emerged to prominence through social networks such as *Twitter*, later invited to join a TV *soap opera*, but he also *tweets* images of his native *Alemão Favela* whenever an armed conflict comes up or shots are heard. Silva was also briefly arrested in 2016 because of his reporting in a sealed-off area, and his prison quickly became news and was protested by members of the mainstream media.[2] As Silva, *Monique Evelle* is another producer from the state of Bahia with similar standing in the media, counting with a personal website and curated images of herself.

Although the producers with whom I spoke did not confirm that they are in search of Silva's kind of notoriety, there are elements enough that allow an association between these "networked" youth with a prototype of *favelado*, which has had a good potential of major publicity via the mainstream media. I discuss this relationship with the mainstream media and grassroots reporting in Chapter 5. Here, what interests me is the extent to which this media exposure as *favela* interlocutors has added up to the "assimilated" image and how this boosts a form of politicization. *Favela* researchers such as Beatriz Jaguaribe (2014) have argued on whether the Internet could reduce the overbearing weight of the *favelado* stereotype, as location would no longer affect online interactions. However, from this evidence, it is not clear if that imaginary distance but also proximity between interlocutors remains as an element that is transcended through the online advent, as *favela* dwellers have sought not to abandon their location as a statement over the online presence. Instead, it is staying in the *favela,* disclosing it publicly and at the right moment that one increases or decreases the eyewitness power that a *favelado* might have in the mainstream media.

For example, some producers have suggested that the trustworthiness of their accounts on conflicts in the *favelas* has increased after they started to call themselves *favelado*. Most said to enjoy this title, at least the young range I focused on. It becomes a new normal, regardless the platform on which it is featured: it could be in fictional dramas such as *telenovelas* or in the news media. It helps them in acting as a source for others that report on the state of communities. Often, both dimensions of power, the soft one: the *favelado* as the successful citizen, informer, and the hard one: the "troublemaker," have appeared together. A few producers claimed that the downsides stemmed from contributing as witnesses for the police. They are never accredited for some information they gave, so much so as "the cops will treat you bad anyway." Otherwise, the *favelado* of the media seems relevant, overall, because it publicizes a character known by all. From the remote conception of a *favelado* as a homeless person (Valladares, 2000:23), the new *favelado* is key to promote a common recognition of belonging, even if a troubled one. Many producers do not hesitate in chasing celebrities and posting pictures of themselves alongside TV and film actors, a practice which becomes more emphasized to the extent that these celebrities share any feature (background, ethnicity, trajectory) with them.[3]

Here, I follow studies that have prioritized the ease and inclusiveness of how technologies are appropriated in the periphery (e.g. Horst, 2011), as opposed to expecting only activism and participation from a "networked cohort" (e.g. Loader et al., 2014). Hence, there is a mix of leisure content and other associations, but which serve producers with a position from which they introduce themselves to the "ordinary" citizen from elsewhere in Brazil. This position affects the way they crave for a new status for the old, derogatory *favelado.* Producers end up gathering a set of local and national, "famous" and anonymous, daily or timeless references that attest to their intention to appear cosmopolitan and connected. This content also leaves me close to what authors saw as the role of "social news," meeting a democratic ideal of allowing multiple self-representations to flourish and improving the number of bottom-up spokespersons (as in Goode, 2009). And yet, there is more than these debates suggest. In the long term, this analysis evidences that, besides these usages, producers try to assert themselves in a more coordinated way, deploying expressions and images within a context of a struggle of which all of them have appeared aware. This happened when the YouTube channel of the *Gatomídia* collective published a video about ICT insertion in the *favelas*:

> The *favelado* 2.0 is the girl or guy from the favela who, [without] training resources and not having attended many courses, gets by with the technology [that] comes to him, becoming an expert in mobile applications. The *favelado* 2.0 films, shoots pictures for his or her entertainment, knowledge, and to guarantee rights, whenever the rights of those living in the community are torn apart by some other forces. (*Gatomídia* Youtube)[4]

The fact that this self-broadcast carried the discourse of one being "2.0" ties up narratives of innovation with those of living a harsh reality, which are not new. To "be understood" by a highly demanding and curious audience is a goal and, therefore, producers have to extend the perception of the *favelado* as conveyor of other subjectivities. *Coletivo Papo Reto*'s producer Thainã de Medeiros, for instance, shared scenes from a cinematographic production based in Favela Nova Holanda in Rio de Janeiro. He wrote: "How is the audiovisual production in the *favela*?—I've myself lived this scene." The scenes showed two teenage boys running from what seems to be police persecution on unpaved streets. His reference appeals to both the wider world of professional production and to the *real* conditions in which the piece was made.

This video and Facebook post couples two complementary narratives (the new *favela* media productions and the past remembrance of an innocent being persecuted). At one level, media producers reinterpret their historical muteness; at another, they place new voices at another post-modern level of irony. This new *favelado* can, at the same time, show an awareness of technology and mainstream media productions while revealing their negotiations with the real constraints. An example would be the below producer, who voiced opinions on environmental issues while also seeking to sell this story to a mainstream outlet:

> There are many cases of environmental destruction that happens in our community, which are not shown by the mainstream media. It is the case of corporations such as *Coca-Cola*. There are cases that this company is using, through illegal means, the water of a nature park. They take the water from this park and divert it directly to their factory for production. (Media producer 36)

This attitude is not only about saying who is a *favelado* or to ground one's abilities based on being a *favelado*, but it is also to review the current affairs in a more critical, counterhegemonic light. Moreover, I found a trade-off with the mainstream, where one sees a growing number of partnerships between the *favela* media (which can raise data and statistics, confirming reports *in loco*) and the major mainstream organizations (which can create bigger impact, increase their resonance). In any case, to cite the *favelado* with no derogatory intent, one has to also reveal good figures, showing the hard-working side of its people, as they published:

> While political and economic scenarios go through turbulence, the favela is reinventing its lifestyle. According to a survey by the Data Popular Institute, published in 2013, the GDP of Brazilian favelas reached more than 56 billion reals by year, but the reality is far from being uniform. (*Viva Favela*, 04/01/2015)

I have questioned producers on the nature of these partnerships that cover the *good* favela. Where do they come from? My point concerned not only the role of NGOs as partner of the mass media, but to what affects their politicization. I inquired about the evangelical churches that have been present in these communities, some for decades. The collaboration between churches, trade unions, and "grassroots" organizations is not a new factor for mobilization (Alves, 1984), where one has seen the prominence of the Catholic Church in this direction. The extent to which evangelical churches could play a different role from other religious organizations remains an important factor to consider for this book's look at politicization, having the evangelicals conquer a power in Brazil's media environment, owning a TV broadcast network and several radio stations, and often engaging in contentious issues (Kramer, 2005; Birman & Lehman, 1999).

Are these churches and their media structure beneficial for a local notion of politicizing the everyday life? By offering technology access and financial or educational support to ordinary dwellers, pastors can form popular media producers. A few producers argued that, in return, these churches are indeed channelling producers' ambitions to fulfil their own religious goals. The extent to which this youth can continue to pursue a socially committed but critical perspective of reality in their publications was in doubt. The presence of a few members of religious organizations has divided interviewees. One producer answered by offering the example of the so-called "Neo-Pentecostal churches":

> There are those who are not up to this [i.e. fighting social issues by discussing inequality]. I think that it is in the religious field in which we see some clash [with this mission]. If we are thinking of it in ideological terms, the way in which evangelical churches play with the issue of jealousy, for example, is very bad. It is hard to work with solidarity in a group, in a community project. (Media producer 41)

I cannot elaborate more on this involvement of evangelical churches, but it is worth remembering the long past partnership between the *favelas*' leadership and the Catholic Church. An example is the *Basis Ecclesiastic Communities* (BECs); in the 1980s, these seemed key to raising the profile of poor communities (Festa & Silva, 1986), but the producers have not cited them at all. Otherwise, they stressed the different purposes of the contemporary evangelical churches. It is not about the media that they may be led to create, but the effects on the youth in general. They gave some examples:

> The financial thing is very much present. They work with the perspective: 'If you donate, you earn it back, but if you donate, don't do it for your neighbour, do it for the church.' In a certain way, this limits the ability of the community's youth to continue the networks that were much more powerful in the past. (Media producer 42)

I could not verify all these claims in every interview. However, international religious NGOs have also appeared as financial bodies for outlets covered in the scope here; the website *Viva Favela*, for instance, acknowledges support from a Norwegian church. On the other hand, this growing interface with evangelical churches echoes recent changes in the demographics of Brazil, a country with a growing evangelical population (Birman & Lehman, 1999). In terms of the politicization of the *favela* media, the fact that religious organizations (like any other) are capitalizing on this communicating will of the *favela* youth creates new opportunities for producers in a more optimistic scenario. We must be careful, likewise, not to discriminate between the kinds of support received—although producers have understandably discussed concerns in these changes in the nature of politicization in the *favela*, whether of sponsorship or in the amount of external attention they recently received.

To sum up this section, evidence has shown the complexities involved in reimagining the *favela* on the grounds of past prejudices and scarcities. The actions of the *favela* media producers span different areas of the community's life, which consequently have become part of their media. I sought to draw an overview on the image of the *favela* and the *favelado* so as to give a clear picture of opportunities to politicize or pacify agendas. I do not intend to settle an expectation of what the *favela* media are or say that these are all the concerns these outlets carry, but producers have certainly shown much will to challenge past stereotypes regarding the *favela*. More than a plural coverage, producers thereby team up to bring publicity to key issues, activities and everyday facts: they end up telling national or international affairs from their perspective or disrupting outdated stereotypes such as that of the *favelado*. Now, I analyze data from the frame analysis that allow us to debate more assertive cases of politicization, in which the above ambiguities regarding the *favelas* are also present.

OLD ISSUES, NEW FRAMES FOR THE POLITICAL *FAVELA*

While the previous section has given a panorama of the contributors and partners of the *favela* media trying to reimagine communities, here I analyze the extent to which the *favela* media has sustained a politicized coverage of its facts than what appears in the past (Kucinski, 1991; Woitowicz, 2009). This coverage reminds readers about the state of deep inequality in the *favelas*. In this section, though, I develop on the way in which new and old facts are remembered, their compliance with the discourse of social justice changes, and the multiple linkages with history contribute to fresh ways of seeing issues that now are no longer acceptable and are in need of further explanation by the authorities.

Amid a varied content, one finds the continuous attempt to reach out to state representatives. Producers admitted using allegations of police violence as one of the ways to call the attention, but there are also other paths, via events tied to *favela* entrepreneurship and celebratory events. Producers seemed sceptical about the possibility of producing *neutral* stories, such as those involving cleaning or public services, which made the research frames about "charity" appear less frequently in my analysis. Below I highlight two examples of a story deemed as "neutral" or under the frame "charity," and another seen as "politicized," which have made the majority of the sample:

> Complaints do not help; it is necessary to do your part. Emlurb collects litter three times a week and, according to the city hall, it reaches remote places. According to Luiz Felipe, the *litter collection service seem*s to be satisfactory. The

> same does not happen with the streets' cleaning. (Frame charity—*Viva Favela*, 20/03/2014)

> Ronald Vaz, a hostage of intimidation through racism. One eliminates and violates the black youth day after day—whether in the periphery via deadly means or in downtown via hostile means, and those who should give us security and ensure the rule of law are also those who violate it in favour of *an elitist society* and who have the profile of *embedded racism*. (Frame politicization—*Mídia Periférica*, 17/04/2015)

A strong correlation appears when we compare the higher recurrence of *politicization* in the outlets that say they follow no professional journalism convention. The case of blogs such as *Mídia Periférica* or *Coletivo Papo Reto* are different from those of the NGO-sponsored *Viva Favela,* with the latter focusing less on criminality issues and more on events taking place at the city's outskirts. Likewise, *Rio on Watch*, another outlet funded by private partners, fits more into the same frame of charity, often telling stories of hardship and success accompanied by analyses and reflections, mostly written by academics and journalists with the occasional partnership with *favela* dwellers.

This correlation is important to understand what drives politicization and what justifies it. The *favela* media is indeed a palette that ranges from the more radical political to a softer, dialogue-orientated narrative, but the extent to which there are narratives that politicize social issues versus those that prefer to prioritize positive aspects seem to follow the structure of each outlet and its potential to attract partners. Some of them have vowed to a certain level of public image that makes their content look milder and curated as opposed to displaying graphic imagery, repeating slangs and non-standard words. The latter is prevalent amidst outlets that are not linked with NGOs or other large institutions. In sum, the more popular and well-funded a website or producer is, the more elements of *charity* and less of *politicization* have appeared in their coverage.

There are exceptions, of course, as well as content that blends both elements. An example would be a well-known *favela* media producer, who has a good space in the mainstream media but who has dedicated his Twitter account to informal explorations that do not lie in any of these frames. His approach to fellow *favela*-based citizens, aimed at knowing who-is-who in the community, how this average citizen lives, and how much he or she earns per month, illustrates this way of approaching citizens with soft language but to bring hard questions. One day, he asked his audience: "To what *class* do you belong to?" This question appeared in the format of a poll on his Twitter account, as follows:

Producer: Your average salary is:
53%—80 to 1,500 reals
18%—1,600 to 2,500 reals
29%—2,600 to 3,500 reals

Producer: Which class do you consider yourself from?
9%—Upper class
41%—Middle class
39%—Low
11%-—Under the low

Reply 1: It is a hard question. I think I was middle class. I have no class at the moment. (Twitter account of media producer 03, 04/01/2015)

I am more inclined to interpret interactions like these as characterizing a kind of candid dialogue framed as *charity*. Yet, would this kind of amicable discussion help to tackle prejudice by confirming a particular dwellers' low income? As seen, it is a distinct form of solidarity that manifests, more pro-active and with a modern language, especially if one compares it to the 1990s' humanitarian focus on saving lives and tackling extreme hunger. This specific participant, above quoted, eventually played with assumptions of income and class by responding: "I have no class at the moment."

At the other edge, politicizing stances also meant serious reassessments of the community's internal settings and demographics, some of them directly aimed at feeding rebellious acts and addressing life-threatening issues. This close presence of criminals and their relationship with ordinary dwellers has been seen as a complex web of interactions that entail living in the "crossfire" (Arias, 2009; Alves & Evanson, 2011). This complexity also appears in moments of crisis and in the positions that producers assume. In this excerpt, bloggers urged dwellers to reconsider their cooperation with the police, likening their potential involvement with officers to being "spies on behalf of criminals," which, in other words, aims to downplay the importance of any collaboration with the officers. According to this stance, dwellers should not film drug dealers at police officers' requests:

1. Monitoring criminals is such a responsibility of the state. The state should take care of criminals, not us. We are a civil society.
2. Criminals are already breaking the law.
3. There is no criminality without help from the police.
4. Efficient security policy is not the one that kills most.[5] (Coletivo Papo Reto, 04/12/2015)

The above evidence attests to an ambiguous intent. On the one hand, dwellers are the "civil society," on the other, they should not help the police. Producers have opposed to collaborate with the mainstream society's military apparatus, due to crimes perpetrated by the formers inside *favela* territory. Even if supporting crime-prevention efforts is frowned upon, the politicization of these dwellers still aims to tackle the *hegemonic* power of the police and neutralize it via dwellers' individual inaction, defining "spying" as the act of "denouncing" a crime.

This approach contrasts radically with the *charity* frames. Overall, this convergence towards politicization is a common impression from the body of evidence discussed in this section. I saw *favelados* fighting for new interlocutions, branding their presence, "showing off" material affordances to gain respect and pursuing attention from mainstream society. Even when this content did not seek to confront anyone, there lied a form of *politicization,* whether by giving names of crime victims to the media or by offering images of their bodies lying on the streets in private *What's App* chats. Sharing such graphic material has seemed a necessary form of exposure, whether to get justice or to establish new alliances with external partners.

These forms of *coverage* have showed how contemporary *favela* dwellers are far from being "hostages of poverty or violence," empowering their discourses to the extent of constructing frames that challenge the traditional news coverage. To the extent that the excess of police presence in *favelas* has compromised the access to basic rights by dwellers of the periphery (Amoroso et al., 2014), producers have seen in the graphic display of violence on mobiles and social networks the easiest way to fight against facts that in the past would have run unnoticed. The fact that this practice may hurt the possibility of having a wider audience (or an audience that is prepared to sharing this content) belongs to a secondary discussion on the appropriateness of this content. I approach a few other sides of this hyper-politicized way of narrating reality.

Speaking as Protagonists, Finding Limitations

The self-confidence that stems from this *new favelado* also reaches other areas of the dwellers' lives, projecting an unprecedented form of leadership. The resurrection of the *favelado* as the new protagonist not only responds to a past in which dwellers could not assume an active role in mediating solutions, as discussed in chapter 2, as it projects a leadership that it is not that candid anymore. I have italicized the key parts of a publication that tells the story of an ordinary dweller that has reached the age of retirement while living and working in a *favela.* I point to some elements and attributions that seem to boost the profile of this dweller based on her real story*:*

> The one thousand faces of Ana Mineira from Carangola: *She came to Rio de Janeiro* to work as a maid and help her aunt, who was living with an ill husband. For decades, she worked and lived in the [employer] families' houses. Over there, *she had the inspiration to create*. 'Sometimes, I was cleaning and had an idea. I stopped to make a note of a poem because sometimes the idea runs away,' she tells us. Once retired, she moved into Maré Favela and started a training course in painting [. . .]. (*Viva Favela*, 06/09/2014)

Although some of the anonymity of the past still exists in part of this discourse, especially with regards to failures of welfare policies, the overall tone is more complex than just a tale of *success*. There is straightforwardness, and positiveness in Ana's life. By contrast, an old model of community leadership would resemble a form of mediation from community leaders, no moral case done. I selected an excerpt from an eviction at Curicica Village:

> Threatened with eviction, residents of the Curicica Union Village are informed that there is no house for everyone. With [regard to] this last-minute announcement, two of the more important resistance individuals couldn't attend. According to residents, the city hall did very little to ensure transparency and send information. Zezinho and Costa used a broken microphone, which made it hard for most people to understand what exactly they said. Although the support from [community leader] Zezinho and the words of Costa as a guarantee, the residents continued to fight for their rights. (*Rio on Watch*, 17/11/2014)

Different from the "guarantees" that Zezinho and Costa seem to offer to fellow residents, what I argue here is that, different from these characters, the new protagonist of the *favela* is less at forefront of these issues, in a physical sense, as far as the 'online' presence is concerned. It is possible to infer that current producers see the latter practice as a more effective way of dealing with the community's issues. It is clear that the nature of the issues has changed as well. It no longer applies only to financial queries, evictions, and public services, but it embeds major agendas as that of racism, sexual minorities, and a subjective form of recognition that is always changing.

The growing involvement of the new *favela* leaders with politics and parliamentary discussions is a telling illustration from micro to macro administrative questions. Particularly popular during this research's period was the possibility of lowering the age according to which an individual is criminally responsible for "serious" crimes such as murder. This law change would specifically affect the *favela* youth, who might be often involved in petty crimes, but then get involved with large gangs, and bear no direct responsibility for the murders and the "serious" crimes. These cases were offered another chance to rehabilitation while in prison. The law change would transform this rehabilitation in a conventional prison term, what would hinder these youth from reintegrating into society afterwards. Many *favela*-based organizations opposed the law change on the grounds that a country that offers no education or opportunity for this youth could not jump straight into punishing them, as this notice said:

> Rapper Fall Classico reinforces that he is against lowering the criminal responsibility age after knowing the reality of the young man who robbed him. (*Mídia Periférica*, 27/04/2015)

The risk of centering at *punishing* the historically marginalized youth has also risked a new re-assimilation of the subaltern condition of the *favelado*. Before as a poor, troubled individual, now a criminal and potentially guilty one. For producers, this constant aim to punish *favela* citizens stems from a pattern unequivocally aligned with the Brazilian history of slavery and discrimination. Drawing on literature that has seen the progressive penalization, criminalization, and militarization of the state toward the poor in Brazil (e.g. Wacquant, 2008), this law change would come as another chapter that would harden the stances in punitive spheres of power, and as result, shatter any chance of return of these citizens to society, where a good job or respect were concerned.

Producers were aware of this broader struggle, especially because they have resorted to anachronistic associations that could cover this recent fact conveying a sense of continuity in the repression and discrimination. They have appealed to remind on Brazil's colonial past by using terms such as *quilombos*. These were hidden settlements that fugitive slaves founded once they had escaped their lord. Here, this term defines precarious homes and relate to dwellers' fears of persecution by the police. To name a meeting location, a media collective, or simply, an event, most producers called it *quilombo* as to raise society's awareness for their seriousness, remembering of their shared isolation from mainstream society. Even though it is a painful reference to the Black slavery past, it helps them to assert the opposite, their position of control over their destiny in modern times. I have italicized some parts of these calls:

> The quilombo talk
>
> Every week, the young communicator invites one activist from the black movement to dialogue about black culture and speak a little bit about a black activist,

enriching our knowledge culture on our predecessors and those who fought for the race recognition. We will post here about all the editions of the interviews (Mídia Periférica, 20/05/2013)

This link to the past also tells us about the present leadership. This role has to do with broadening up the mentality of dwellers by politicizing "history," as well as stretching the borders they can cross, the places they can show themselves in. Many *favela* media outlets referred to the Facebook page, *Favelados pelo Mundo*[6] (or "Favelados around the World"), which is an initiative that gathers qualities visited early in this chapter: the personalization of producers' narratives, the intersection between poverty and sophisticated narratives, and the historical bonds of present exclusions. As context, I position this process in which I credit producers for the creation of a public "personality" of the *favelado* alongside habits, tastes, and routines as one aimed at denouncing a broader reality of oppression, but which also involves some generalizing assumptions on individuals and their subjectivities, similar to what happened with the Afghani girl *Malala* (Rahman, 2014).

In this case, the media outlet started out after a handful of producers had decided to post daily updates on their trips around the world. What would be a travel blog has become an instrument to target the old middle-class stereotype that states that *the poor cannot travel*, which often reads as: *the poor should not travel* (see Nascimento et al., 2008 or Freire-Medeiros, 2013). As their cover image, they placed a stereotyped *favelado*, the poor, black man taking a ride on the rear of an old bus. This picture assembles the portrait of the extreme poverty of those dwellers who used to have no money to pay the bus fare with further cosmopolitan intents. The content of this page shows young *favela* dwellers taking selfies in front of tourist spots and visiting mainstream capitals, such as Paris and New York.

I contend that outlets such as *Favelados pelo Mundo* deliver a coverage of inequality that could fit in as the *charity* frame I analyzed, particularly due to their proposal of crowdsourcing images in peaceful connotations rather than only from crime and disruption. However, they are also focused on the gaps between the poor and the travelling middle class. This imposed *contrast* wrestles with a more subjective kind of hegemony over *favela* citizens. It is the idea that *poverty* is no longer an obstacle to material affordances as such, it does not stop them from living other experiences. They attack the hegemony of deprivation, as well as travelling as the middle-class *rituals.* They seek, instead, to state their knowledge of the world. There is a counterhegemonic intent in the broad intention of this page, but it is undoubtedly politicization that we see. As the *favela* may be the occasional stop for tourists aiming to visit poverty, *favela* dwellers can reverse this relationship by taking the *favela* to mainstream locations.

This example helps me to summarize this section, in which I brought both examples of the bloody, violent struggle against state agents, but also subtler ways to display new affordances and challenging middle-class prejudices. This approach of having "*favelados* around the world" is only a smaller part of a whole frame that connects with the new *favelado 2.0* seen earlier, and to the *rolezinhos* visited in chapter 3. These cases teach us how one can see poverty, inequality, and consumerism placed altogether, but not to establish the socially-accepted associations of affordance and prestige. These adjustments of representation aim, otherwise, to politicize the *favela*'s presence in a number of different ways. I would not say that this is only aimed at showing inequality, as it fights other kinds of stereotypes, impressions, and issues that are also hegemonic. Next, we see that *life* is a recurrent discursive resource that forms a comprehensive repertoire for producers. They strategize their framing by *individualizing* everyday facts and forging a new counter-hegemonic order in which everything in their life has to demonstrate social change. This strategy will be proven particularly powerful when dealing with the murder of *favela* dwellers, which is a fact that used to have little repercussion until recently.

Individualizing Murder and Getting Support

The *politicization* of inequality in the peripheral media has led intimate aspects of one's *life* to come at forefront. As already explored in the interview data, violence is a part of this frame. Available data grounds the concern to one's security as one of the top priorities in the *favela* and a decisive perception to judge one's life experiences. According to *Amnesty International*, in 2014, from the 244 murders by the police in the city of Rio de Janeiro, 68 were in the *favelas*, where mass murders are not rare. In the 1990's case of the 29 dead in *Baixada*, where 11 young men died after a mass shooting in Acari Favela, no one suffered any prosecution. Likewise, 65% of *favela* dwellers have said that they fear police violence.[7] In any case, violence in the *favelas* or in poor areas is hardly a new phenomenon (Vianna, 1990; Huggins, 2000; Huguet & Szabó de Carvalho, 2008; Penglase, 2014), nor should we assume that it is entirely due to the inequality context. To this book's points, producers have politicized this scenario of violence through many other aspects—I would highlight crime under-reporting, the community's fears, and the investigation of crimes practiced in *favelas* as their key concerns.

Whereas not all crimes have appeared on the *favela* media, I found these outlets a handy resource to create more impact. Producers got to transform the reporting of murders by focusing on the victims, their profile, and their personal history. It might seem an obvious tactic, but for decades, murders in the *favela* limits were an event of little significance, in which the press rushed to other stories, while not returning to ask for inquiring into the investigation's outcomes. When producers started to individualize the victims in their reportages at length, whether by printing faces and names on posters or by paying for online posts with provocative messages, this situation has seemed to change. By *individualized*, I mean their relentless focus on the names, biographies and socioeconomic conditions of violence victims. Outlets have mixed a brief log of the victim's past information, to stop the association with the victim with crime, a frequent trick to reduce the importance of the crime, then producers started to link the murders and connect with other similar examples to prove their point on police's negligence. I propose a contrast between this diligent approach with the anonymity that existed in earlier coverage.

I sourced my mainstream examples from the leading portal, *G1*. When reading both the mainstream report and the one from the *favela* outlet, both made use of the same photograph of the victim, though the differences in their discourse are evident. Whereas the former gives a generic headline, the latter presents the crime in straightforward language to include many elements that relate to the identity of the victim. The headlines reveal distinctions in what elements they prioritize, which can epitomize the fundamental differences of the peripheral media and the mainstream media, in these and other cases involving this kind of reporting. I have italicized some of these parts:

> Relatives say the *dead young man* in Babilonia, Rio, was arrested by police officers. (G1, 27/08/2015)

> One more, Clayton da Silva Modesto, *black, poor and favelado*. (*Coletivo Papo Reto*, 27/08/2015)

In another brief comparison with the mainstream media, it is possible to question the criteria of mainstream press reports. I found the *favela* media extending the understanding of every single murder as a *massacre*. The "group" being victim of a *massacre* was not necessarily only the murdered individual, but the whole community that appears as being under attack. In this case, the inappropriateness of past mainstream reports finds a landmark case in the graphic imagery of corpses lying on the floor during the *Carandiru* massacre.[8] Otherwise, by individualizing these crimes and transforming them into a case-by-case approach, the *favela* media producers reversed the angle of the *Carandiru* massacre by forging a greater display of the victims' past and by dwelling on their identities, thus appealing against a perception that crimes against the poor go unpunished, unremembered.

The *Carandiru* case also sheds light on how, at the mainstream media level, no profile of each of the murdered prisoners has mattered enough for their coverage. Twenty-five years later on, Brazilians live with a broad remembrance of the case. Because there has been such overlooking to who were actually the victims from these catastrophic events, the lasting reference to event is the stage of the massacre, the *Carandiru* jail, which the State of São Paulo had demolished in 2002, despite its historical significance as the place where 111 victims lost their lives.

Another example of the same kind of bulk-framing happens in the use of the term *traficantes* (drug dealers) or *presidiários* (prisoners of the judiciary system), which are fine for journalistic reports, but which, again, fail to recognize names, identities, and profiles. The main territory of action for media producers is this vacuum perceived in the mainstream media. Where newspapers have limited their naming of individuals involved in armed conflicts in the *favelas* (where only a handful of drug dealing leaders' names is known), or those wounded during police operations, arrested at police checkpoints, the *favela* media, due to the proximity to these characters, have got closer to the experiences on an individual level, often using first accounts of those involved in such incidents. It is from these ways of reporting that *favela* media designs its approach, not only wishing to make a broader point and improve representation, but taking a strong stance to warn against the violence that still affects dwellers on an everyday basis, as this report has memorialized the aforementioned facts:

> *A decade of anger* in the *Baixada*: 10 years later after the *Baixada massacre*, parents, relatives, and friends of the victims gather to pay tribute. On 31 March 2005, eleven police officers, which were unhappy with the administrative changes in many of their battalions, met in a bar and planned revenge. The murder of 29 people has substantially changed the everyday of the victims' families and the lives of dwellers in *Queimados* and *Nova Iguaçu*. (*Viva Favela*, 04/02/2015)

In 2015, episodes of urban robbery or pickpocketing provoked a reaction from middle-class and urban *vigilantes*, who took revenge on black young men (who then appeared in anonymous videos tied to lighting poles).[9] As the images circulated in the mainstream news portals[10] and on social networks, again, seeking to anonymize the punished individual, the *favela* media outlets sought to denounce the occurrence of such type of cruelty over Brazil, reflexing the fragile position of poor individuals (invariably black or brown) in Brazilian society. During these days, the mainstream coverage was slowly catching up with reports on the criminal attitude of the middle class, although it still did not bear any consideration for the personal identities and lives of the victims.[11]

Without much support in the present state of affairs, media producers once again invested in the comparison with colonial portraits. They collated Debret's[12] painting *Pelourinho* with an anonymous image of the youth attached to the lighting pole. The YouTube video had this young man tied-up to the pole and besides him, there is a woman who tries to help him out. The scene was enough for one to start drawing parallels between past slave punishment and these attacks. They likened the revenge taken on the deviant black youngsters to Brazil's past of punishing fugitive slaves. This frame was particularly powerful, which many commentators on social media argued that it characterizes the revival of a *pelourinho*, the historical slave lashing spot. While the mainstream media have not bought into this idea, this case served to assert—with precision—what producers really aimed for. Either as a vague reporting standard, vague when it involves the disadvantaged, that intentional disassociation links with the generic criteria for the denomination of massacres,[13] where one misses to have a further grasp of the real profile (poor, black or brown) of the victims that figure as central victims from the *criminality* in the country.

A last example of how crime reporting has benefitted from recent tactics of politicization lies in the *Cadê Amarildo?* (Where is Amarildo) controversy. This campaign marked the disappearance of the builder Amarildo de Souza on 14 July 2013 from his neighborhood in the *Rocinha Favela.* This case earned extensive coverage from the *favela* media; it started as an activist campaign but later emerged as stand-alone coverage. In terms of the activist campaign, Amarildo's face became the main illustration on t-shirts and on outdoor signs, carrying discourses that were later the basis of the *favela* media coverage.

The *favela* media had, for weeks, re-published a banner that read: "A builder, father of 6, Rocinha dweller, where is Amarildo?" As the first sentence insists, he is "a builder" and a "*Rocinha* dweller." Part campaign and part coverage, the initiative tried to reconstitute Amarildo's routine and constraints while living in the *favela* until the point of his avoidable death. Producers offered evidence that Amarildo was no drug dealer, but the latest victim of what they saw as a *genocide* targeting black, poor and *favela* dwellers. They also linked this to the failure of the controversial *UPPs*.[14] These police-manned kiosks were installed at the heart of Rio de Janeiro's *favela* hills after successive military campaigns to occupy and restore civil normality. Despite these measures have proposed an approximation between police and the civil population, they were met with much resistance due to the disappearances and murders that continued to happen at communities (Granja, 2009).

Producers have posed an interesting moral dilemma, in which they protested that this apparent "normality" for the mainstream society came at the cost of the *favela* dweller's peace and privacy. Therefore, *politicizing* the *Amarildo* case was, eventually, about challenging the efficacy of these security policies, which, for some dwellers, controlled their lives but did not end violence.

Amarildo's case has triggered coverage that later came to lay bare the subordination of the *favela* dwellers to the permanent control by armed men. In this case, those of the Brazilian Army. They argued that, in the meantime, the city's center ran free. Though I am not drawing more on this tension, it is important to keep in mind these parallel realities—i.e. at the local level, the distrust of police surveillance and, at a major level, the suspicion of the Brazilian judiciary, fuelled by claims that a biased justice system would ignore Amarildo's case. These parallels made a crucial repertoire that led to the politicization of *life* as an instrument to remind the public on the glaring inequality that marks what one understands as "justice" in Brazil. As weeks passed and no news of Amarildo's whereabouts appeared, the *favela* media reporters went further to investigate the conditions in which the family of Amarildo lived. A campaign started to use a picture of his family standing in front of their house in the *favela*. Meanwhile, *favela* outlets continued to cover the daily news of this investigation:

> Amarildo's widow asks: 'Where are the remains?' (*Brasil 247*, 14/07/2015)

Whereas the mainstream media was also covering the case at this stage, international, notorious actors such as Julian Assange joined the campaign by holding signs with the campaign's motto: "Where is Amarildo?"

If one sees the case as a successful networked activism case or as a critique of how inequality affects the population in a wider range of aspects, producers have dwelt in every angle of the case, offering their readings, personalizing it, and individualizing the stories. On the campaign's Facebook page, the historical link has also existed, when producers appropriated tales of Brazil's enslaver past by showing an image of prisoners dragged out by a collar chain, the type of those used for fugitive slaves during colonial times. This continues the anachronistic linkage earlier seen, coupled with the fight against the old anonymization of the victims that became frozen in their condition of subjects to power. Furthermore, video reporters interviewed Amarildo's family members,[15] where peripheral media reporters visited Amarildo's home to use it as a backdrop for a documentary.[16] The material was later broadcasted in Rio de Janeiro's parliament.[17] These multiple linkages with history, life, politics, and affectivity matter to the extent that no similar strategy appears in the past literature on the *favelas*, nor is such a strategy part of the common practice of the alternative media. Would this case have attracted such attention in the mass media if it weren't detached from Amarildo's personality and class?

Contemporary literature on multiple aspects of life in the *favelas* (Perlman, 2010; Penglase, 2014; Jaguaribe, 2014) has set up a clear position of affectivity and group solidarity in daily activities, memorialization, and resistance against external threats. These data contribute to enlighten the case as a rather comprehensive coverage strategy. The frames deployed during the search for Amarildo and for his killers helped the public's perception of "all or nothing" in the everyday routine of the *favela*. By narrating Amarildo's death not as one more, but as *one* individual *less*, the coverage has achieved to make poverty images popular in a context that could receive the support from the majority of the mainstream society, underlining the argument of inequality that exists at multiple levels (judicial, state, and society).

In anticipation to the court verdict, producers' coverage correctly pointed out that the victim was not a specific police target but ended up as such due to the long record of impunity in cases involving the assassination of poor people from the *favelas* like Amarildo. Officers who took part in the torture of Amarildo and the disappearance of his body faced justice,[18] and the state had to pay compensation to his family.[19] In 2018, the murder of the city councillor Marielle Franco has shown the same characteristics of Amarildo's case, the assassination of a woman who had as her main mission to eliminate the underpinning inequality that affects the periphery. The national and international resonance of this case has also drawn much from the mobilization and content that appeared first on the peripheral media.

In the final section of this chapter, I discuss which political opportunities stemmed from these cases. I apply Benford and Snow's (2000) model of political opportunity so as to tie together the range of innovative discourses analyzed here. What do they all mean as a single movement to politicize inequality? I start by looking at many instances to read it as a single attempt to forge and mediatize their everyday struggle, and accordingly, push for politicized discussions on rights and citizenship. The implications from seeing *life* as such prominent element in the *favela* media, and transforming it into dwellers' main weapon, comes down as a risk taken by dwellers, who act against decades of indifference and prejudice from mainstream society.

REFRAMING LIFE IN THE *FAVELA*

Throughout this chapter I showed how little from the tradition that forged the newspaper *A Voz do Morro* (Morel, 1986; Souza & Barbosa, 2005) has remained in the contemporary *favela* media. Consonant to this book's purpose of mapping "politicization," I investigated the extent to which producers approached hardship with soft stories and how they do transform them into politicized frames. If *A Voz do Morro* had become a paradigmatic example of *favela* communication (Morel, 1986), in contemporary Brazil, producers have not hesitated before investing in the "media" in all of its potential for publicity. So, how can we interpret early 21st century's *favela* producers' efforts in a time of massive campaigns and international repercussions? What is the significance of politicizing producers' diversity for the public's understanding of inequality? To understand this change, I have to look at the different context that has surrounded producers. While not immune to the commercial pressure that stems from social media platforms, they are no longer suffering the immediate pressure of having their house demolished,[20] so they are free to, at least, explore new opportunities and change in their media representation, despite ongoing constraints.

What I saw as an appropriation of *life*, either to promote solidarity or to cover actions of community resistance, fit both 'feedback to power' and 'adjustments of representation' ideas of politicization. For instance, Holston (2009, 2009b) investigated how forms of citizenship can resist in places of uneven rule of law and criminality. These "forms of citizenship" have also encapsulated the use of *life*. While the category "citizen" is elusive to a population that still face dire issues, this term had appeared to logically escape the victimization seen in past portraits of *favela* dwellers. In other words, it is about building another portrait of themselves if, in the past, the notion of "citizenship" failed to give them dignity. These news pieces, instead, gave them the case for adjusting their media, socio-political representation. Because many producers appeared proud of their insider's knowledge—of what happens in the *favela*—the digital media have allowed them to frame themselves as "those who are being read, listened to, and then respected." This consciousness draws on both universe of the police and of criminals, as it appears in the thriving media production from these areas (see Mattos Rocha, 2013).

In Benford and Snow (2000:624) we learn that *frame bridging* is part of a strategic process to successfully promote "ideologically congruent but structurally unconnected frames" (Ibid, 2000:624). This process happened in the case of *Amarildo*, as it also explains the *favelado 2.0* or *traveller favelado*, images that stem from the personalization of the life in *favela*. Producers then connected loose facts and traces of contemporary life to a representational system that centered the attention at their primordial condition of *favelado*. In all these cases, frame *bridging* happened in different ways. Firstly, it occurred by bridging the use of ICTs in such a way of displaying new material affordances (the *favelado 2.0*), those which were previously limited to the middle classes in the context of Brazilian inequality. In the case of *Amarildo*, it was the absence of justice for the disadvantaged alongside the difficulties for the poor in paying for prime access of expensive lawyers. The coverage then tried to reverse traditional impunity by bridging a personal tragedy and later transforming it into a new politicized frame.

Furthermore, by claiming that a *new favelado* was born, producers have acknowledged other social issues that stem from the use of frames. For instance, illiteracy, criminalization of poverty (frame amplification), or it linked life stories with skills (frame extension), and "isolated" injustices to become mass causes (frame transformation). To a greater degree, these cases and respective linkages were able to get the awareness of external allies (whether artists or the mainstream media), revealing *favela* dwellers dwelling on the same strategy. Without this, the new *favela* would have hardly echoed so different aspects within a single political strategy, which is the opposite of the old depoliticized lyricism seen in the *Voz do Morro* newspaper. To another degree, normalizing the term *favelado* has also disrupted the hegemonic sense of isolation imposed on them, dwellers felt they were no longer "imprisoned" but their stereotypes (Valladares, 1978), these terms were alive and theirs. The *favela* media have thus confirmed that the citizens can now move across to other parts of the city and around the world (as in the *favelados pelo mundo*).

Having set these two framing paths based on private lives (life as an asset to stop hegemonic discourses and to politicize new frames), the media producers' main aim was to take over the role of the protagonist. This new spokesperson has talked crime, has drawn associations with history and, as an interlocutor, this individual is not afraid of including unpleasant experiences, and to a lesser extent, the facts related to crime and violence. By covering their life but privileging such intimate interfaces in both negative and positive aspects, they dwell on an imaginative, post-materialist aspect observed in other cases involving the South American youth (Blasco & Krausen Hansen, 2006). *Self-designing* life can have profound counterhegemonic impact as it showed the permanent display of both soft and hard aspects of one's expectations: at the same time that it surprises its viewers and broaden their outreach to meet celebrities, it is also about crime and joblessness.

To allow this new radical fluidity, producers vowed to set themselves free from the moderating influence from activists or NGO volunteers, or churches, and even from that of the mainstream media. Both ways of publicizing dwellers' life as an individual resource to show inequality differ from the model of collective "popular newsgathering," that much relied on an equality and communion among citizens (Atton & Hamilton, 2008). The role of the external agents has, none the less, continued as one of "partners," some of which have been present in past case studies (like in Rodríguez, 2001; Davis, 2015;

Custódio, 2017). Through this new individual fluidity, they also explored their "cultural opportunity," which is an important pillar of the concept of political opportunity as a whole (Benford & Snow, 2000:629). Culturally, this fluidity conveys an ability of knowing what no one else does, allowing them to bridge the *particular* way in which the *favelas* understand the facts. This change is disruptive, as said, because no other actor can mediate that on their behalf, and alters a scenario where institutions (NGOs, politicians) or individuals (celebrities, sociologists, priests) have had, literally, more weight than dwellers did in solving their issues (as discussed in the first section). Ultimately, this shift creates an internal dynamic that invites many other dwellers to also "embody the *favela*."

Finally, I associate this fluid way of politicizing the *favela* life with an existing informality that has existed in the *favela* discourse. Segre (2009), for instance, discussed the notions of formal-information contentions in these communities. The point I raise in this chapter is that, where *formal* or *informal* were used to depend on the engagement of institutions and mainstream society or merged with organized activism, now *favela* reporting can call off mundane activities, so images appear together, the pictures of a team lunch or of a corpse can appear consecutively on a Facebook news feed. It is possible to contextualize this fluid *favela* production from an audience-forming perspective (Medrado, 2007), but I would argue that the value of this fluidity resides in the ultimate revitalization of the *favela* toward mainstream society, potentially emerging as a bottom-up consciousness of power.

In any case, many other angles are still available to analyze this nuanced politicization of life in *favelas*. It is possible to understand a practical refusal to accept weeks-long occupation by the state (Granja, 2015), and to engage with new aesthetics of protest in Brazil (Soreanu, 2015), or even choose to compare it to the double standards of the press regarding the *favelas* (Lacerda, 2015). My inclination here is to point out on the centralization around the individual from *favelas*, a pattern that has not only sought the "collective of anonymous people," but had poverty and precariousness confirmed on the basis of the individual experience.

In sum, the *favela* media has first fulfilled a major goal of helping dwellers and outsiders to adjust media representations, brokering with this coverage a more effective feedback to power. And yet, a landmark achievement was to propose a new image for the *favelado,* introducing a new institutional and civic expectation from this actor, perhaps enabling new political aspirations. As *favela* dwellers have recently organized to launch their own political party, they start connecting with black movements and other *favela* dwellers to forge partisan representation.[21] This section's conclusion deserves indeed more development in future research. To what concerns visualizing the "peripheral media" in action, the *favela* media has contributed to the generation of collective frames that deepen and politicize discussions about inequality in Brazil. Other than that, it enabled the action of media producers and *favela* dwellers by blazing the trail with highly politicized discourses and angles that could get further resonance in the media, tested among a vast set of collaborators.

CONCLUSION

This chapter approached two levels of the coverage of the *favela* media producers. Firstly, it presented how producers' discourse has reimagined the *favela* and the *favelado* by revitalizing concepts that fit into a new landscape of ICT access and new material affordances. In the second part, I reviewed evidence to sustain that, by investing in the leadership within the *favela* or by individualizing crime victims, producers shared images of their communities and raised the awareness of their profiles. In these developments, producers have politicized the image of the *favelado* from that of an underestimated and stereotyped "black man of the margins" to that of a citizen that claims rights and protests violence. Then, I analyzed scenarios where peripheral media outlets have shifted their representation into an identity-based model, previously anchored in a historical type of community representation. I defended that by reframing the *favela's* decades-old conflicts with such imaginative self-representations, dwellers emerge as protagonists of their own political narratives. In the next two chapters, I dedicate the analysis of the peripheral media according to its alignment with the discourses of the mainstream media.

NOTES

1. This aspect has appeared clearly in many interviews, but also it is easily identified in mainstream media content when reporting on the favelas.
2. "René Silva is arrested in Alemão," as reported by *O Dia*. Available at https://odia.ig.com.br/_conteudo/rio-de-janeiro/2016-10-01/rene-silva-fundador-do-jornal-voz-das-comunidades-e-preso-no-alemao.html. Accessed 31 December 2016.
3. Actors Taís Araujo and Lázaro Ramos, who have become prominent thanks to their works on Globo TV, have recently joined a part of the militant mainstream, especially on race and inclusion, who appear in the peripheral media as role models.
4. "Who are the favela makers." Available at https://www.youtube.com/watch?v=jOvLn6RZOqQ. Accessed 20 December 2015.

5. "Ten reasons for not denouncing criminals," as seen on Mídia Periférica website: https://100ko.wordpress.com/2015/12/04/dez-motivos-para-nao-denunciarmos-criminosos/#more-322. Accessed 23 December 2015.

6. Profile not originally included at research, but website Rio on Watch reproduces its content. Original story at http://rioonwatch.org.br/?p=20388. Accessed 10 July 2016.

7. According to research reported by the *Data Popular* institute, as stated by the portal G1 at http://g1.globo.com/rio-de-janeiro/noticia/2015/06/violencia-policial-65-de-moradores-de-favelas-do-rio-temem-diz-estudo.html. Accessed 10 July 2016.

8. The Carandiru Massacre happened in 1992 as result of a police intervention during a riot. This episode caused the death of 111 inmates. Recently the police officers involved saw their jail conviction overturned as lawful murder. See Leite (2006) on the multiple narratives for this episode.

9. According to press reports in G1, Extra, and Folha, this was the case of a teenager tied to a lightning pole with a bicycle lock, after the suspect had committed a robbery. A passer-by man discovered the case thanks to neighbors and then called the police, later posting the case on Facebook.

10. "Teenager tied to a lighting pole by group of *vigilantes* in Flamengo" Jornal Extra, http://extra.globo.com/noticias/rio/adolescente-atacado-por-grupo-de-justiceiros-preso-um-poste-por-uma-trava-de-bicicleta-no-flamengo-11485258.html, 18 September 2015, accessed 30 October 2015.

11. The prevalence during the period of early 2014, when such occurrences started to gain prominence in the media was to call the victims by subjective references, such as 'teenager' (jovem) or 'rapaz' (young man). My point is that at that moment the peripheral media was already disclosing details of his life, or at least, its condition of black, and marginalized as the key feature of this crime. As this story from Folha de S. Paulo confirms it. Available at http://www1.folha.uol.com.br/cotidiano/2014/02/1407239-adolescente-e-agredido-a-pauladas-e-acorrentado-nu-a-poste-na-zona-sul-do-rio.shtml. Accessed 31 March 2014.

12. Jean-Baptiste Debret (1768–1848), French painter who lived in Brazil.

13. As it is the case of the Carandiru's Massacre, in 1992, named after the prison in which it took place, or the Realengo's massacre, in 2011.

14. *Police Pacifying Unities* in Portuguese.

15. Much of the video coverage counted on testimonials from Amarildo's family, the object here is the non-mainstream material made with the participation of Amarildo's wife or several members of his family, as well as with activists, human rights lawyers, and witnesses. An assemblage of this material resulted in *Uns,* which is a documentary available on YouTube at https://www.youtube.com/watch?v=ITUfXc0ySvA. Accessed on 30 November 2014.

16. "Amarildo's family speaks about the Somos Todos Amarildo project." Youtube at https://www.youtube.com/watch?v=ITUfXc0ySvA. Accessed 30 November 2014.

17. This is reference to the interview with Anderson Souza, Amarildo's son, filmed by undisclosed media producers, which was a material made freely available

on Youtube, access at https://www.youtube.com/watch?v=zCXWaAZxp90. Accessed on 30 November 2014.

18. As reported by Amnesty International, which is a summary of these developments on its website. "Punishment to policemen involved in death of builder Amarildo is exemplary to break with impunity." Available at https://anistia.org.br/noticias/anistia-internacional-punicao-aos-policiais-envolvidos-na-morte-pedreiro-amarildo-e-exemplar-para-romper-com-impunidade/. Accessed 30 May 2016.

19. "Justice concedes pay to builder Amarildo's family." G1. Available at http://g1.globo.com/rio-de-janeiro/noticia/2016/06/justica-concede-indenizacao-familia-do-pedreiro-amarildo.html. Accessed 18 December 2016.

20. This is not to deny that eviction continues to be an issue for contemporary *favelas.* I refer specifically to the context of dwellers who were interviewees in this book, most of them live in old communities, therefore those seen as stable communities in that sense.

21. "Black movement and peripheral movement launch *Frente Favela Brasil* political party." Agência Brasil. http://agenciabrasil.ebc.com.br/politica/noticia/2016-07/movimentos-negro-e-de-periferias-lancam-partido-frente-favela-brasil. Accessed on 30 September 2016.

Chapter Four

Challenging the Mainstream Media

Known in Brazil as the "big media," the country's largest media organizations occupy a significant space in the coverage of the peripheral media. It is no surprise that producers with whom I spoke were centered on Globo TV, as it is said to affect a specific type of communicative inequality. Producers have seen Brazil's leading media organizations resembling a monopoly, in which independent producers have neither the space to grow nor the conditions to access the market. In this same direction, authors have also researched the extent to which these players can manipulate public opinion and, overall, divert the press from modernization towards their own gains (Amaral & Guimarães, 1994; Lima, 1996; Waisbord, 1997; Fox & Waisbord, 2002; Paiva et al., 2015). It is none the less true that such big groups have otherwise promoted socially-conscious discussions and dialogue, from which democratic frames could favor a form of citizenship (e.g. in Porto, 2007). Therefore, if there is any consensus about the role that Globo TV and of a handful of national dailies, it is one that points to their contribution to democracy (Waisbord, 2000:87; Matos, 2008).

Having presented this backdrop, this book does not focus on the role of the mainstream media for democracy. However, it is not possible to ignore the opinions that all producers have expressed in interviews about the media environment. This book's interest is in the extent to which the peripheral media responds to the weight of the mainstream media through the politicized discourses it helps to spread every day. I dwell on two specific aspects that appeared on the evidence. First, I reflect on producers' expectations of building a more "democratic media" by increasing the politicization on the communicative inequality, or the ability of small-scale producers of having their outlets, using their language, and culture. I also stress that while producers might see mainstream coverage as superficial, they work to identify opportunities of partnerships with these outlets. By contrast, I also assess the importance of grassroot initiative of *educomunicação*, a practice that trains disadvantaged people on the critical role of communications in light of a few mainstream-sponsored programs of the same kind.

In the second section, I debate the results of the frame analysis that showed producers leaving the *big media* paradigm in search of excellence for their practices, politicizing their journalism through new formats, but also responding to the mainstream's influence over the *watchdog* journalism practice. I start by reviewing the debate on media democracy, linking this continuous ideal with the advance of the peripheral media. I end this chapter by discussing the extent to which producers can contradict literature that has seen the mainstream media as the ultimate and hegemonic standard.

TENSIONS FOR THE RIGHT TO COMMUNICATE

Most producers with whom I spoke revealed they had a position on the mainstream media. Whether supporting or opposing Brazil's biggest media organizations, it became clear that they were increasingly abandoning binary opposition or full compliance and moving towards a notion of conditioned partnership with the country's biggest media players. Although Brazilian authors have voiced the "absence" of the mainstream media in the studies about the country's redemocratization (Miguel, 2000; Abreu & Lattman-Weltman, 2006), the general opinion from media producers with whom I talked was that there is a contribution from the main organizations. Fewer opinions revealed total dissent, but in which case producers repeated accusations of media monopoly and criticisms about the "conservative" nature of the mainstream media. Most producers, in fact, have spoken about the possibility of a limited partnership, especially regarding technical cooperation, as long as this does not affect their agenda, frames, and ideology. When questioned on the direct consequence posed by the mainstream media for the people's understanding of inequality, producers argued that such large and powerful media apparatus leads to less visibility of the everyday scale of social issues. They still accused large conglomerates of draining their possibilities by limiting their chances to create new audiences and diversify the agenda.

This first exploration matters because it informs on existing communicative barriers according to media producers, a subject which is rarely seen outside the mainstream-dominated scholarly debate. What do producers bring as novelty in the face of their criticism of the media establishment? I centered this book's approach in Globo TV first because of the myriad of case studies directly focused on this player (Lattman-Weltman, 2007; Rego & La Pastina, 2007; Wilkin, 2008; Gomes, 2008; Moreira, 2009; Androvandi, 2010; Porto, 2012; Souza & Dalberto, 2013; Grijó, 2014; Mauro, 2014; Rêgo, 2014; Champagnatte, 2015; Soares, 2016). The second reason is to reflex the fact that interviewed media producers have nominally made reference to this organisation. For example, references to Globo TV attack "the media's" institutional weight and how it "corrupted" Brazilian media democracy through market exploitation. Its name is what most frequently personified the "cosy ties with the powerful." I do not imply that these allegations are only in respect of Globo's activities, but to this book's purposes, its name may as well illustrate a reference to the broader media environment.

When asked what the best solutions for this media turmoil are and how their outlets aim to change it, producers have argued on their purpose of delivering the real "voice of the periphery." As far as it seems a vague statement, I see producers' repertoire as pointing to the "conservatism" of the media in Brazil, much based on the decisions of a few media "patrons" (Fonseca, 2003). Thus, they point to this decisive process of what gets published or broadcasted and starts to go through a real popular process. These same producers have argued on the differences of depending on the media broadcasters and having their say directly:

> Here we have, for example, two big newspapers, historically owned by two conservative families. Our local TV channel only broadcasts Globo TV and we have another network that broadcasts the *Bandeirantes* [media group]. The space is therefore very difficult to dialogue with; we do not have many alternatives. Therefore, we have been trying to face that discussion. (Media producer 38)

> Let us talk specifically about Globo, which was born in 1965, a year after the military coup [d'état]. It [Globo TV] must follow its own interests, but it cannot deny [that] it has spectators; therefore, it must [occasionally] talk with them. The same Globo that denied it, supported the dictatorship. It [did], one of these days, apologise [for its support]. [. . .] To talk about this would be to concede and propose the democratisation agenda inside Globo. This would be very difficult for them, as it would be for Record [TV]. (Media producer 37)

Another producer saw that the only antidote to all kinds of inequalities that stem from Globo (both in terms of media access and of limited portraits available) was to build a strong consciousness that informed the public about this media imbalance. At the same time, they are admittedly unable to refuse a sort of relationship with Globo TV, irrespective of its agenda, practices, or current programs. This producer pondered other issues deriving from the technical supremacy of the former, which turn out to be not entirely negative:

> I think that the economic aspect [of domination] defines the ideological one, because who pays more is who has the space, and this naturally touches upon this pedagogical process of market ideologisation. [. . .] We, unfortunately, have no economic power, and economic exploitation not our interest. [. . .] I shall recognise that sometimes [social] movements create barriers for this dialogue; therefore, when you start to think about these [private] institutions as the main responsible agents, you start to demonise these private institutions—you end up shutting these doors. (Media producer 39)

Otherwise, criticisms continue regarding the entire system of license distribution in Brazil:

> We don't have it [license to broadcast] because it's all sub-divided. It is all split among the business people, and among very few families in Brazil that rule the communications and, not by chance, a good part are also politicians. Jangadeiro TV's proprietor, the second biggest here [in Ceará state], is Tasso Jereissati, and Verdes Mares's TV is Edson Queiroz. They are a media conglomerate and, during a certain period, wanted to join politics. We have to take this out of the hands of these people, otherwise it'll be always the same thing, and they'll only speak of their interests. (Media producer 36)

It is an ambiguous relationship because there is criticism about the lack of diversity in ownership, but producers also confessed that they need this mass outreach to get stronger publicity for social issues. In that case, to this book's question on coverage and repertoire, I wondered if they still get to develop a stronger counterhegemonic coverage (as they assumed sharing content with larger media producers). Moreover, this ambivalence towards the mainstream can also be seen as they look for models amid professional journalism. While some left-wing players are cited, they are also virtually considered as part of the mainstream, as this producer mentioned:

> We were journalism students and were involved with left-wing militancy. And, of course, they expected [that] we had contact with people from *Caros Amigos*, *Carta Capital*, and *Le Monde* in Brazil, which [are outlets] with more critical perspective. And because we know a lot of people from São Paulo [who went] through these experiences, I was starting to understand how it is that thing of militant media in Brazil, and, I could say, the background [of it] during the dictatorship, the fight through the clandestine scene, the difficulties [. . .] And, always, we [have] had a lot of this. We had a certain will in seeking to know how that was the 'historical' and that influenced us for sure, very much. For example, the *Movimento*, the *Sol* newspaper and all these old outlets—we had contact with [them]. (Media producer 14)

A more positive account on the mainstream media does not want to give up their views or original work. Rather, it is about seeing themselves as *insider antagonists*:

> [. . .] To be honest, *Globo* has invited us to talk many times. Our producer goes there and she talks about subjects they do not like to touch upon and debate. For example, *Globo* has recently spoken about gender: how can we debate gender in a *Globo* programme? They have sought us, and we are not taking any profit for us, but we are glad that we can send our message through. (Media producer 44)

> Well, we've done things with the *Roberto Marinho Foundation*[1] as well as for *Futura TV*. Our editorial policy is like: 'we can do it; if you want to fund us, [that] is fine, but we will do whatever we want.' If in case one wants to change what we do, obviously, we won't accept. (Media producer 36)

Therefore, the point of departure for seeing any politicized coverage is not at looking for opposition, but seeing *how* producers can deliver better quality, and *demonstrate* their attempts to stop the continuity of an unequal media system and its effects. This book contributes more by exploring how producers follow this purpose, and this review on *Globo* and the mainstream media aimed at what is more urgent and wherein the criticism lie. Hence, I go through some evidence that shows that producers have discussed their notions of *equality* and how to reach it on their level.

Forging Critical, Bottom-Up Pluralism

Producers who criticized the media concentration have said that the insistence in this topic connects to the extent it favors inequality. Their overall impression is to agree on a common view that "monopoly" means concentration (Baker, 2007), and concentration means having "families" in charge of deciding which media programs will be produced, and social issues and human rights issues they will be discussing. But even if they do agree with this, they point to a bigger threat, that of a prevalent entertainment-driven agenda that meets profit intents. Producers believed that because it is a private media system, some subjects would never receive proper space in the media. Moreover, the system's regulation does not consider this issue (lack of representation) as a formal limitation or something that must be imposed on broadcasting companies. They said that the Brazilian government should offer mass media alternatives that contemplate these missing items as an agenda of its own:

> There is no public channel [through] which we could talk about human rights. Meanwhile, three channels bomb us with crime news during lunchtime. There

> is no quality; there is no democracy in communications. They may have [channels]; even the religious fundamentalist people might have their channel. But we have to have the channel to speak differently. (Media producer 36)

> We're fighting hegemony, but, at the same time, we're becoming mature. This is our fuel [for] life. That is why our work makes senses. It does not make us afraid because [ours] is not a big work, or because [there are assumptions that] society is not ready. The balance is at continuing the work even knowing that you have to go against yourself. (Media producer 45)

Producers' criticism of large conglomerates about these persisting issues of representation is often down to their failure to address the indigenous, black people and other minorities, besides the poverty issue. Such minorities would be the *victims* in this failure to represent. Partly because they, being "poor and excluded from mainstream society," are unaccounted in a "commoditised" system. Being fair towards this excluded layer would mean rescuing them from the media obliviousness and bringing forward their political points:

> Their representation is often not really nice. It is as [if they were] folklore, or they talk about them [the indigenous] as if they were disrupting the development of some real estate. This appears in a prejudicial or 'cultural' manner, as if it were culture and not part of the population. The *Indigenous World Cup*, they broadcast. So, if they find [interesting to broadcast the indigenous games, with all that beauty and everything, why not show the reality of the indigenous people, as some of them may still fall victim [to] slavery? In some cases, they are killed for land. (Media producer 28)

Looking at the above case, this opposition comes up when one analyzes the coverage of the mainstream with that of outlets such as *Agência Pública* and the *G1* portal. While the former has consistently explored the pains and the daily struggles of indigenous communities, the latter has featured the indigenous prominently due to its "Indigenous Olympic Games," in which images are of festive congregation. It is not to argue that the agenda for the Brazilian indigenous tribes should always bridge suffering and degradation, as producers recognized the "mix" of news as the ideal. However, if this mix is not achieved, it is the replacement of one agenda for the other—*leisure* is replaced by *conflict*—that strikes the producers most. It is a dichotomy that transforms the meaning of every indigenous presence in Brazil's capital, Brasilia into something contentious. For instance, every presence of indigenous tribes in that city is received as a fighting for rights,[2] but which entails conflict and "invasion." This absence of pluralism drives the associations of mainstream media complacency with inequality.

In a second part of this discussion, I see producers also aiming to politicize discussions over soft portraits of the periphery. They have argued about the de-politicization especially promoted in Brazilian *soap operas*. As a result, the website *Mídia Periférica* has produced what they call "Postcards from the Periphery" with pictures displaying the reality of seeing from one's window the unfinished brick houses and streets in which garbage lies apparent—these images correspond to an ordinary scene of any city outskirt in Brazil, but for them, it is the one that deserves highlight. At the same time, by naming it "postcards," the initiative also communicates a sense of distance with their interlocutor, but which does not sanitize the images as seen in the well-watched soap operas.

Once producers agreed and acknowledged that telling this *counterhegemonic* truth lies in their hands and that it is possible to publish more about it, they have designed strategies to make it more resonant. It became clear for many of them that the politicization or criticism of mainstream portraits is not enough. The responsibility to improve the *feedback to power* and the *diversity of frames* becomes a challenge on its own. In a way, they must improve reception from a public that has, for decades, been conditioned and, therefore, limited, to mainstream media formats.

To ensure this message can come through, they discussed professionalized strategies and content production that does not exist in "popular" institutions, such as in social movements. This interface for social movements is an interesting input. Over the past decades, researchers were fascinated by the media success of a few social movement organizations in Brazil, as it is the case of the Landless Rural Workers Movement (MST), which left from a position of invaders and criminals to master their insertion in the mainstream media (Gohn, 1999; Bertol, 2003; Hammond, 2004; Lima, 2006; Carneiro, 2006; Fonseca, 2007; Gomes & Nascimento, 2008; Vanden, 2017). This ability is by and large not the reality of most movements across the country, despite recent changes and modernization (Hochstetler, 2000; Guidry, 2003), and as these producers also point out their interest in sharpening their language:

> The social movement language is too much of a pamphleteer, very hermetic. They tend to do things for themselves, and we started perceiving that our role was making them [able] to speak out, that they should start to speak to other people [. . .] Although, I am saying that social movements are tough with language, at [the] same time, we have learnt a lot. They have a political background; there were things we did not know why they were fighting and then we later understood. (Media producer 36)

> Our magazine has been always very concerned with the language we use. We never got close to making a text, for example, a kind of reportage to tell the

> history of some place, but we [very] much respect the journalistic standard. On the other hand, we aim to make the most accessible language possible, [whether it] is a text [or] a photo, but it has to be mainly accessible for the people of our age. (Media producer 48)

Otherwise, the mainstream media can also be a barometer for quality, as producers conceded that they occasionally targeted mainstream columnists and asked them to publicize some of their causes, issues, or materials, depending on whom showed empathy:

> There are interesting things on [the] mainstream media. The *Fantástico* [Globo TV programme] was doing good things [in] those days. The biggest issue is really the monopoly, the group of executives; there is no issue in having channels owned by the business group. The problem is having a channel owned by the society; only business people own it. (Media producer 36)

> We are all volunteers and there is some contribution from outside, when we ask some columnist or renowned writer, such as *Xico Sá* or *Cora Ronai*, if they could write about something, but all collaborations are voluntary. (Media producer 36)

Others resorted to remember the long radio heritage in Brazil. In fact, many studies have also supported the view that radio continues a major source of news and culture to a wide range of the population, especially in the countryside (Nunes, 2004; Marinho, 2006; Oliveira, 2007). According to them, radio has had a historical role especially amidst the poorest, who used to get informed on politics and local affairs. As alternative media, radio has thrived as a platform for the gathering of small communities (e.g. in Anderson, 2015). Aware of this backdrop, producers argued about the necessity of using the radio platform to dodge the digital divide:

> Our outlet has to reach a poor boy from the Marsilac [São Paulo neighbourhood]. Perhaps he does not know us from the Internet, maybe he has to run a printed magazine. [. . .] We have a radio show on the community radio of our neighbourhood. If you think, what is a community radio with a two-kilometre-reach? This is nothing, but we must use all the tools to pave a bridge. We reproduce our show on the Internet later. We fully upload the radio show on to our website. We are looking to articulate through many tools. (Media producer 08)

The issue of the mainstream media not reaching all locations and not talking about all its people, despite its large breadth of technical infrastructure, is another unexplored opportunity for them. This producer argued about the relationship between "visibility" and "effectiveness" in their production, as both concepts do not depend on each other:

> The mainstream media are spaces in which we want to arrive. We want to occupy the space of the mainstream media. We do not want just having visibility through the mainstream media. If that happens, it will happen because of our performance or to give more visibility to something interesting [that] we did. (Media producer 36)

Producers from Brazil's northeast are most likely to resent the incomplete coverage from the mainstream:

> We know we live in such a plural country, rich in culture and diversity. The media headquarters, nowadays, unfortunately, are in the Rio and São Paulo axis, as if all [of the] country could be summarised only in two federative unities. This is something that not only our project, but all the sectors, all social movements, are mobilising [and] articulating through many meetings; [they are] trying to end this and democratise the media. (Media producer 44)

> We are talking about why a certain magazine would worry about articulate[ing] the northeast. My experience working in a southeast-based blog showed me that if we do not set our own agenda, the people from São Paulo will not do it. There are many things to talk about, but there is a lot of neglect. Let's be honest. (Media producer 14)

An aspect of this "effective" coverage of inequality, especially at the broadcast level, also lies in the uneven attention given to issues of violence, land disputes, and the protection of indigenous tribes. Those are urgent representational needs, linking "human rights" not only to the basic needs (i.e. water, food), but also to a wider context of inequality and public services:

> They wanted to make a campaign on the public lawyers. You know, in Brazil, those to die the most are those connected with human rights. Especially in rural areas and, these lawyers, they are invisible. Nobody knows about them. Once in a lifetime, when someone like Dorothy Stang dies, who was an American missionary, the people come to realise it. An American missionary died in Pará [state], so that is news. So, they came up to do a campaign via the Internet, but we said we thought it better to use part of the money to make a film, travel across Brazil, and even [though] the budget is low, as we think that this is important, we fit in that sort of thing. (Media producer 36)

The above producer weighed in on the press's double standards when reporting a case of murder in the Amazonian hinterlands. Full exposure, or "politicization," was given to the case of Dorothy Stang, the American philanthropist who was murdered in north Brazil. The underreporting of similar cases involving ordinary Brazilians triggers criticism. The admiration for mainstream professional efficiency clashes with criticism for its failure to incorporate a popular language and focus on local cases. While "these mainstream media organisations have enough infrastructure breadth to include Brazil's large territory," their failure to do so becomes the basis for their general wish to go "beyond" in this coverage. That goal includes fulfilling the current insufficient interest in other publics and fighting against the prevalence of entertaining over a politicized coverage. The extent to which that shifts in representation could involve what is not currently deemed as newsworthy for a mass audience summarizes much of the discontent.

As we leave the old debates, I find that the opposition to the mainstream concentrating less on its size and commercialism (as in Kenix, 2015), and more on its hegemonic way of framing reality and its results for the periphery. This hegemonic pattern is not so much credited to mainstream players, neither the latter appears as the only blocker of improvement, at least not as much as current scholarship faces it (e.g. Paiva et al., 2015). For producers, what has really failed was not to *forge pluralism*—not the kind of existing pluralism as soft representations and commoditization (e.g. the *favela* as a soap opera), but the "critical pluralism" that is not afraid to show the real conditions of the periphery (e.g. the peripheral postcards). A change in the draconian media's code could speed up that transformation and force a new realism within media coverage, but as producers have shown, they prefer to *start* by choosing amid forgotten voices. In brief, if for the mainstream media, the peripheral media might have seemed obscure and detached, producers have acknowledged that and recognized they need to produce content that is more accessible and part of the so-called public interest.

Before fleshing out what these initiatives are, and what public interest comes to be in this case, I have also reflected on other circumstances that entail the generation of a more critical pluralism. Producers also mentioned a strong inclination to *educate* while *covering*, a responsibility often refused at mainstream media level (Schudson & Anderson, 1989). My intention is not one of advancing the media literacy literature, which has debates of its own at the global level. However, it is possible to address the Brazilian context of *educomunicação* using parts of the evidence collected, problematizing it as a form of discourse among media producers. I highlight two cases that mirror this repertoire of "educating" citizens, flagging up the limits between mainstream and grassroots reporting where the possibility of their politicization is concerned. I contrast similar programs, sponsored by the mainstream media organizations in Brazil and in the UK.

The 'Citizen Journalists' and the Role of Educomunicação

As I approached media producers, I became aware of the role of many organizations, NGOs, and university programs that train young people from disadvantaged backgrounds to produce online media. These interactions led me to question the extent to which these organizations could exert some influence regarding the politicization of inequality at a strategic level. This effort of *educomunicação*, or educating for communications, connects with a long-standing tradition of media literacy that appears in literature through multiple approaches. It actually refers to an enterprise that has approximated media users from popular culture, promoting a critical analysis of the media from the streets to the "classroom" (Kellner & Share, 2005; Alvermann et al., 2018). It is a "movement" which has set different questions for different realities regarding "the ability to access, analyze, evaluate and create messages across a variety of contexts" (Hobbs, 1998; Livingstone & Graaf, 2004), a necessity in times of new technologies (Livingstone, 2004).

I am unable to provide further context based on this scholarship on what stage or what questions the Brazilian tradition of media literacy aims to achieve. However, due to the large number of interviewed producers that said to engage with activities of *educomunicação,* my idea is to approach it to the extent that this activity could relate to this book's aim to see politicization in their discourse. For instance, even producers with no media experience or those who are not in journalism schools, have said to receive teachings from classical works in Brazil, such as Paulo Freire's *Pedagogy of the Oppressed.* Indeed, the 1980s' MacBride report did cite the absence of local communicators as one of the biggest issues in Brazil regarding "media development" (MacBride & Abel, 1984). In a straightforward manner, I ask in this section, would this *breeding* of new producers lead to more politicization, being consonant with the change sought in the peripheral media? How could *educomunicação* later translate into *coverage*?

Most producers argued that, after realizing the mainstream media's failures to report on the periphery, they decided to "act." Secondly, they have seen this effort as a "natural" consequence of their "role," as both words are pieces of their repertoire. Media producers, educators, and journalists had already gathered together in the 1980s with the same purposes (Festa & Silva, 1986) when their aim was also to give "critical thought" to new media practitioners, the "microscopic revolution" (Guattari & Rolnik, 2008). What differs in contemporaneity is that producers have refused to engage with this side of "grooming" citizens as a structured process, as suggested by the media literacy scholarship; they have framed it here as a voluntary effort. Fewer of them have seen it as, regardless of success or failure, "preparing the ground" for future market possibilities. Eventually, instead of drawing on the literacy that sees multiple questions in this practice, I also came across similar kinds of *training* initiatives from the mainstream media's side, to which I contrasted what producers have told me.

On the mainstream media side, I selected two pioneering programs: one in Brazil, sponsored by the *Folha de S.Paulo* newspaper, and the *Guardian*'s *Rio Voices* in Britain. Regarding *Folha de S.Paulo*'s *Mural*, the scheme's idea was to cover everyday issues from peripheral communities, which would create reports published online in a blog hosted under the newspaper's main website. Young collaborators would generate their material and receive supervision from a *professional* journalist who was a member of staff. In Brazil, this scheme produced a blog that first appeared in 2010, led by Brazilian journalist Bruno Garcez. After five years, 650 posts appeared on *Folha de S.Paulo*'s website, where one finds the following description:

> *Mural blog* is produced by some dozens of community correspondents—on their majority, they are students or those who already graduated in journalism, but overall bloggers who are interested in telling what is happening in the region where they live, in São Paulo's periphery and surroundings.

Looking at some of *Mural*'s publications,[3] there are familiar topics to the peripheral media. These are urban concerns, such as the lack of public transportation and healthcare, as well as reports of racial discrimination and inefficient public policies. In 2015, the blog counted 50 correspondents based at the Greater São Paulo. One participant reported that his willingness to join the project came after living in the periphery and perceiving that what he was living "was not shown on television."[4] Five years since its beginning, *Mural* has fructified into another news agency.[5]

The second project featured here happens in Rio de Janeiro, part of the British *broadsheet The Guardian*, which has developed its own "professional training" with community journalists in Rio de Janeiro, Mumbai, and Johannesburg. This initiative started in 2010, receiving funds from the Bill and Melinda Gates Foundation, and appears within the "*Guardian* development" section. Yasir Mirza, one of the *Guardian*'s representatives, has written about the main foundations of this program:

> So now we are making this a regular part of what we do, by launching the *Guardian*'s Citizen Reporting Programme—for Marginalised Voices. The aim is to work with marginalised people around the world, empowering and amplifying their voices with training and support. We'll cover how the news life cycle works, how to help verify a story with evidence, where to find this evidence, what constitutes local, national, and international news, and how to pitch and connect to us digitally.[6]

Published under *Guardian Witness*,[7] this scheme brought out stories on disadvantaged communities, including evictions and development issues, as well as reports of Rio's *favela* violence. The *Guardian* has promoted workshops with selected citizen journalists. *Michel Silva*, a young reporter in this project who comes from another media project in the Rocinha Favela,[8] has taken part in the *Guardian*'s coverage. I tried to contact Silva for this book, but multiple attempts received no reply. On 14 December 2015, a piece signed by Silva in the *Guardian* reads:

> A teenager called David was killed today during a firefight between drug traffickers and police. It barely makes the news. This month, Rio de Janeiro focuses more on the Olympic test events, which are taking place in the richer areas of the city. Shootouts and killings in favelas are all too common and rarely appear in the newspapers. However, thanks to smartphones and Internet access, residents are filming the shootings and publishing the images on social networks. It is an attempt to draw the attention of society to violence in Rio's favelas.

These articles appeared initially in English, later translated into Portuguese. Leaving aside any potential translation issues, the articles followed the newspaper's style and were therefore edited before publication. Even though the news organization has agreed not to interfere in this content, Mirza suggests that they may still be subject to further review and approval:

> We can't turn around and say, 'that's really interesting and a really serious issue but it's not a story for us.' So you have to finesse it and approach it in such a way that you empower and train people.

Having been given the main guidelines for the mainstream media's programs of citizen journalism, many producers with whom I spoke were keen to collaborate with large media organizations. For some of them, this interaction could be a successful "win-win" partnership, though they emphasized individualization and personality. When analysing similar initiatives to forge community journalists through training programs sponsored by NGOs, social movements, or universities, one finds a universe of activists, university members, or psychologists giving lectures on a kind of media practice that fits the needs of the disadvantaged youth.

The literature details many successes of communication for "empowerment projects," from which one harvests good results. Many studies have actually drawn on the potential that springs from *teaching* media producers to "find their voice" (e.g. in Riaño, 1994). With that in mind, I spoke with a coordinator of the *Associação Imagem Comunitária*, based in the city of Belo Horizonte, a charity that trains and enables small-scale media projects. One representative told me about their core activities:

> What we do is to support and strengthen the media production or community communicative processes put out by groups, collectives, and sociocultural institutions. These are their outlets, not ours. An exception was a programme

associated to the *Rede Jovem de Cidadania*, one of our biggest projects. The production was ours, [in] partnership with groups and youth movements based in the greater Belo Horizonte. It was broadcasted for more than 10 years in the *Rede Minas* network and Brazil TV [national chains]. (Coordinator, Imagem Comunitária)

What this contributor's testimonial also sheds light on is the wider *social value* of the media and communications, which leads us to the differences between both kinds of programs. While Brazil's *educomunicação* arises from the Paulo Freire's pedagogic tradition (Freire, 1970), which seemed influential for all interviewees (to the extent that they receive no backing from a major funding scheme, but the ideal sounds strong), there is no mention of such broader values on the mainstream media's side. Programs have appeared tentatively and not for the long term. That situation is the opposite to grassroots initiatives, such as *Renajoc*, a network of young communicators of Belém and Manaus in the north. The same is true for the *Desabafo Social*, which gathers young media producers from Alagoas and Bahia. The involvement of academics has revealed the degree to which universities can play an important role. This partnership can either happen directly (I visited the *Coletivo Rever* from Sergipe, formed by ex-university colleagues) or in modules taught at the university level (in Minas Gerais for instance, a program of community media is part of the curricula from the University of Viçosa).[9]

I spoke with *Favela News*, which receives support from U.S.-based NGO *Shine a Light*. While working with the communities of Recife, this NGO's aim is to pursue a middle path between education for professional fluency and the self-awareness of the disadvantaged youth. For them, the latter should have nothing but their own efforts to develop as a small media organization. The NGO has offered ICT access and training infrastructure to young people to create content at first; they can also operationalize tools and, more importantly, reflect on what portrait they want to create for themselves in the media. The project started in 2005 from field research conducted by anthropologist Rita de Cácia Silva and American-born Kurt Shaw, along with the NGO *Shine a Light*. They argued that encouraging this population to access new technologies, as well as encouraging them to follow the routine of publications, was a major challenge:

> Of course, we had to work a lot on training, but the biggest challenge was the everyday discipline. Knowing that they had to know that and there is no excuse. If we wanted people to see it, we have to send out things to the Internet every day, or many days per week [. . .] One of the difficulties is getting the people from the periphery to access new technologies. At [the] same time, there is an immense creativity in this population. Training people in this area is challenging. If one is up to [it], he can do it on [his] own.

Here, the concept of community journalists does not refer to those who are granted space by the press amid the *hard news*. Rather, it lies upon the reporters' lives, as participant producers said they felt counted as "full individuals" and not as operators of an exceptional kind of reality. The biggest difference between these grassroots projects and those by news organizations is how the former prioritizes professionalized commitment over the other complexities that stem from inviting young media producers. Silva and Shaw told me that dealing with multiple cultural or conceptual backgrounds has not always been easy. If not a clash, it is a tight competition with other entitics that surround disadvantaged communities in Brazil, including that of other NGOs and evangelical churches (see Chapter 5) and the appeal of cheap, widespread "popular" news—mostly crime and uninstructive pop culture. Producers were also aware that assuming journalism as the best platform and language for this youth is another way to limit other possibilities of their expression:

> This producer, for example, is a young man who works with us. He is an autodidact in breakdance. He is a perfect dancer, and he can win contests. [To fit in our training,] you must recruit the right person and his or her interests for things [to] run all right. I think we find a lot of resistance in this sense. We, [for instance] have struggled a lot to find a right girl from the periphery that could take part in this project and who could have this curiosity.

Another *educomunicação* group called *Gambiarra*, from *Vitória da Conquista* in the state of Bahia, told me of the challenges of competing with this popular press while "educating" their audience:

> I think here, in Vitória da Conquista, those who consume Internet news seek for news related to crime reporting, and this is an approach our outlet does not follow anyways. We try the opposite. We aim to include the debate on 'rights violation,' on 'image rights' for example, that relates to the image of a dead individual that one sees in some newspapers. The most accessed blogs are those which have this 'police news' approach. (Media producer 50)

When comparing both kinds of training programs, the common preoccupation is with improving technical skills, but there are other distinct aims and expectations. Both similarly try to increase the reporting abilities of communities, as said earlier, in order to address the lack of voices in the media environment. While mainstream organizations can boost the *favela*-based youth by promoting short-term publicity, which is an unthinkable target by many other disadvantaged producers, *educomunicação* initiatives can boost long-term counterhegemonic communication. Following Paulo Freire's (1970) theories on liberating the oppressed by making them understand the "causes of reality," the small-scale but widespread presence of *educomunicação* makes this dissemination of values more relevant by seeding critical values that do not take the supremacy of media organizations for granted, as they do introduce new concepts of *fairness* in the media representations' arena.

Otherwise, by forging "community journalists" through making them attend a list of workshops and by sending their texts to editorial reviews, the mainstream editors could create hierarchized partners.[10] This youth's media potential could thereby suffer constraints from an exogenous policy, which may be at odds with the criteria of their own. The risk of inviting community journalists who work for themselves, even though their actions are still in favor of their community, is depoliticizing them only to enrich the variety of constantly actualized and potentially *paywalled* news websites. As said, *educomunicação* seems to follow distinct purposes, it is less tied to publicity and more to value dissemination at the grassroots level. For this book's purposes, it became clear that *educomunicação* is aimed at communications in a slow fashion, whether because it explores topics such as language or because it promotes an understanding of communication as an ongoing "right." Instead of tying down producers by offering them a privileged space in the media, *educomunicação* does not seem bound by formats, but in discourse.

In sum, both programs have formed scenarios that are not necessarily complementary. *Educomunicação* is a strategic process to form counterhegemonic communications, and "citizen journalists" schemes are fit for the purposes of the news business but do not bear any relationship with the past or present of communities or with the long-standing, social mission to challenge narratives. In the next section, I present results from the frame analysis, which add to this discussion by informing on how these initiatives could collaborate to sharpening producers' discourse, taking them through classic journalism formats, such as that of so-called *watchdog journalism*, but aiming to improve these practices in search of a new accountability.

REVITALIZING STORYTELLING

In this section, I draw on the content from media producers in their ability to propose alternatives to the deficiencies producers have spotted at mainstream media level. The content analyzed showed that, from the 120 articles examined, only four offered politicized—in the sense of "confrontational"—discourses against the mainstream media companies. Amid these occurrences, a smaller number tried to politicize stances against the media's omissions when reporting sensitive events or, instead, its excess of "bad news" in a time of optimism under the leftist Workers' Party government (as in Branford & Kucinski, 1995). In the next two sections, I explore this *politicization* by competition with the mainstream media news. While producers are moving away from the criticism against media ownership and concentration, and instead focusing on improving their skills of storytelling, they also draw on the insufficient language they see at the mainstream level. Overall, there is a continuous attempt to create alternatives for the mainstream media, but my interest is in how the peripheral media may operationalize its media criticism by centering it on politicizing inequality rather than treating counterparts as purely *enemies*, a tendency which I discussed earlier in the first section.

Developing a New Notion of Balance

Although at a lower rate, attacks against mainstream organizations are still recurrent. Producers have targeted companies such as Globo TV to accuse it of insufficient coverage of inequality. This accusation responded to the major climate of political instability that stemmed from Brazilian presidential elections in 2014 and which would worsen after the impeachment of Dilma Rousseff. I do not discuss the deep settings of this specific polarization, neither focus on Rousseff's campaign development, which would entail to engage with her opponent's too (see Jaenisch & Borelli, 2011 for a framing comparison). To what concerns this book, though, it is important to assess the prevalence of such vocabulary that cites Globo TV as a "dangerous institution" or "champions of inequality." Where does it stem from? How strong is the reluctance to accept this organization's central mediating role?

In fact, confrontational vocabulary such as this has appeared almost exclusively in the radical newspaper *Brasil 247*. As the intensity of Brazil's politic and economic crisis increased, attacks focused on the "family-owned media." I place some examples from *Brasil 247*:

> Pessimistic, the family-owned media sector sees inequality. (18/09/2014)

> *Folha*'s columnist defends inequality. (14/06/2015)

The case of *Brasil 247* is still controversial because police investigations later found some of its editorial staff involved in allegations of corruption.[11] Secondly, the outlet's support for the disruptive activism against Globo TV on its daily coverage also stood out when comparing it with other outlets included in this book. During weeks, the portal supported radical activists that stormed into Globo TV's live transmissions, with demonstrators holding messages such as "Marinho family's mansion in Paraty" (a luxurious estate reportedly owned by the conglomerate's controller family). On one occasion, the portal had the following favorable headline to these flash protests:

> The little-beard man informs: Globo TV, we will not give you a rest. (16/05/2016)

In fact, it is important to put these factual demonstrations in context according to the other sampled outlets. Not all of them have turned to this confrontational tone against Globo or against the mainstream, nor did *Brasil 247* do this on behalf of the "periphery." My finding regarding blogs written from the periphery of large cities (which is not the case for *Brasil 247*) is that one finds more general accounts relating to the mainstream (cited as *mídia global, grupos de mídia*). In these blogs, consequently, there is less confrontation because of their expectations of collaborating with major players. Being in dissent from the mainstream did not mean dissenting from media organizations. Instead, producers sought to voice messages against middle-class privilege, racism, or opposed stereotypical images that appear in the international media. In that sense, *Brasil 247*'s coverage is an exception in data, which otherwise confirmed more partnership and less antagonism in a confrontational sense.

One example of tackling the narrative but not the narrator lies in this post from the *Mídia Periférica* blog (05/04/2013). The blog approaches the way in which foreign journalists tend to frame poor communities negatively, rather than giving a normalized account of their ordinary life. As a result, they fight what they see as journalists transforming their lives into permanent episodes of confront:

> Sensationalism: The periphery is not a stage, nor are the young actors in this theatre. What makes a foreign journalist come to Brazil and prepare a story for Reuters, a globally known website, and spread sensationalist images from Salvador's peripheral communities? We are not here to say that there is no [drug] dealing. We know that deaths and everything else exist, and we know why they exist; it is because of the lack of public policies and government's help within the communities. [. . .] Beyond this journalist's take, there are young people spreading out in their communities with emerging cultures and local artists.

The above criticism refers to a story run by the news agency *Reuters* regarding what the agency saw as the rising criminality indices in slums from Salvador. Entitled by "A World Without Smiles," this piece highlighted the prevalence of drug dealers in poor communities. The illustration that accompanied that story showed an individual with a gun in each of his hands, crossed arms, as his face appeared hidden by a cap. This tone of banal violence, somehow staged, tied to a poor neighborhood of Brazil as a background, has shocked the editors of many peripheral media outlets, leading them to place criticisms against the so-called "global" journalism. In other stances, blogs such as *Viva Favela* have published critical analyses of what they see as a wasted chance to appear on global news outlets.

Again, instead of criticizing the *power* of international news agencies, producers have adopted a strong disapproval of showing violence with no other sides depicted. The coverage of the 2014 World Cup had somehow intensified this pattern, with recurrent images of police officers carrying snipes while walking in the *favelas*' narrow streets. For producers, that way was a partial perspective, which failed to connect dwellers to the broader landscape of their lives, submitting them to a stigma of crime and alienation. In fact, the truth is that mainstream media editors (or those in charge of such publications) are expected to act in this way or, at worst, be misguided in their choices and frames.[12] This sort of media treatment remains unacceptable to producers as they also play the role of media watchers, what appears as a more active pattern in producers' discourse than it does the militancy against Globo's power carried out by *Brasil 247*.

As a result, media producers, even though broadly and experimentally, end up rewriting the rules of professional journalism to suit fairer purposes. Producers argued that their notion of *balance* is more accurate, for instance, because it includes the obligation of not criminalizing and victimizing dwellers of Brazil's periphery. An example of this new *balance* lies in the portal *Rio on Watch*'s campaign and toolkit to guide more proper media coverage of the *favelas*. The website has offered extensive criticism on the way in which mainstream media organizations should refer to these and other low-income areas in Brazil (for example, by avoiding the term *slums*), a treatment that, they argue, stems from a general disregard. The terminology would reflect the fact that journalists, alongside tourists and visitors, have patronized dwellers with their own vocabulary and interpretations:

> The strength of a word: The Slum Stigma around the world. Most of the English language reports on Brazil, during the intense spotlight of the World Cup, have translated the word *favela* into *slum*. This is not so surprising. Every single journalist or editor [will] find examples of colleagues employing the same term, as Google translates favela into slum and slum into favela. (*Rio on Watch*, 20/07/2014)

The preoccupation of producers with reporters phrasing *slums* instead of *favelas* is due to the limited degree with which big news organizations are prepared to consider the history and the affectivity that exists in these communities, founded in their terms and languages. I contend that by elevating the priority of the native coverage, producers want to *recolonize* the ground lost to the mainstream way of doing things and that includes producing a data-rich discourse and conquering new readers, though no equivalent distribution structure exists. Their main contribution to paving alternatives is, as we shall see, conceptual and discursive.

Politicizing Transparency: The Case of Belo Monte

The case of the *Belo Monte* dam is a good example of these attempts to re-colonize formats and show "reliable journalism," which is a contested title. It is key for this book's purpose to lay out the reasons why the contemporary periphery is more politicized than in the past, and here we find journalism providing good reasons and arguments for believing it is. It matters to understand this context of *politicization* because it dialogues directly with the so-called journalism conventions. It is not because journalism conventions are important *per se* to producers, but because of its role in giving them a platform to create and improve their own protocols of reportage.

The construction of the mega dam in the Amazon was a widely covered topic in the mainstream media during the period of this research. It was controversial, as it touched upon environmental, economic, and social variables in the city of Altamira, in the state of Pará, in the heart of the Amazon forest. Among all peripheral media outlets which have covered the social impact of *Belo Monte*, *Agência Pública* carves out a position that is unique. It moved towards a civic discussion, publishing reports that approached many of the undisclosed issues behind the project, some of which appeared very briefly in the country's main dailies. Producers worked based on what they saw as absences of the news. There were details of the work construction and environmental impact that ran undisclosed even amid prominent columnists, they said. I drew a quick comparison of the verbiage that appears in the coverage by *Folha de S.Paulo* and that of *Agência Pública,* in which I italicize some contrasting repertoire:

Looking at the above coverage, it is possible to perceive how both approaches differ—for instance, from "minimising" the damage to pointing

Table 4.1. The Belo Monte coverage by Agência Pública and Folha de S.Paulo

Agência Pública	*Folha de S.Paulo*
"Shut up in Belo Monte: This the story that opens the 'Cards on the table' series, in which citizens criticise [the political] candidate [and] the biggest construction of *Dilma's government*—40,000 people, mainly indigenous, have suffered the impact of this project." (*Agência Pública*, 09/04/2014)	"The urban population increases from 100,000 to 140,000 in two years and transforms the city in a chaos of traffic accidents, violence, and expensiveness. On the other hand, this place will receive *thousands of houses and sewage structures*, which have never existed. Read on this report everything that has been done and what is *missing to minimise the impact* of this work in the city's life." (*Folha de S.Paulo*, 16/12/2013)

out "huge social and environmental" impacts. If the situation in the city of Altamira is damaging for the population, the *balance* that seems to guide the broadsheet's language obfuscates the due pressure on government and authorities. Distinct from the less urgent tone in the story found at *Folha*, *Agência Pública*'s report highlights environmental damages and uses clear language to *politicize* the lack of clear explanation for the misuse of the "vast resources" dedicated to this work (by calling it *money*). *Pública*'s media producers have given to an average reader a stronger sense of what is going on out of the construction plant, linking it to the lives of affected citizens (most of whom are poor and indigenous).

As later revealed,[13] *Folha*'s special report received funds from the company in charge of building the dam. Although this factor does not need to affect the quality of the latter's reporting, neither does it compromise the well-intentioned purpose of the latter's pieces, this information on the newspaper's sponsorship is weaponized so as to allow producers to claim publicly what is *really* an independently-funded piece, as *Agência Pública* did at the time. Their reporting has meant to reveal the consequences for the public-drive of the report when one faces constraints of access, as their reporters have alleged to, as opposed to the comfortable settings that a sponsorship from the building company has given to the so-called "professionalised" coverage. In brief, assuming that one has no special access would appear as an advantage for an expected independence and legitimacy.

As seen above, *Folha*'s emphasis on the inevitability of the dam sheds some light on the newspaper's constrained position where one expects them to delve into the work's real impacts and escalating dangers. The newspaper has somehow done it by offering a glance on the impoverished reality, but it could have done more. This dilemma also reveals the degree of idealism in any idea of *watchdog journalism* when applied to South American journalism: familiar organizations vs liberal journalism, independence vs political clientelism (as discussed in Waisbord, 2000). *Agência Pública*'s coverage has claimed a deeper commitment to journalism's social mission, which translates into interviews conducted with Altamira's residents and fine videos and animations where the message to taxpayers is straightforward and provocative: "Brazil National Bank of Development in the Amazon: How our money funds [infrastructure] works in the Amazon" (*Agência Pública*, 09/12/2013). They convincingly argue that "our" money is misled to these purposes, appealing to democratic premises of taxation and return. One could argue that this is not an angle commonly found at alternative media level, often proud for being detached from any dialogue with middle class taxpayers. Eventually, this material also resulted in a *fine* media product, a professionally made animation and didactic explanations on public budget and return of investment.

The contrasting conditions in which each outlet has covered *Belo Monte* maps onto the different degrees of what one understands by watchdog journalism. In terms of what concerns this book, this *genuineness* politicizes issues that are key to understand the mechanisms of inequality, as it contests the mainstream media with provocative questions such as "who is more realistic?" and "whose *reality* is the big media more interested in?" These questions connect to past scholarship that saw the typical alternative media stance as result of an *open* process of reflexivity (Harcup, 2005; Rauch, 2007). But here I argue that while it was certainly meant to reinforce the daring conditions of the reportage, as it says: "*proudly* produced with no support," the process *is* tailored to confront the hegemony of the mainstream counterparts. Even if it did not bring the Belo Monte's works to a halt, the coverage and language employed in *Agência Pública* reports still developed a huge effort to place the dam's damage at the forefront in a dramatic way. To sum up, their work was undeniably more about the surrounding neighborhoods than about the *dam* itself.

The main takeaway from this evidence lies in the new ways to dodge *hegemonic* imperatives of what is *coverage*, both in terms of production guidelines and a sense of priorities. First, it tackles the counterhegemonic position of the mainstream media as a unique narrator in such a remote location. Second, it goes against the assumption that the mainstream media's production methods (and sense of balance) are the only one way that might lead to reliable and superior reporting. Third, it conveys transparency to the reader regarding the process without giving away its degree of radical discourse. The necessary formality of reporting, in the sense of seriousness, continues to exist so reporters are well positioned to analyze a work that costed the public billions. Now, I wrap up discussions present in both above sections to analyze the sense of renovating journalism standards, but which happens to be the emergence of an entirely new model.

TOWARDS A BOTTOM-UP CRITIQUE OF JOURNALISM

This chapter analyzed producers' interests in tackling the mainstream media's views of the periphery by engaging with public interest journalism or framing what they do as such. While it is not my aim to discuss who is inside and who is outside of journalism as a profession (as in Schudson & Anderson, 2009:89), there are clear efforts in politicizing the limitations of professional reporting. The duality of not abiding by journalism rules but also aiming to evoke it, mock it, or even assume the position of "journalists" is well addressed in literature (e.g. Forde, 2011). The same critique of journalism has historically been present among "grassroots" media groups from South and Central America (Rodríguez, 2001:21), but here I dwell on the discursive side of this critique. The peripheral media differ from these groups because it responds in a more nuanced way. What stands out in this book is how this duality does not apply to invalidate what the mainstream media do (no claims of elite alignment or corporate construction of reality, for example), but it does translate into more throwing the latter into obsolescence, while there is the politicization of existing social and reporting issues.

The literature on political opportunity has seen "opening media access" as one of the ways in which movements could create broader avenues to broadcast what they see as social change (Gamson & Meyer, 1996; Tarrow, 1992). In this chapter's cases, I see that the assumption of "seeking media attention" as problematic, and therefore hard to apply to the case of the peripheral media. If producers have, as seen, advocated against the *big* media, they have also voiced no wish to join or replace, but to shadow the frames of an imagined better mainstream media (fairer, and focused on social issues). The producers whom I interviewed were ready to collaborate with powerful Globo TV, but they also preferred to act primarily based on their own discourses and websites, which meant the total rejection of the big organization. Likewise, they have recognized the value of the mainstream media's own formative programs, but still not abandoning the decades-old, grassroots concept of *educomunicação*. As a resource to politicization, these educative programs have opened what is like having a common language with the mainstream media as far as they mobilized *their* audience as *their* publics to *their* politics.

The discourse against Globo TV organizations expectedly departs from the deep-seated image of a "monopoliser" (Amaral & Guimarães, 1994) but evolves into a less-important category of opposition. For instance, only two producers remembered the company's ties with the military dictatorship (1964–1984). In the 1970s, Globo allegedly received funds from American investors to guarantee a supportive agenda to the right-wing regime; it was when the Marinho family had consolidated their hegemonic presence with a TV network (Amaral, 2002). Researchers such as Bernardo Kucinski (1998) have also raised arguments about the enduring ethical dubiety of Globo's journalists, what he called the "parabolic antenna syndrome."[14] By contrast, *Globo*'s problematic dealing with democracy has appeared marginally in producers' discourses. Likewise, neither the personal accountability of mainstream journalists, nor disguised interests of the broadcasters were much at stake for most producers.

The "ideological" aspect to which the producers have related to are the decades of literature hailing Globo TV's technical and professional supremacy. Straubhaar (1984, 1991), for instance, has often quoted works on Brazil's "asymmetric interdependence" towards the United States, but pointed out that Globo TV's *telenovelas* could create a less dependent relationship. Fox and Waisbord (2002:1–21) firmly defended the group's local and regional power, although concluding that this power is peripheral and not one of a "world media player." Other authors have discussed the soft power of Globo TV as a contributor to national identity (Mattelart & Mattelart, 1990; Porto, 2007). Radical perspectives also placed such importance by casting doubts on the viability of a media democracy while the mainstream media had such a central actor (Kucinski, 1991; Amaral, 2002).

As a result, the politicization verified here is subtler, but gets none of these points. I prefer to translate it as a *tension,* a sentiment which is also demonstrated from the mainstream media's side. In defence of their history, Brazil's media moguls have lately[15] compared Brazil's media experience with that of other countries such as the United States, coming to publicly apologize for past commitments with non-democratic forces. Commercially speaking, Globo TV's grandiosity and ability to export goods such as *telenovelas* has not been that different from other media organizations (Rêgo & La Pastina, 2007; Thussu, 2006:166). Likewise, it is fair to concede that no evidence has ever proved that the mainstream organizations have blocked producers' prospects of developing a more inclusive and bolder media. Instead, they often appear as a role model for some instances of professional journalism, as it did elsewhere (Bardoel & Deuze, 2001; Wilkin, 2008). And yet, producers have taken the mainstream media factor less seriously than the media studies literature have done it.

Why does that happen? First, I would be skeptical about notions of the "rejection" of the mainstream media and would engage with ideas of *balance, continuum* or *hybridity* (Harcup, 2011; Kenix, 2011 and others) to describe the relationship between the periphery and the mainstream media, while the latter have been key to "create" many aspects of the former's public image. In brief, we cannot reduce this cohort of producers into a small amalgam of dissenters that create a mirror of the "main" thing. A new reporting reality is otherwise a unique model based on producers' specific interests and affordances. Based in the far southeast, producers from *Agência Pública* have travelled to cover an agenda that is far away from them because they believed to be of *public* interest. There were, apparently, no press relations department or media agents. The same is true for the videos that *Nigeria* produced after visiting public prosecutors in the countryside of Brazil explored in chapter 2. Outlets such as the online magazine *Vai da Pé*—a self-funded online magazine based in São Paulo[16]—have underlined their inclination to follow an idea of *impersonal public* (as in Haas, 2004), in which they envision a less institutionalised and conservative type of audience and reaffirm their "interpretative" scope (Harcup, 2003:371; Rauch, 2007).

In effect, many producers have also argued that part of their mission is to reach an interclass, interracial collaboration (via *educomunicação*) in which producers from privileged backgrounds can share technical skills with other producers, in editing in expensive software. In this way, *Vai da Pé* and *Nigéria*—formed mostly by middle-class white producers—can talk on behalf of other producers or activists with less media formation, as this may also happen the other way around. At one level, this collaboration starts to mingle productive with discursive standards; on the other, that integration leads to a working collaboration, which produces alliances with the professional media, as it constitutes far away from the mainstream. The middle class, *favela* residents are together with media producers of other profiles to afford an occasional breakthrough in the so-called media market (e.g. as the example of the *Voz das Comunidades* blog).

All these intersections are enough to claim that the politicization around the mainstream media have illustrated less of the dominant presence of big media players, as far as it reveals more of the new challenges that emerge directly from the communities and their media producers. My reading of the real counterhegemonic shift from the 1980s' agenda of the alternative media (Festa & Silva, 1986) lies in the greater diversification of the media environment and readership from *favelas* and peripheral neighborhoods, consequently leading the debate on the media monopoly and media regulation to a certain obsolescence. It is not true, at the same time, that peripheral media producers assumed that the current institutional framework is no longer important. It is relevant and urgent, but so it is to put up new media products in this market.

As producers migrate away from directing attacks at the mainstream media, they started seeing these issues as too engendered to tackle and easier to make something better. This strategic thought is seen in a film produced by a *Nigeria* film collective, in which the group criticizes media representations of beachfront dwellers, but the group's main concern is in delivering the finest product they can. Watching this online short-length film, *Subdivided Sand*, one finds no direct references to the mainstream media, as if the group aimed to *overlook* what the public sees from Globo TV, and, otherwise, convince their spectators by placing their narrative as the only reasonable viewpoint.

While it is true that this increasing proficiency is not enough to discard the tradition of public service and responsibility by Brazilian mainstream journalism (Medina, 1982), this collection of films, reportages, and online content bypass the bargains and relations with power holders that have been typical of journalism in South America (Waisbord, 2000:182). The harsh market reality in the region feeds the pressure for media change and media convergence, not entirely approached in this chapter. Here lies another motivation which I interpret within the same wave of politicization of inequality as promoted by the peripheral media. What I intended here was to acknowledge not only the growing limitations of the professional sector, but to introduce how the dimensions of this constraint also confirms the growing scope and creativity of the peripheral media.

CONCLUSION

In this chapter, I reviewed evidence that confirmed producers' struggle in fighting portraits and practices that have affected the coverage of inequality in Brazil. Even though mainstream practice can indeed influence them in different ways, there are new ideological frontiers. I aimed for more clarity on what are considered unacceptable media portraits by them, trying to unveil new initiatives and projects related to a critical consciousness on the media (via *educomunicação*), as well as analyzing how old agendas against the mainstream media dominance have appeared. The contribution of this section was to move away from the "colonisation or collaboration" paradigm, claiming that such binary terms no longer corresponded to the opinions collected from producers or reflect their relationship with the mainstream media. For example, producers have opened up new ways to politicize inequality based on enhancing the media practices in their favor. Challenging the perception of a public service journalism is dependent on the circumstances seen in the mainstream media organizations and that means producing new quality content on independent basis. In the next chapter, I end this book's empirical parts by stretching the discussion on the image of the periphery according to the Brazilian State, which after decades appears up for a contestation by peripheral media producers.

NOTES

1. Connected to Globo TV as non-profit organisation.
2. As in the following story published by G1, "Indians insert arrows in front of the Brasilia *esplanade* in protests for land distribution," where the main feature is the violence of the protest. Available at http://g1.globo.com/distrito-federal/noticia/2016/11/indios-fincam-flechas-na-esplanada-em-ato-por-demarcacao-de-terras.html. Accessed 18 June 2016.
3. All content references are from the blog's website http://mural.blogfolha.uol.com.br. Accessed 18 April 2016.

4. As quoted by Folha de S. Paulo, available at http://www1.folha.uol.com.br/cotidiano/2013/09/1341989-jornalista-do-blog-mural-lanca-livro-sobre-maior-favela-de-sp.shtml. Accessed 12 January 2015.

5. The project seems to continue via crowdsourcing, their website is at https://agenciamural.com.br. Accessed 12 January 2015.

6. According to interview in the News Rewired panel. Available at https://www.newsrewired.com/2015/07/16/how-news-groups-use-citizen-journalism-to-give-a-voice-to-marginalised-communities/. Accessed 31 December 2015.

7. Available at http://witness.theguardian.com. Accessed 31 December 2015.

8. According to his account on the Guardian's website. https://www.theguardian.com/cities/video/2015/jan/06/guardian-citizen-reporting-training-programme-india-video. Accessed 01 February 2015.

9. More information on this program is found on the initiative's website: http://www.com.ufv.br/noticias/34-gerais/835-museu-da-comunicacao-realiza-atividades-nas-escolas-de-vicosa.html. Accessed 20 October 2014.

10. While no specific dates of workshops or evidence from this text review process have been found, by contrasting the testimonial of both schemes' sponsors, seeing their social media invitations to potential participants, and reading the final language of these publications, it is expected that these programs have followed bureaucratic procedures, which have not been seen in *educomunicação* practices.

11. As widely reported in the Brazilian media in 2015. Brasil 247 editor, Leandro Attuch appeared as beneficiary of a corruption scheme, according to whistleblower Milton Pascowitch at https://www.cartacapital.com.br/blogs/parlatorio/site-brasil-247-recebeu-propina-de-vaccari-diz-lobista-1677.html. Accessed 12 December 2015.

12. Editorial staff's decisions are not generally open to scholarly or non-scholarly scrutiny, as journalists have generally treated their own options out of public gaze. However, in the case of *favela* reports, and perhaps due to the campaigning for a better coverage, has achieved some public acknowledgement of these pitfalls, as in this case of journalist Jo Griffin, *The Guardian*'s contributors. Citing newsrooms concerns, it was argued that editors did not know what term to employ when reporting from *favelas.* This opinion was found in this media criticism website. Available at https://ijnet.org/en/blog/rioonwatch-launches-guide-encourage-nuanced-news-coverage-rio-de-janeiro-olympics. Accessed 15 December 2016.

13. In December 2015, the Piauí magazine, one of the leading monthly magazines in Brazil, has revealed the close ties between PR agencies and the Brazilian press, in which the former facilitates deals to promote certain clients, which in return, sponsors some of the press pieces. Folha's reporting on Belo Monte was one of the examples. "O sujeito oculto," available at http://piaui.folha.uol.com.br/materia/o-sujeito-oculto/. Accessed 14 February 2016.

14. Name given after a backstage conversation mistakenly broadcast in which the Globo journalist Carlos Monforte appeared in conversations with a former minister from Fernando Henrique Cardoso's administration contradicting the version just debated live in the program.

15. The owner of Brazil's most influential daily *Folha de S. Paulo,* Otavio Frias Filho, argued in his defence a comparison with the *New York Times*, which is also

owned by a traditional publishing family. Brazil's leading left-wing magazine, *Carta Capital*, is also property of the Carta family, which saw itself recently involved when its close relations with ex-president Luís Inácio Lula da Silva came to public attention. These arguments came up during a conference in London, 24 June 2016 at https://www.youtube.com/watch?v=usPgv2M4ZlE. Accessed 08 October 2016.

16. When I spoke with them, their improvised newsroom was at one team member's home in a middle-class suburb, west São Paulo.

Chapter Five

Challenging the State

In the last chapter, I explored the extent to which peripheral media outlets have absorbed different influences from the mainstream media as strategic resources to attack current media portraits of the periphery and build a more engaged and counterhegemonic coverage of inequality. In this chapter, producers also appear to associate their practice with notions of public interest, but in a way that tackles discourses specifically inherited from the Brazilian State, interacting with its swaying power. I use interview data to identify this historical influence, seeing where their will to change the discourse resides. In the frame analysis part, I discover a set of *linkages* with contemporary inequalities and its relationship with state intervention. It is important to obtain a full grasp of these state-citizen-media interactions, as they could reveal a break or continuity with past discourses—especially seen during political campaigns—in which the poor are portrayed as inferior and naturally dependent on the state's (or politician's) mercy. The common perception of Brazilians regarding inequality, which adds to this panorama, has expected the state to solve all sorts of social issues, as this allows them to assign full responsibility to politicians, and justify their indifference (Boschi & Diniz, 1991; Reis, 1999, 2000; Henriques, 2000).

On the other hand, this section allows us to engage with other correlated debate involving the alternative media and the state in Brazil. As leftist governments came to power in South America during the 2000s, a few authors discussed the potential "ideologisation" or the action of small-scale producers in favor of these governments' views and policies (Kitzberger, 2010, 2013; Villareal, 2015). For example, in Brazil, many media activists and media scholars became government allies or part of its staff (Castro et al., 2014) during president Dilma Rousseff's terms (2011–2016). This government has also boosted public policies orientated towards funding and expanding the alternative media. Were these developments aimed at reversing the historical dynamic of persecution between state power and the alternative media (Sodré, 2008)? Would this state boost change the perception that the peripheries were overdependent on the state (*assistencialismo*)? These questions are fundamental for this book, to the extent that they allow us to stress how the periphery reacts to such decades-old instances, being the *periphery*, arguably, a creation of the state and the "elites" (Valladares, 1978; Souza & Barbosa, 2005; Souza, 2005).

As this book spans across a period when left-wing ideology sold Brazil as leaving the stage of underdevelopment to finally become a prosperous society, the idea is to contrast producers' opinions, testing their views on this benevolent state that supposedly "helped to relief poverty." Moreover, we can also contrast producers' engagement with state policies aimed at the "alternative" media and analyze to what degree the hypothesis of "politicization" can be true to the extent that producers receive funds from the state, which requires them to comply with a set of professional and content criteria. I start by reviewing the ways in which non-mainstream coverage has historically opposed or engaged with the state.

INTERACTIONS WITH THE STATE IN A BOTTOM-UP COVERAGE OF INEQUALITY

I found two strong patterns that positioned producers' discourse regarding the contemporary Brazilian State. The first one viewed the state as responsible for correcting the country's record on inequality, which protests the lack of public services, and campaigns for welfare policies. Another pattern opposes the latter's attempts to change the scenario. In this second convergence, producers viewed with suspicion the definitions given by the state, finding populism where politicians have tried to help the "needy." In the first, to protest the government's lack of attention to public services, producers made use of anachronistic references, as they linked current state negligence and the failure to support its representatives with the memories of an authoritarian Brazil. In this first pattern, the producers have engaged with the state in attempt to get support for funds to feed their media production. Aware of the unprecedented effort from Dilma Rousseff's left-wing government to "develop" the alternative media in the country, producers enjoyed the existing opportunities but, at the same time, voiced critical stances against the state handling of the overall media environment.

Both points relate to this book's topic for two reasons. They help us to understand the ways in which the state is a part of producers' coverage of inequality, but not necessarily only through what I call here politicization. Secondly, it helps to see that, while not always in opposition to the state, producers still confront politicians, authorities or institutions using radical repertoire, engaging with the bureaucratic environment of procedures and government support. This way of relating to the state outside the framework of "begging" for help or bribing politicians is a major shift for a historically clientelist country where inequality was not considered everyone's responsibility, neither has the state taken its share (Barros et al., 2001; Galeano, 2013). Next, I start to outline notions of distrust and hopelessness as a first symptom of a further scepticism regarding politicians.

Distrust, Public Services, and Dialogue with Power

The series of government failures and the relationship between unfulfilled electoral promises and needy marginalized communities have a special highlight from the peripheral media. At the same time that producers blame the state for not acting on basic public services, such as the lack of power or public health care, there is also a place for remembering its incompetence for having "provoked" the illegal trajectory of some communities, from squatting to their first establishment, as it is the case of most *favelas*. Media producers said that they tried to move on out of this conundrum of blaming the state by checking what the propaganda says and sticking to what has been promised. For instance, what are the health care provisions and the extent to which the government has lied in campaigns. I italicized some of these emphases:

> We try to show this [issue of] neglect, the lack of access to basic things. Going to a health centre and not having the right to take the vaccines; *the government is advertising [these] on TV* and they do not exist. Or the school wherein you want to study and there is no electricity, at least to drink fresh water or to be able to see what the tutor wants to teach, what he is writing on the board. (Media producer 36)

Even when some of these public projects in communities do start, their distrust also extends to the ability of the state to deliver works and facilities, especially as governments change and, in the meantime, policies tackling social issues do not move forward:

> Unfortunately, we have a huge difficulty in keeping up a policy; whenever a government or political party wins an election, that policy is discarded, and we no longer have it. (Media producer 39)

Most producers have had the clarity to assess the roots of such neglect, as well as the roots of their inherent distrust. Most of them have considered it a by-product of the many interruptions to democracy in Brazil, which, at the same time, provides them with stories and an agenda:

> When we talk about the re-democratisation period of Brazil, we are talking about a period in which some people try to erase what happened. Until a few years ago, [there was a] book called the *Revolution of 1964*, which the supporters justified as stopping a communist coup—this is one of the widespread versions. They taught it as if that was 'for your benefit' or 'this happened but it is over.' What happens is, the people do not stop to think about it, on its leftovers, on what is still here. For example, I speak about the criminalization of the graffiti, which is one of these leftovers that we find. Why can't I do my graffiti? Because I can spread any message, even things from the media. (Media producer 38)

The persistence of such authoritarian time stems from a time that many in Brazil have associated with having excellent public services. The above producer mentions the attempts to move forward from the military regime, as far as it was also during this period that Brazil's decade-long lack of orientation to forging quality of life in the cities' outskirts has started. Appropriately, on many occasions, producers likened public services to the flaws in the country's institutional democracy. In this sense, there is a strong perception that by *communicating* with the government directly, issues are more likely to be resolved, coming from an idea of "participatory" politics that have been strong since the re-democratization (e.g. in Avritzer, 2000).

In Baixada Fluminense, an impoverished area of Greater Rio, producers of the self-funded newspaper *Voz da Baixada* have tried to create dialogue directly with the City Hall's representatives. The newspaper has proposed a monthly meeting with one of the government officials, in which one of the editors discusses issues that affect the *Baixada* region. They believe these meetings could improve the local community's perception of democracy and perception of state power. A leading producer told me:

> An idea we have started is to promote the 'Baixada Dialogue,' which is an initiative in which we bring up pragmatic solutions previously proposed by other city mayors. We set up open meetings, in which we call the people to join us, and it is where we talk about current issues, such as health, the sewage system, and security. We invite a specialist in the subject or someone from the *Baixada*, who could be very involved in this subject or social movements, depending on what we discuss, and the public manager or one of the mayor's assistants. After ten [editions of the] 'Diálogo da Baixada' meetings, we can write a document with the citizens' proposals and deliver it to future mayor candidates during the next election.

This initiative got to assure readers that media producers were indeed committed to taking social issues beyond—in this case, towards a practical acknowledgement, thereby reducing the gap between an imagined government and a real one. From a media perspective, this outlet's initiative transformed their role into one of real community leaders, which could be otherwise unnecessary had the state built visible and effective channels for such issues or had the state taken these inputs into serious consideration.

These producers have, nonetheless, meant not to abandon the lobbying at the municipal instances of power. This improvization in reaching out to officials has just sought to create another moment of democratic listening. Another degree of this relationship happens when producers receive funds from the federal government. Despite the above example, I have found only a few other interfaces with the local power, despite an increasing number of producers cover Brazil's countryside, with high indices of persecution of blogs and independent journalists.[1] In terms of sponsorship, most producers have argued that their councils and municipalities are cash-strapped to invest in public grants, whereas the major programs were those put out by the Federal Government. Therefore, what we see next focuses on the relationship that peripheral media producers have established with federal bodies in which they apply and receive grants, discuss public bursaries, and on top of it, criticize government and the state. I stress with them the possibility of becoming, after all, partners with the state.

PUBLIC FUNDING: JEOPARDIZING POLITICIZATION?

Most producers have said to use or have used public grants to fund their media production. Knowing this led me to further examine how attractive federal policies that funded the "alternative media" could be and the extent to which, if any, this advent could undermine the politicization I sought to analyze. The point at which I start to research these policies is when they give continuation of Lula's first policy, *Culture Points*[2] (2011–2014), later implemented in Dilma Rousseff's first term (2011–2014). It went further to increase funding and organize the networking of media groups that were focused on reporting agendas from ethnic, sexual, and other minorities.[3] Different from other contexts in which drawing on a concept of "ethnic" media was enough to satisfy a conceptual conundrum on who to include or not when incentivizing the "alternative" media (Deuze, 2006), the innovative call to "create media" in the *Free Media Points* program had an emphasis on delivering digital access (a computer and Internet kiosk).

In that sense, this policy saw citizens, especially young people, having ICTs and Internet access for free, a feature that it is in itself an advance, but also a limitation, as debated in past studies (Pretto & Assis, 2008; Pretto & Bailey, 2011). Regardless of the size or outreach, and as the figure below demonstrates, producers engaged in other formats, those with whom I spoke to, said to expect more. For example, they have participated in these programs as entrepreneurs, and as users in a time of uneven Internet access (though growing). However, what invited them to subscribe into these initiatives in most cases was the possibility of receiving an amount that could be reversed into media production, not only into access, as this was scarcely funded field. They had also, and inevitably, started to have new opinions about the government, especially those who had joined the initiative.

Opinions varied within a vast range of subjects, from government officials to incentives for big media organizations. I aim to concentrate here on reproducing evidence that sets up a clearer scenario about the effects of this close interaction with initiatives from the federal government to understand what politicized discourse they could still produce in these circumstances. I had to challenge the mechanisms of this interaction with the government and then analyze how producers altered, opposed, or accepted certain conditions imposed.

One of the ways in which producers commonly referred to their interaction with government requirements was by scrutinizing published *editals*, checking for opportunities for themselves and their groups. These official publications have appeared as the easiest bridge with the government. Producers interchangeably used the word *edital* to mean resource opportunities and, at the same time, "see what was going on" in their area:

> Our project has no financial resources; we don't receive anything from anyone and have not received recently. The most we can do is resort to crowdfunding. We made [enough] now to fund a trip. We try to apply for *editais*, we try to get funds in cash. (Media producer 50)

When I shifted my focus to approaching how funds increased effectiveness in covering poverty and inequality stories versus publishing about other subjects, most producers relativized the importance of these programs as another source of support, mentioning that it did not provoke a shift from stories on poverty and inequality. Some of them even pondered if these grants could mean a distraction for the whole category of alternative media producers. A few of them pinpointed on the contradictions of the government dedicating a small amount of resources to fund the alternative media while having a large budget to dedicate to its advertisements on the mainstream media. Producers argued that, because their goal was increasing a socially critical coverage, they should be eligible to similar funding levels and not be underrated due to their limited outreach:

> The logic of governmental advertisement, which is based on the audience of each outlet, is also arguable. It is complicated because this logic does not include emerging initiatives, as it does not consider network articulation. For example, a story from our group has been published by *Opera Mundi*, *Carta Capital*, *Carta Maior*; therefore, it is not possible to measure only the reach of these publications. (Media producer 49)

On the other hand, the issue of funding as state benefit has shed light on a competitive context in which producers have seemed concerned with their own survival as professionals, citizens, and households:

> If you look at the government's latest *edital*, those who won were the same ones who had other chances of funding. I believe they will have to create a barrier—those who have never had the opportunity of focusing 100% on a magazine, for example; of not having to split oneself in other jobs and masters. One doesn't have time to focus on a magazine. (Media producer 16)

While no further opposition existed against the criteria adopted in the *Free Media Points* program, they noticed that the government primed for its relations with so-called *progressive bloggers*. This group of political blogs had at its core ex-mainstream journalists, who made an impression over producers (and over the public opinion, as seen in mainstream media reports) that they are supporters of Workers' Party policies (Guazina, 2013; Castro, 2015). While this study has sought not to test the likely involvement of these bloggers with the government, their great popularity is said to have overshadowed the activity of those outlets only focused on social justice.

Looking at specialized *editals,* the participation of peripheral media among the awardees over the years (2013–15) is rather reduced. I found Internet platforms and service providers, such as social networking websites for entertainment, and cultural and artistic groups. This list might have confirmed producers' accounts that the policy lacked the focus on those practising the online "coverage" of social issues. For them, it should favor not the "digital connection," to the extent it means the "ICT-access" mentality, but media production that can play a "real" role over fragile communities, associated to the Internet-based outlets. On the other hand, although a high percentage of producers have only published on the Internet, a considerable number has also invested in alternative formats, such as film, radio, print, exhibitions, and conferences, as I have shown below. It is evident that these alternative platforms matter for most of them, but a robust online presence remains the most valuable resource for media producers; therefore, any potential fund should address this need to put up websites, produce content, pay subscriptions, as long as it is a more suitable support for their reality.

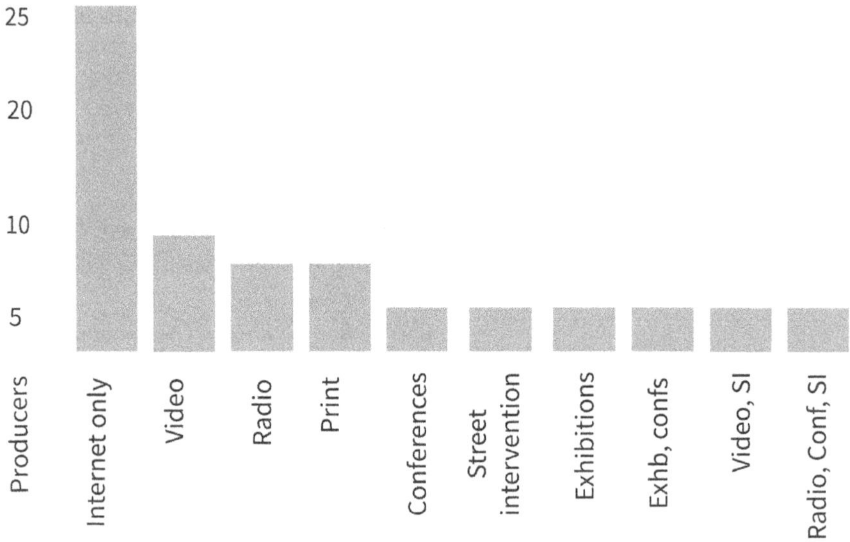

Figure 5.1. Main platforms for media producers.

Once this funding frustration was voiced out, I moved on to question other reasons to support the government with their media outlets. I came to focus, instead, on what producers have mentioned about the issue of partisanship and its relevance for engaging or not with these policies for the alternative media. Was there any ideological or partisan inclination expected from them that could weight for the government's decision on who will get the grant? In advance to this question, producers said to act in favor of an inequality agenda even if that meant they had to go against their partisan or political orientation. But for twelve years, Brazil was governed by a left-wing, socially orientated coalition, which is said to have changed the country for the better. That fact could naturally gather more support to this government. I anchor the following discussion on these two scenarios, trying to position these arguments in a way to dialogue with past research that saw the alternative media either challenging or allying with these governments, not only in Brazil, but in the whole "Latin America."

Partisanship and the Social Justice Agenda

When I asked producers about the left-wing government's policies about poverty, inequality, they have agreed with some of these policies and disagreed with others, but most of them preached an ethical detachment from the world of institutionalized politics. These same producers have not denied, however, that some alternative media producers had, indeed, partisan ties. To report on the government negligence discussed earlier, producers agreed it is problematic if one is partisan in one's goals, especially under the popular Workers' Party government of the time. Ambiguously, a greater number of interviewees feared that their readers could confuse their interest and eagerness in denouncing social issues with a supportive (and for some, blind) leftist agenda, which could throw into doubt the veracity of their coverage. I highlight some of these partisan experiences, as well as the ambiguity that stemmed from the interviews:

> Some [alternative] media around are very [much] 'government supporters.' My criticism is that because you have a political position but one you will support, you will have to be honest with your content. For example, during the last election, Dilma was in the first place in the polls, and [candidate] Eduardo Campos died, and [candidate] Marina started to run ahead, and out [of nowhere], some 'Internet famous' outlets started to blame Marina. Why are they blaming Marina? [This was] only because Dilma was doing badly in the polls. *Then I think it is not fair. It is political, intellectual dishonesty*. You're criticising Marina for something that Dilma also does. (Media producer 12)

> We worked with Telesur, a state TV from Venezuela, which has been organised in Brazil. They recruited some collectives to produce content for them but, after a while, they changed their editorial policy because of the World Cup. Amid the World Cup, we were doing political pieces. *Then the government said we cannot talk about bad things* about the World Cup anymore . . . [it seems that] they were '*hiding something,*' so we decided to leave it. (Media producer 15)

According to the above testimonial, the government expected grant-applicant producers to comply with reportages that showed the 2014 World Cup in positive light. In other words, they should portray it as a smooth event, respecting the inclinations of the left-wing government that decided that the country should host it. Many producers, though, preferred to confirm their critical stance against the event. Producers did protest the political choices that led to Brazil hosting the World Cup, but they did not protest the masterminds of these decisions. This paradox leads us to inquire into the legacy of approximation of the alternative media to left-wing characters.

To what concerns this legacy, that of the 1970s' alternative press, to support a political part of the left was not only obvious, as it also involved nominating dissenters or consenters. At that time, that would involve nominating those in favor or against the dictatorship. Back then, unionist leaders such as Lula, who also appeared on a cover of *Movimento* magazine in 1970, counted on support mostly due to democratic reasons (to be for him was, after all, to be against dictators). In the contemporary peripheral media, the same form of leftist support occurs, but, as said, for other reasons. Forty years later, Lula is a popular ex-President accused of corruption,[4] but as a display of affection, one media producer posted a selfie with Lula in a 2015 event with the following caption: "With Lula for democracy!"

This intention of posting affinities with famous politicians of the left does not allow me to deepen on ideological or partisan preferences any further. Nonetheless, I return to the last producers' testimonial to lay out what was rare episode of dissent, amid ideological grounds clearly aligned with left-wing agenda for the periphery. In the case of Lula, as far as his political discourse has spoken about hunger, privilege, and prejudice in a "paternalist" mode (Chagas, 2007), that still resonates strongly through producers' opinions, whether on the left and the right. This kind of admiration seemed for them something different from siding with or following specific commands from these political forces or changing the focus of their coverage. In other moments, they seemed to condition this partisan support to the inclination of the leftist party in solving social issues covered in their outlets:

> While we have a government from the centre-left, we will share the same premises. If a government from the right comes into power, in this moment, we will see what happens, because there is a conflict of interest. This happens in many places, in many states. (Media producer 40)

> I think the government is important; of course we are not going to want a government [from] the right, which does not think in human rights or equality, etc. But I think the question is on human [values] really, not only right or left, but whenever you think you should say some things to people, start to accept it. (Media producer 41)

This continuum between left-wing ideals and the peripheral media agenda is well studied if we go deep in the discourse of *mídialivrismo*. Some of the participants of the *Free Media Points* program described what they were doing not as *alternative* media but as *mídia livre* or "free media." Later, I found out that this term baptised the government's program focused on training alternative media producers. While challenging the label "alternative," producers were happy in calling themselves non-hegemonic and non-traditional—in sum, *free media*. In fact, the Brazilian government had sponsored a couple of meetings in Rio de Janeiro under the same title, where the training would cover *mídialivrismo*. On the government's website,[5] the *Free Media Points* program meetings appear as a way of "not being restricted to the big communication outlets, supporting and feeding ways of [having a] free communication." This announcement was signed by the Communications Assistant of the Culture Department of the time, Cecília Coelho. Each producer had offered a distinctive opinion on how *mídialivrismo* mattered for their practice:

> Mídialivrismo came with [the media activist group] *Fora do Eixo*. I [was] made part of this group for a time, as well as of *Midia Ninja*. This was a concept with which they worked a lot; it was initially 'collaborative coverage' and, more recently, it became 'mídialivrismo.' It is about using the journalism and communication languages, using the mobile for live broadcasting, using hashtags. [It is] not necessarily [related] to a media outlet, but [refers to] being able to do things with less resources. (Media producer 15)

> It is the appropriation of the platforms by people who aren't necessarily communicators, communication specialists. It is about giving the possibility for [a] people community and exert[ing] their right to communication. (Media producer 17)

Fora do Eixo is a media collective that played a key role in publicizing the 2013 nationwide protests via Internet livestreams (Peruzzo, 2013; Vieira, 2014; Wainberg, 2015). Although the group started in the early 2000s in the city of Brasília (Morais, 2013), before Lula's first administration, the group came to notoriety once their ties with the Workers' Party grew and some of its activists joined Rousseff's government.[6] In fact, producers have also likened *mídialivrismo* to an ethical conduct, such as holding politicians, society and the media to account once it is necessary. As a discourse against various kinds of hegemony, *mídialivrismo* was meant both as an opportunity to try new formats and to change (the mainstream's) tougher publication rules that prevents some publics from entering in its programs, as these producers described:

> The hegemony of this [mainstream] media makes people [live] in a country that does not reflect ourselves, and, today, every story with more than two pages blocks us, in a time of [the] Internet in which things are fast. (Media producer 14)

> We come from the student movement, from the social movement for communication. Therefore, the way we make our point is a way to make it clear to our reader what is the process behind the content production. Normally, the traditional media is far away from this; it is impartiality in disguise. (Media producer 45)

I asked producers if the *mídialivrismo* meeting in Rio de Janeiro had helped them increase their coverage on inequality—if there was any specific boost in that sense. I found positive accounts, as it seemed that producers from different parts of the country enjoyed the chance to work in partnership. On the other hand, producers who disagreed with this particular role of networking, described the meeting as "inevitably" partisan, meaning the favouring of a few colleagues:

> This meeting was thought [of] by the people from *Fora do Eixo*, because a meeting took place last year, then they invited us to share again experiences of [the] alternative media in Brazil. They wanted to do a public hearing about this 'call for projects.' That was a certain mapping, but also co-optation. You know how those spaces are. There were people from *Fora do Eixo*, from the Youth National Secretary, which is also from the *PC do B* [political party . . . In the meeting] they thought about this call for projects [*Free Media Points* programme], alas the result was [published] today. The first ones were the usual ones. (Media producer 14)

> I was in Rio for the mídialivrismo meeting; the Youth Secretary has managed this meeting, and they had priority tickets for those from the north and northeast. Then this opened many paths to us. Today, for instance, I can talk with collectives from the northern region more easily because we had that contact, and it also allows us to articulate our actions. As I said, we are a collective, we walk through these spaces and it is important for us [to have] this communication. (Media producer 38)

Producers from the north or the northeast highlighted that meeting with enthusiasm. They argued that such chances of meeting producers from other regions were rare. Producers from the southeast tended to otherwise compare it with other big events, such as the *World Social Forum*, an event that used to happen in the city of Porto Alegre and which congregated social movements and members of the left around the world (see Santos & Santos, 2006).

With some of the attendees, I explored whether laying out this scenario of government support for an agenda would undermine the strength and accountability of their personal views. More precisely, I asked if the governing party's visions or priorities could drive their agenda, making them prioritize key issues and not others. As a response, those who also had been at the *mídialivrismo* meeting reaffirmed their ethical values, occasionally clarifying further limitations of these programs. Most of them saw them as limited solutions if one thinks of feeding the alternative media's development in Brazil as a "major challenge":

> If there is any situation in which the government says: 'You will receive a resource that comes from the [government sponsored] *Belo Monte dam*,' we will not appreciate it, we will not receive it, we will refuse it. We will always assess, otherwise it is a conflict with what we are proposing. (Media producer 14)

> One of the critiques is regarding the requirements. Because at one point, you will have to be a *Culture Point*. We, as a collective, have never discussed al-

> ternative media as a 'culture point' [. . .] Some groups present themselves as culture points, which means that they do not deal only with communications, but create events [and] articulate [through] festivals, as some have [the] ability of hunting public funds. (Media producer 12)

As the above producer pointed out, there were differences between those groups, which led to part of them comply with the targets of sustaining a *Culture Points* policy (maintaining a small facility with Internet access, for example) and those which were not totally in agreement with government's idea of investing in platforms and content alike.

To summarize this section, this cohort of media producers has not seemed much seduced in the face of the state unprecedented openness to their work. As seen, left-wing partisanship and the historical social justice goals have also resonated as in the 1970s and 1980s (Festa & Silva, 1986)—as it still seems a common denominator for the alternative media in general (Peruzzo, 2008). Producers' discourses against inequality does not necessarily dwell on this attachment. Otherwise, what we see is that a number of politicized stances toward leftist political parties and politicians (as a class) but reaffirming that the interests of the periphery remained intact. Next, frame analysis will allow other sides of this relationship with the state to come up, in which content sheds light on the representational side of inequality. A shift in media images was particularly desired having in a mind the stereotype of benefit-seekers and chasers of politicians as "godfathers," which are images that still lie upon some young people's minds.

DECONSTRUCTING MYTHS OF STATE DEPENDENCE

Back in the 1950s, the poor appeared as victims, but they are also those more likely to figure in political campaigns and personify official discourses, especially those living in the *favelas* (Cardoso, 1978; Fischer, 2008; Gay, 2010). In the peripheral media, 87 out of 120 articles analyzed have framed news or stories on poverty or inequality in relation to what the public administration has said or discussed the expectations that politicians have generated with their discourses. By contrast, producers have also mocked politicians' statements and denounced their inability to tackle crime among the poorest. Even though I have not included articles on corruption or the economy in my analysis, as they seemed out of the scope, the politicization found stems from an anger against the state. There is a strong perception that government officials jeopardize what would be an equal society by threatening human rights and media democracy. For example, by politicizing issues such as *abortion*, the state punishes those at the bottom[7] and creates more inequality.

It was the same regarding parliamentary bills that threatened communities of indigenous in the north of Brazil.

In the below table, I have delimited the main discursive patterns that show how both frames which I proposed to study have manifested in producers' repertoire. First, I found "agonistic" standards of deliberation which I interpret as a resource to *politicize* their discourse (as talking to the state demands strong rhetoric and voicing issues aloud). On the other hand, the frame that sought the reproduction of *charity* in their discourse leaned more towards negotiation and occasional alignment with authorities during crises.

The identification of these different, but somehow converging frames shows how complex is the crossroads between inequality, the state and the discourse against inequality in Brazil. At one level, the peripheral media politicizes the state's failure to uphold the rights provisioned in the 1988 Constitution; on the other hand, producers develop a positive discourse of change that has the state as a partner. I chose to problematize this ambiguity by employing the *assistencialismo* discourse, which politicians have used for decades to personalise state aid given to the poor. It is an idea that has framed public benefits as *aid* deriving from a politician's personal will and benevolence. Historically, the charitable politician used this idea to improve their chances during elections, in which politicians used it to call themselves "the fathers of the poor,"[8] a frequent claim during presidential campaigns of the 1950s, but which, somehow, still resonates (D'Araujo, 1999).

Overall, what this section shows is the reaction to these patronizing stances, in which politicized frames were to critically attack these past misconceptions on the role of the state to the life of the periphery. I break this section into three different and interdependent parts. First, I approach how producers have rejected the *assistencialismo* narrative by changing the people's understanding of state *benefits* as inherited rights, not as favors from

Table 5.1. Ways of interpreting the peripheral media discourse

Frame Politicization	*Frame Charity*
"Agonist" over "deliberative" rituals about rights and welfare benefits.	Directs attention to social issues from the people's perspective.
Holds government to account on historical issues (e.g. racial inequality, constitutional rights).	Aims for public funds, helps to create new media spaces, expands coverage, and attends events sponsored by the government.
Campaigns for more progressive laws.	Occasional partisanship, alignment with left-wing parties.

politicians. Secondly, I show how the peripheral media content goes beyond the "suspicion" of populists, where producers' coverage is concerned with spreading information about ongoing parliamentary bills and seek engagement with democratic institutions. Third, I approach how producers link crime to a consequence of a failed state. Producers tried to develop headlines that dismantle the idea that crime is a natural consequence of poverty, denouncing authoritarian state measures taken against marginalized citizens. To create such politicized frames, producers deployed strong narratives based on several attempts to recreate a repertoire of the past, mixing it with that of the everyday issues.

Unmaking the Assistencialismo Narrative

The extent to which the state needs to intervene and change people's destinies appears as a controversial point in the peripheral media. There is a constant return to the old saying that builds on the image of a *pai dos pobres* or the "the father of the poor." In fact, producers seem to respond to a constant threat from the political communications that put at stake issues that are serious and entrenched in the public imaginary such as food security and the lack of subsidies from the state for the poorest. For more insight into how *assistencialismo* still manifests in the late 2010s, it is enough to capture the Dilma Rousseff's 2014 presidential campaign. If the "father" has existed in the past, the "mother" is the role that we find in Rousseff's political trajectory (Dos Santos & Jalazai, 2014). Also, in her TV ads during her running for the second presidential term, spectators watched a video of a middle-class family whose dinner suddenly vanishes as an outcome of her main adversary's potential win. In sum, these images drew on the deep-seated values of Brazilian society by likening the right to eat (in a society with a history of extreme hunger issues) to the election of a president and, to another extent, to the state.

The peripheral media coverage challenges this tradition by using sophisticated and persuasive ways. They tackle the shame that some feel when receiving state aid, to replace it by images of an active and entrepreneurial periphery. Rather than building upon narratives that show its positive results of policies, which is the common frame of justification for such measures, they reimagine the advent of the 'benefit' as a necessity; in which the disadvantaged receive these amounts to *correct* the country's wrong course.[9] Therefore, to challenge these ideas of *assistencialismo* is to portray citizens as active characters that *do* things to deserve the state's support. Indeed, we find producers engaging in the very idea of what really is a public benefit, as to modernize the understanding and the fair application of constitutional rights, as we read on this website:

> Líntia also recognises the developmental benefits of Bolsa Família, praising the programme's emphasis on school attendance. School attendance has substantially increased at Fogueteiro. She finds the monetary motivation to educate the new generation somewhat unsettling, however: 'Bolsa Família is a way for [the government] to force education. Some families have little interest in educating their children, so the government pays to stimulate that interest. Now [parents] have a reason to educate their children: money.' (*Rio on Watch*, 25/10/2013)

As a successful conditional cash transfer (CCT) program, the *Bolsa Família* paid a sum to every low-income family in exchange for them keeping their children in school and ensuring their progress.[10] To modernize the coverage of such social programs is to give more insightful views that do not allow top-down appropriation from politicians. There are a few examples of how dwellers see these state benefits with a special regard, an area where women are the most outspoken (Marques, 2008). I pinpoint this program's coverage in the peripheral media much to give continuation to these bottom-up impressions. Secondly, because its presence is a paradigmatic event to reverse the problematic consolidation of such social programs as part of an agenda of rights and not as favors from politicians. Producers seemed to agree that the good understanding of programs such as *Bolsa Família* is key to leading the people into a more autonomous position regarding the legality and the impersonality of state benefits.

As a backdrop, it is useful to remember the process of writing the 1988 Brazilian Federal Constitution. It triggered thousands of letters to the members of Congress, in which ordinary citizens expressed their will to have jobs, cars, and houses. There was also an overall consciousness that they also needed better labor rights and women's rights, and less of a clientelist state. As Monclaire (Monclaire et al., 1991) showed in his landmark content analysis of these letters, citizens wished for a country of equal opportunities. This woman, in her 30s, no income, and resident of the impoverished state of Maranhão, wrote back then:

> I wish that job opportunities [are taken away] from the city mayors, as they use it as a vote weapon. We are in democratic times; I expect the government do something in favour of women. I believe in the government and in the opportunities of being happy. (Ibid, 1991:61)

There is much of these lines in the peripheral media. The change is, however, from *expecting* social change towards *participating, creating discourses.* This model of citizenship, which historians such as Carvalho (1999) have foreseen it, fights for rights but does not fall for clientelist politician. The politicization frame is thus not one of agreeing or disagreeing with the government or praising its policies, but about the conditions of citizens who are making a living despite the lack of benefits to which they are entitled. While the mainstream press used to depict the beneficiaries as standing still at their doors in the *favelas* the actualization of such portraits is an advance regarding the awareness promoted among a population that was not used to know the commitments owed to them. The change in this portrayal is visible and it speaks to the opportunities of renovating such interest in disadvantaged communities not as receivers, but as participants of a social project.

Nevertheless, I still saw that these outlets can also weaponize the good use of government benefits to sell their own partisan stories. The radical newspaper *Brasil 247* has credited the success of these programmes to the recent leftist governments, favoring an over-optimistic perspective,[11] compromising what would be a politicized perspective. Otherwise, most peripheral media coverage has focused on the state failure to promote social justice and stop the spread of inequality, far from hailing the welcome, but limited effect from these policies, as these italicized excerpts show:

> Community leaders in Cascadura demand action from the city hall. The neighbourhood in north Rio de Janeiro has serious economic and commuting issues due to recent changes in transportation lines. They *face* issues on leisure areas, education, and healthcare. Locals and leaders *are demonstrating against the lack of municipality investment in a public school*, for a park and a local health centre for the Cascadura community. (*Rio on Watch*, 20/06/2015)

> More schools. Less jails. To throw an adolescent into the Brazilian prison system means to throw this youth into *forgetfulness with no intention to recover*, re-socialise and, in most of the cases, socialise someone who has always lived at the margins of society. It is a proposal fed by vengeance, to assign responsibility [to] all under-age individuals because of the mistake of a few ones based on a take on social issues, or [in] better [words], it is very *dark*. (*Mídia Periférica*, 04/04/2015)

In sum, this link with the way Brazilian society tends to go straight into punishment of its deviant youth is also another break from *assistencialismo*. According to this excerpt, a deeper political consciousness of the population is also born out of allowing the population to realize the merits of joining a common social purpose, developing in them the notion of responsibility. Once hunger and extreme poverty were at a historic minimum after the 2000s (Pinto, 2005; Ferreira, 2006; Hall, 2006), producers migrated from such issues to discuss strategic decisions taken in the name of the nation. I am not arguing that, eventually, inequality has appeared less or is less politicized, but I assert that part of the coverage I found seems to target the middle-class reader more than in the past alternative press. The *assistencialismo* narrative seems to die because of the focus shift from highlighting the benefits that a low-income population enjoys, bouncing back to the well-known politicians' unfulfilled responsibility. By eyeing the latter's power to change the law, producers seem eager to speak "as equals" and take the ownership of this debate. I discuss next how producers tried to bring the knowledge and concern for law changes closer to the periphery.

Connecting the Periphery to Institutions and Parliamentary Debates

Another strategy that has to do with producers' "politicization" lies in having the periphery aware and encompassing complex stories such as new infrastructure projects, landmark constitutional changes. Producers have succeeded in seeing failures in what seemed before a total "consensus," while existing serious gaps in the country's coming to term with itself. For instance, the former indifference regarding the fate of threatened communities, or budget cuts that only affected social care but not the wealthiest classes. During these three years of coverage, I found that the same story could be covered multiple times and with an evolving sense of slowly catching up with strategic political events. Producers had also the consciousness of translating these debates parliamentary acts for an audience that is not familiar with government rituals. I italicize some parts. For instance, we find the *favela*'s opinion on the state's military budget, a type of feedback that seemed rare in the past decades:

> In Ceará, land of the Tremembé [tribe] is *threatened by a Spanish resort*. For almost 15 years, the indigenous fight for delimiting their lands in Itapipoca; coveted by a touristic enterprise, *Funai has delimited the area* three years ago, but it is yet to be homologated by the Ministry of Justice. (*Agência Pública*, 30/01/2015)

> Maré Favela's activist questions the spending [of] the military. (*Brasil 247*, 15/07/2015)

For producers, this *new engagement* in politics is less aimed at immersing in the deliberative routine of politicians and more focused on creating other forms of commotion that leads to a broader engagement from the community. In the past, radical reporters were involved in congress proceedings, but they were busy denouncing conjectures that were too big to tackle, such as the "international capital conspiracy" or the exploitation of national resources by "foreign groups," much cited in literature that has addressed historical debates in Brazil's media (Sodré, 1998; Woitowicz, 2009). The radical press saw, perhaps counterintuitively, Brazil as a counterbalancing actor of "the international capitalist order" (Sodré, 1998:386, 374). Not only the peripheral media outlets have not embarked in these debates, but their approach is tied-up to a tailored interpretation of the institutional decision-making proceedings, whereas they do not refrain from naming ministers, secretaries, and representatives, along with a wish to articulate responses from these actors:

> *The responses from Rio City Hall*: A report from Pública has questioned the situation of the real estate project with view to the Olympic Golf Camp, as shown in the story 'The sun is set for everyone, but not with that view.' (*Agência Pública*, 23/02/2015)

> [The Secretary] Maria do Rosário defends the National Policy of Social Participation. (*Brasil 247*, 18/06/2014)

Many reports have privileged bills or law projects that had major impacts on the disadvantaged but respecting the parliamentary order (the "debate of the day" in the Congress). As earlier discussed, controversial projects such as the *Belo Monte* dam received unprecedented linkages to the life of the poor and of small cities. Other projects that directly affected the population, such as the *2014 World Cup* or the law that lowered the age of criminal responsibility, also triggered much controversy (Levy, 2017). Politicized frames included phrases such as "We want *FIFA standards for schools and hospitals*," but with plain and clear explanations so that the message could reach readers of many profiles, as in this report:

> We from the *Mídia Periférica* blog are against the reduction of the *criminal age* and, together with other movements and people, we are waging a guerrilla war against the conservatives. We need more schools, theatres, soccer fields, *Pronatec*, quotes, all this will strengthen the prevention against the youth going into crime, because thinking on this basis is essential. (*Mídia Periférica*, 01/04/2015)

Lowering the age of criminal responsibility to 16 years old received a special level of attention due to its implications for young people living in the peripheries. The protest against it based on the fact that adolescents could already face long sentences for a series of crimes, such as murder, which I also discussed in chapter 4. This argument divided the country.[12] Producers have unanimously defended that the poor Brazilian youth have had no proper education or chances to develop themselves. Their headlines suggested that this youth deserved another chance before facing jail with longer terms, even in the case of serious crimes. This takes came in during a time when Brazil saw the sudden emergence of more conservative forces that were much supportive of increasing punishment and hardening criminal law, reversing the civil code that aims to protect the youth.[13]

Indeed, most Brazilians in jail are already male, black, and from the same socioeconomic conditions.[14] While the mainstream media has arguably hesitated to cover this issue more assertively,[15] this campaign received total support from all outlets included in this research. Other actors have joined it with hopes to sensitize the public and pressurize senators to block the bill, such as the then-president Dilma Rousseff, as well as authorities, artists and leftist militants. Below I list the parliamentary debates that have attracted most attention, and which led to producers' intervention. They wanted to have their say on the changes these bills, if approved, would provoke, whom they would affect, and remember the country's past of indifference to inequality to justify their positions. The agenda producers have chosen to encompass with their coverage is also tied to so-called "progressive" causes, but, to a great extent, because these causes are a reality or also belong to the poor periphery.

The engagement with this particular debate repeats a standard seen in consecutive years. In the last chapter, I analyzed the case of the distinct coverage of the *Belo Monte* dam by *Agência Pública*, but here I present this same sort of engagement with the same sense of pushing the state towards further accountability on social issues. In the 2014 series, *Agência Pública* questioned the legitimacy of the *Belo Monte* dam due to the series of legal and environmental risks, where producers paid much attention to the state's failure to provide welfare, housing, and healthcare for the affected populations. This line of argument was true to other cases, how could the state be efficient in

Table 5.2. Main parliamentary debates covered by the peripheral media (2013–2015)

Year	*Bill on Discussion in Brazilian Congress*
2013	Belo Monte dam operation in the Amazon forest
2013	State police violence bill
2013	Bus fare hike approval
2013	Gay marriage approval
2014	Funds for FIFA World Cup stadiums
2014	New law on environmental protection
2014	The Internet Constitution
2015	Lowering the age of criminal responsibility

doing things that involved the market and investors and incompetent in caring about people. I italicize the key parts of this coverage:

> From the work [on what] the Dilma government calls its 'biggest project,' the Belo Monte dam, more than 40 thousand people [have been] affected and *complain of the passivity of the state*. Social movements cannot dialogue [and] the police violently repress public hearings, they argue. Even *those who accepted the project* [now complain]; they articulate [that this is] because of unfulfilled promises and environmental impacts already perceived in the region. (*Agência Pública*, 04/09/2014)

> Occupation Solano Trindade celebrates successes and draw[s] *strong criticism to the Federal Housing Programme*. (*Rio on Watch*, 12/09/2014)

These pieces of coverage are sophisticated because they politicize such issues, without necessarily breaking with the government or discrediting the democratic process. Producers wanted to disrupt the logics of silence and passivity that reminded the *assistencialismo* narrative, but their approach is more down to budget or sewage expansion, or to protecting the right to schemes such as *Bolsa Família*, than it is to the appeal for compassion or for rejection of state. As I explored the case of *Ocupa Estelita* in Recife in chapter 3, their idea was to tackle *hegemony* of the decision-making level, here they have escalated it to the federal level, which is a reversal of the *assistencialismo* as an acceptable angle in modern Brazil. In the following section, I review the issue of violence, i.e. beatings, repression and murders of the poor, as other forms to denounce state authoritarianism that affects those with a so-called "low" position in society, while working for a new kind of accountability.

Framing State Violence as "Genocide" of the Poor

The fact that the state has a great share of responsibility for crime and violence in Brazil, which is particularly harmful to peripheral communities, leads to frequent efforts from producers to denounce the former's military action. What happens in such fragile environments such as the *favelas* has inspired producers to increasingly promote flashbacks that remind society of the country's authoritarian past, even though it does not entirely explain the continuity of this reality. Producers' repertoire reads as: Violence is *mainstream*, but they have to reduce the complacency against the *type* of violence that has in the peripheral populations its most obvious effects. If violence does affect more black and poor citizens, or if that is what the media say (e.g. Penglase, 2007), producers have then criminalized the state due to what they see as complacency and agency.

This selective law enforcement, which is a deadline for the poor, but a lighter rule for the white middle class, gives them a permanent repertoire. They say it is the state's *choice* to decide who is going to die or survive. One powerful example lies in the reporting of the UPPs[16] or pacifier unities installed in the Rio de Janeiro's *favelas*. Kept by the state and funded by federal budgets, these are police kiosks where permanent staff are on a mission to stop drug dealers and restore the rule of law in Rio de Janeiro's *favelas*. These initiatives have quickly left their primary model goal to serve the community on emergencies, sadly migrating to surveillance, resulting in the centralization of public life around these government officials. In 2018, the federal government has assumed the role that would be that the state government patrol and provide urban security for the population in Rio de Janeiro. During the period of this research, this movement was just at the beginning, and the police workforce slowly grew in *favelas*, as it began to upset the locals, as this report shows:

> Leaderships question the legacy of the UPPs: José Mario tells that some improvements [have occurred], even with some issues and initial adjustments. Police officers were those to manage some projects, particularly the sport-related ones. Alongside the community, he fought for, instead, enhanc[ing] existing local projects in Santa Marta. José Mario thinks that, in many situations, no dialogue happened between the police, dwellers, and community leaders. Nowadays, according to him, the main problems of the community are the stuck cable car, the garbage on the streets and high electricity bills charged by *Light* [electricity company] after the installation of a new chip. (*Viva Favela*, 04/01/2015)

While producers have voiced the need for state intervention to guarantee public services, they have also claimed that they do *not* need state control of the community. Unlike in other parts of the city, there was an excess of monitoring the lives of citizens as a disguised determination to punish lawlessness. Not surprisingly, the everyday life in communities started to become inflamed with episodes of injustice. Rapper *Rashid,* in a video published by the magazine *Vai da Pé,* criticizes the lack of opportunities for the youth in opposition to the monitoring and punishment to which they are subject:

> Boys and girls have no way to burn energy. They look around and see no one who could stand for them. They have no place to play and to distract themselves. They have no place where to burn their energy, to focus their thoughts on. They look to the TV and do not see themselves in [any] one. You give nothing to this youth and then this youth will do something wrong and then *you will punish him or her*.[17]

The term *punishment* stands out as *the* punitive measure of the state and a frequent byword in many pieces of content. By politicizing the population against what the producers saw as discriminatory policies of spying on them, a few reports have turned to side with the criminals in controversial posts. Outlet *Mídia Periférica* used the case of a criminal in jail to illustrate their point that puts less emphasis on crime and more on the perpetuation of inequality that the discourse of crime enables. The state "stimulates society's reprisals against young people" who may not necessarily be offenders. For dwellers, the state's measures seem focused on "an ultimate and secret goal of keeping poor people in jail.[18] I italicize some key parts of this discourse:

> The robbery that this boy committed meant the aggression of the 'system' against him. The true victim is only himself, with no opportunities, forgotten by everyone, but, as *Marcola* [a drug dealer] said once: 'Nowadays I'm *assisted by many government benefits, I weigh in on the budget, the state protects me, but I had to be noticed so this could happen.*' I write this text in outrage with such brutality with which they treat ours,' and [as] a way to exorcise my fear, because I may be accused of robbery on the streets, of being poor, of being from the periphery, also because of the clothes I use. I am not only defending this boy, but also protecting us.
>
> Enderson Araújo is a black young man, poor, who they [would] also find suspect if he [was] walking down on the streets after 10 pm. (Mídia Periférica, 30/06/2016)

The first excerpt quotes one of the most famous drug dealers in Brazil who, it is suggested, receives more help and protection from the state once he is in jail than when he was free. That kind of reverse logic manifests through metaphors that express disillusionment with a welfare state that sees the "protection" of the middle class, who seeks protection from those who are just their fellow citizens. In sum, if people happen to find themselves surrounded by people who are black, poor, and from the periphery, this layer of society should keep an eye on and be careful, making the burden of proof to those whose appearance is suspicious for them. This subtle, but repeated kind of association, regarding this engendered and pervasive repeated behavior in the everyday of the black or brown citizens, becomes another leg of a major repertoire. It aims to battle the control and surveillance imposed against these "improperly dressed" individuals.

I see both aspects of this particular coverage not necessarily sticking to data and *documented* murders, but rather to a general position that aims to contradict the public's impression that the poor are the danger, and the state presence is always *welcome* in the *favelas* and in peripheral regions. Locals have said to be uncomfortable with the idea that one might be recklessly supporting any intervention in their communities, as far as it is deemed as necessary, urgent and justifiable, ignoring the deadly effects over its people. Their concerns have roots in many episodes of top-down decisions that have "managed" the populace according to the risk they posed to the mainstream society living at the town's center (Gay, 2010). That focus on so-called mechanisms of control also appears while the news of police abuse becomes more frequent, as *Brasil 247* reported in many instances:

> Allegations of police violence in Jacarezinho Favela. (*Brasil 247*, 13/07/2015)

Extreme police methods that cracked down on street protests have also been under producers' radar. While the 2013 demonstrations were notoriously violent, the police in the periphery has deployed ruthless tactics against demonstrators and dissenters since long ago (Huguet & Szabó de Carvalho, 2008). However, only recently the mainstream media has perceived the phenomenon, perhaps because its reporters have come to also suffer from the consequences of the excessive violence in central areas during disruptive protests.[19] In brief, producers have seen in it an opportunity to explore what they do know on the police actual performance in *favelas*. To report on the use of rubber bullets and non-justified prison episodes is as priority for them, as it is to describe persecutory events that led to dozens of murders in suburbia. One of the producers' methods was to liken such episodes with totalitarian states or those in war, again using the anachronistic metaphor, as in this report:

> We are all Douglas Rodrigues. He is another black youth that has [had] his life taken away by the *armed wing of the state, the military police of São Paulo*, that one that kills more than in the Iraq war [. . .] The *military police kills with no mercy* and the only explanation is that they killed by accident, but this is a true *genocide, extermination* of us, the black youth from the periphery. (*Mídia Periférica*, 29/10/2013)

This link with the past and with broader events such as *dictatorship*, *genocide* and *extermination* does not ignore what these historical events mean. *Agência Pública* has constantly compared present's violence to the military dictatorship of the 1960s because producers knew it is still a sensitive image for the public opinion. Reporters have dwelt on it because of society's apathetic positions. In some events of public life, producers have stated that it is part of society's intention to display such deliberate ignorance of the widespread torture practices employed until recently.[20] In a Facebook event, the *Coletivo Papo Reto* invited dwellers to understand the present struggles by reflecting on the past dictatorial developments in their community:

> The *Coletivo de Pesquisadores em Movimento* and the *Raízes* [collectives] invite you to a conversation about dictatorship in the favela.

> The purpose of the activity is to reflect together on the institutional violence in a historical perspective, giving special attention to the period of the civil-military dictatorship (1964–1985). We will use the research made by the commission on the true state of Rio de Janeiro regarding repression in the slums and racism. During this period, to reflect on the state of violence these days, the aim is to use documents of repression located by the Commission of the Truth [Dictatorship investigation], in which we find testimonials collected [by the Comission].

While I do not further analyze this or other visible remains of the Dictatorship in Brazil, nor on the relationship with poverty, what is interesting here is the ability to associate the times of authoritarian rule, therefore, past state violence, with the influence of inequality to guide the relentless violent state. In other words, two kinds of violence are clear for the periphery: one that has received more media highlight, and the one that results from citizens' actions as a reply to this backdrop,[21] which producers see as *general criminality*. The mention to the Dictatorship in this case is tied to the former, which helps to sustain the perspective of state distrust, where the worst evil is submission to a kind of power that punishes the poorest and acts to hide off its past or present crimes. This high level of politicization deriving from this frame has had an effect over producers: it made them careful with every word they employed to report the conflict. I highlight below some alterations that subtly, criminalize the state and to place it as an armed force against civilians.

Figure 5.2. Main frames for the Brazilian State in the peripheral media.

Tracking these linkages and patterns is important to identify other branches through which questions regarding inequality and social justice still can appear.

In fact, dictatorship, censorship and the military control of society are not topics that faded from Brazilian debate in the past few decades (Fleury, 2012). In 2014, one of the most used images by leftists to support the re-election of ex-president Dilma Rousseff was of her sitting in a military court in which the judges cover their face and she rests on a chair.[22] I do not aim to entirely credit the peripheral media for the use of such memorialization and linkages. It just does not seem that producers offered such images for the purpose of forging political communication in an ordinary sense of mediation with politics. Rather, they offered a useful guide to understand Brazil's great divides and how they cost lives. To include violence is to mention the failing legislation and the broken social programs, as all of them stem from the lack of political will.

Leaving aside other implications from the use of such strong words, in terms of what concerns this book, the attempt to change the official narrative of what is going on is the ultimate strategy to deal with the indifference of decades. As seen, producers have resorted to maximizing a single narrative with the use of an extensive taxonomy. This effort might resemble a performative effort to create big facts, call up press support, and, overall, lead the community to see itself in different terms. In conclusion, however, I look at the extent to which these alignments and oppositions not only reflect debates that happen in communities, although borrowing several of its internal images, as it suggests a broader change in the way the periphery covers inequality and promote adjustments of representation, overcoming its brutal stereotype through the *creation* of alternatives to deal with the state. In sum, there are multiple ways through which they have sought to erase the populist trace left behind by generations of politicians, as I shall discuss next.

FROM THE PASSIVE TO THE ANGRY PERIPHERY: CHANGING THE FEEDBACK TO THE STATE

Based on the cases assessed in this chapter, both prepositive (*mídialivrismo*) or reactive (on violence) forms of discourses have meant broader changes in the interactions between the periphery and the state. I start by reflecting on these changes at the level of collective framing literature, namely, through the notions of frame resonance (the support that echoes through the social classes, both middle-class and peripheral preoccupation with violence), frame linking (state punishment versus the opportunities given to young people), and frame diffusion (multiple formats and languages sourced in the past and present). I would add that, as fresh political opportunities arose, a series of new frames also came up: e.g. the appropriation of momentum to boost support or rejection of new law bills in the Congress, the transformation of protest chants into lengthy, reproducible content, and the labelling by using slangs of the *favela*. These new frames are the peripheral media's contribution for changing the feedback to the state, as these collections of occasions make them move from *passive* subjects into an image of an "angry" periphery. I shall discuss what this means for this book's purposes.

From the perspective of collective framing, Benford and Snow (2000:613–14) debated the "variations of interpretative scope and influence." They describe how a "master algorithm colours and constrains the activities of other movements." Thus, I see these "variations of interpretative scope" acting on three different moments. First, when producers have navigated through public grants, but tried to keep their stories untouched. Secondly, when they demonstrated their distrust of authorities, politicians, in general, while still engaging with the latter aspect of negotiation; and third, when they asserted their independence to judge what actually is the state irresponsibility regarding social issues. In this way, producers did fight the historical narrative of state dependence, as they yet acted with democratic maturity to carve out further positions.

The peripheral media have invested, as per collective framing, in bringing new "colours" to the relationship of the disadvantaged with the state through questions about the quality of democracy and the truth behind every politician's discourse. These are *practical* aspects of democracy, but which have yet to yield *results* for their communities in terms of policies and welfare. On the other hand, these questions have also channelled memories of authoritarianism by a generation that was born in democracy. Young producers get to memorialize the past of non-participation in government, the time of an imposed government which they might not have experienced and this we will be seeing again after the impeachment of president Dilma Rousseff. To limit the analysis for this chapter's cases, I ask why they do cover that the "men came to the community" to "impose" measures, what if they have not seen them? This permanent suspicion of the state and distrust in democracy may be the answer as these main "algorithms."

Another layer of analysis emerges when we look at these aspects as "adjustment of representation." For instance, Young (2002) argued on different modes of citizen inclusion. She defined *external* inclusion as that of involving citizens in the policy decision-making process by showing that their thoughts are determinants for government action. *Internal* inclusion would characterize receiving a level of consideration in which authorities would be considering their "familiar experiences" and shaping new public policies and procedures after them, proving that people's thoughts can be relevant and influential. Considering these types of inclusions for our case, I can see much of this in producers' permanent dissatisfaction with the state. By checking if "there were vaccines available," the producers showed the attention to the government's lack of alignment and awareness. So, they have demonstrated that the state's input does not address it according to the *internal* needs of the community. On the other side, by invoking Brazil's authoritarian past, they remembered the time when they had no right to *perform* as citizens at all. Therefore, they lack more *external* inclusion, as they are not present as "decision-makers" and that non-participation has affected their internal understanding of the process and of democracy.

From these two types of inclusion seen in the evidence, the way in which producers have acted consistently to achieve *external* type of recognition, either by the state and, indirectly by the media, is what invites more reflection. While fighting real-time developments in the streets of the periphery (as in the case of the UPPs in *favelas* and violence) or by engaging with facts at national level (as during parliamentary debates), producers do know that these points may already appear in people's minds, but they must frame it in a way that the deficit of inclusion must be remembered by society (as in Schneider, 1992). It is necessary that we move from seeing such frames as a generic adversarial tool only (e.g. Gamson, 1995), to see them as bridges to communicate their expectations for new democratic rituals; namely, the role of the periphery in public decision-making and policy creation.

Both layers presented in this analysis—both acknowledging the repeated representational exercises in search of more inclusion—have meant a move against the past idea of passivity. Producers ended up tackling *assistencialismo* narratives by unmaking assumptions that they "are on good terms" with politicians, reversing Getúlio Vargas' (the "father of the poor") and other politicians' instances, some of which deriving from the discourse of the "lazy" periphery (Fischer, 2008:95). More significantly, producers' proposals of inclusion delivered a stronger feedback to the state even when producers have cautiously joined grants and bursaries. In other words, even when the state invited producers or helped them through incentives, this acceptance was still subject to conditions that must have met imperatives of not framing themselves as dependent, co-opted people.

Early in this chapter, I reviewed a series of funding opportunities and state-sponsored meetings based on an idea of *mídialivrismo.* That case can much clarify the extent to which this conditional acceptance—the state by the alternative media—happens. As far as these government policies could give producers some visibility and contribute to their common purpose, this incentive has failed to introduce the peripheral media as part of a larger media ecology, and as a result, producers have continuously felt like outsiders. By falling short in terms of strategic outlook, these schemes did not help them with ICT skills or abilities of professional journalism. Instead, it made them look at these opportunities with a certain degree of suspicion. Besides this, the "cultural policy" of Rousseff's years was object of many controversies during her first term, which brought her criticism from within her party and its supporters (Silveira et al., 2013; Turino, 2013). These policies have not advanced in media regulation as well (see Hintz, 2011 for background on regulation in Latin America), nor did the public budget do anything to expand the environment by investing only in mainstream media ads (see Mattos, 1984). Even though there was a well-intentioned wish to connect with the alternative media for the public interest, there was no success in pushing the producers' agenda to beyond the government's limited vision.

Therefore, this attempt at inclusion receives as a *feedback* the difficulties to engage and promote the work of producers that develop a socially-committed drive to their content. This evidence takes us back to the book of ideologization of the alternative media in South America. For example, Kitzberger (2013:129) argued that, in the wake of left-wing parties in power in South America, these governments could co-opt the grassroots media to boost their image, so "ideologisation" is "beyond discourse," or that "ideology impacts the aggregate repertoire of government practices, defining government in a more inclusive way so that it comprises various formal and informal allied or co-opted." My interest here is not in necessarily probing this contention, but, based on the evidence, to stress if this notion of "ideologisation" could not be really easy, even if focused on social justice.[23]

For producers whom I interviewed, the truth is that many of the left-wing politicians in power were also icons because they had defended the poorest. However, this did not mean these politicians should remain unchallenged. In fact, this cohort of producers have developed a robust defence of some left-wing icons while not being totally supportive of their policies. This is the case for ex-President Luiz Inácio Lula da Silva, who said to embody the struggle against Brazil's record on hunger and for the poor, presenting himself as the symbol of class mobility and social transcendence and in 2018 he was convicted—under protests—due to a minor corruption allegation. Even in his case, most producers have voiced nuanced views and those who have appeared to support him on social media are those who do it for historical and affective reasons, an aspect furthermore tied to their identity. Definitely, *ideologization* has not meant the abandonment of the perspective of external and internal inclusion that lies in the heart of producers who are involved with the peripheral media.

To finish this analysis, I must ponder that it is not possible to tell from the evidence how these movements contribute to the politicization closer to an idea of "civic practices," as other studies have approached it (e.g. Custodio, 2017). In Brazil, the discussion *on* citizenship has been tied to many other variables, including one's factual participation in politics, the funding of political parties, which are not in scope for this book (Carvalho, 1999; Correia, 2012). In any case, there has been enough data to support that the peripheral media can lead the abandonment of stigmas originated from official authoritarianism. No producer mentioned, for example, the time of the "communist" media, as preached by dictator Getúlio Vargas (D'Araujo, 1999; Konder, 1983; Figueireido, 2013). I conceptualized this way of dealing with state imagery as an *angry* coverage, as it takes place under the terms of the distrust of government and feedback to power herein analysed—it becomes, at least, a convincing case for producers' inclusion in politics, state practices, and personal resistance, conveying a robust intervention on national issues.

CONCLUSION

In this chapter, I visited episodes in which the peripheral media have contested state narratives and initiatives, while seeking to adjust to the public's awareness and engage with state public schemes for funding. In the first part, I discussed the peripheral media's persistent distrust of the government, their relationship with partisanship, and the role of official support, stressing the embedded discourse of *mídialivrismo*. In the second part, I found the growing rejection of the old *assistencialismo* narrative, in which the periphery pursues more accountability by engaging with parliamentary debates. By linking specific episodes of violence and exclusion to broad terms such as *black youth*, *periphery* and *genocide*, this coverage defied and opposed decades of the state's "stabilising" narratives, as producers have associated police repression with the poverty and inequality that surrounds what the mainstream society fears as "marginality." This chapter contributes to shedding more light on the new dynamics between the periphery and contemporary political institutions in Brazil, in which producers have used elements such as distrust or "anger" as ways to achieve more inclusion in political debates, then improving their feedback to the state. In the next chapter, I conclude this book by discussing the broader contribution from the peripheral media to the politicization of inequality in contemporary Brazil. I revisit the coverage discussed in the empirical chapters and add conclusive arguments that cover the whole research.

NOTES

1. The Committee to Protect Journalists (CPJ) has registered 41 journalists killed in Brazil from 1992 to 2018, most of them worked for small media organizations, some of which could fit the "peripheral media."

2. I translated this and the following policies' names because of the straightforward meaning and perfect correspondence once translated. That also makes it easier for an international reader to refer to it in English, rather than in Portuguese.

3. According to the edital released in 2015, the year after Rousseff has been elected for her second term. Available at http://www.cultura.gov.br/o-dia-a-dia-da-cultura/-/asset_publisher/waaE236Oves2/content/edital-pontos-de-midia-livre/10883. Accessed 12 December 2015.

4. Not completely unrelated to Lula's corruption charges, the support for famous figures of the left has apparently had its side of demonstrating support to what activists saw as a persecution from the right-wing justice against the ex-President. Many of these pictures have come captioned with phrases of support. For context on Lula's case, the news media have provided some background, as in this Guardian report. Available at https://www.theguardian.com/world/2017/may/10/brazil-lula-president-court-corruption-charges. Accessed 05 July 2017.

5. Available at http://www.cultura.gov.br/noticias-destaques/-/asset_publisher/OiKX3xlR9iTn/content/encontro-no-rio-busca-unir-e-fortalecer-midia-livre/10883. Accessed 15 December 2015.

6. As for example Fora do Eixo's leader, *Pablo Capilé* joined the Ministry of Cultura, as other collaborators came later to do the same. This report from Folha de S. Paulo unveils some of the details of this approximation between the Workers' Party and Fora do Eixo actually happened after Rousseff's first term. "Fora do Eixo inside the MinC." Available at http://www1.folha.uol.com.br/fsp/ilustrada/203624-fora-do-eixo-dentro-do-minc.shtml. Accessed 15 May 2015.

7. Abortion research in Brazil has constantly linked its implications with social class. In both Rocha (2006) as in Machado (2000), which have analyzed the demographics behind it and the media portraits in evangelical media, respectively, we learn that the failure in addressing it affects more disadvantaged women.

8. As did later president Getúlio Vargas.

9. Although there is an inclination to see *assistencialismo* as much focused on the rural populations of Brazil, its discussion (or assumption) is present also in urban settings. Scholars have debated ways to tackle this discourse, especially by feeding civil society organizations, and stimulating "voluntary" effort. Still, these initiatives did not seem to respond to the core argument of *assistencialismo,* which is the commendation for the "needy" over addressing the roots of social dysfunctions. See Sanglard (2003) for historical context and impacts of *assistencialismo* initiative on the health care sector. Available at http://www.scielo.br/scielo.php?script=sci_arttext&pid=S0104-59702003000300017. Accessed 12 January 2016.

10. "Brazil's Bolsa Familia scheme marks a decade of pioneering poverty relief" at https://www.theguardian.com/global-development/2013/dec/17/brazil-bolsa-familia-decade-anniversary-poverty-relief. Accessed 20 December 2016.

11. By for example inviting government staff to defend policies, as in this story in which a minister of Dilma Rousseff's government appears interviewed but no downsizes of the program are discussed as well as opinions from citizens. "Lack of information leads to prejudice." Brasil 247 at http://www.brasil247.com/pt/247/brasil/201526/Bolsa-Fam%C3%ADlia-'falta-de-informação-leva-ao-preconceito.'htm. Accessed on 31 December 2015.

12. The discussion on lowering the punishable age in the law has divided the country not only in relation to this issue, but linking both positions to the left (against the change) and the right (pro-lowering it). That reflects a deep polarization of society. A background of this constitutional change is provided in this Guardian article. Available at https://www.theguardian.com/world/2015/jul/02/brazil-age-of-criminal-responsibility-16. Accessed 31 December 2015.

13. At the center of this politicization of the criminal law lies Jair Bolsonaro, an icon for the right, and defender of tougher rules for criminals in Brazil, not envisaging the unequal settings of crime in Brazil. Full background at https://www.opendemocracy.net/democraciaabierta/pedro-henrique-leal/bolsonaro-and-brazilian-far-right. Accessed 05 July 2017.

14. Most of Brazil's jail population is young, black and poor, according to this report from Justice Department states. Available at https://www.justica.gov.br/noticias/mj-divulgara-novo-relatorio-do-infopen-nesta-terca-feira/relatorio-depen-versao-web.pdf. Accessed 10 March 2016.

15. As in this article published by portal G1, in which the pros and cons of this bill are weighed in by lawyers and judges. "Check out arguments of those who defend and criticize lowering the age of criminal responsibility." Available at http://g1.globo.com/politica/noticia/2015/08/confira-argumentos-de-defensores-e-criticos-da-reducao-da-idade-penal.html. Accessed 10 December 2015.

16. UPP means Unidade de Polícia Pacificadora or Pacifying Police Unity in Portuguese.

17. Available on the magazine's Youtube channel at https://www.youtube.com/watch?v=BTWpUXVpOS4. Accessed 06 November 2016.

18. This post appears signed by the editor of Mídia Periférica blog, an outlet in scope for this study, and this story later appeared in Bahia's main daily *A Tarde* and in other blogs such as the *Favela Potente,* available at https://favelapotente.wordpress.com/tag/midia-periferica/. Accessed 30 June 2016.

19. The mainstream media have covered police violence in the Brazilian streets with considerable attention. Folha de S. Paulo has one of its reporters, Giuliana Vallone hurt in her eye during the 2013 demonstrations. As this report shows, "I often never found he'd shoot on me." http://www1.folha.uol.com.br/cotidiano/2013/06/1296077-jamais-achei-que-ele-fosse-atirar-diz-reporter-da-folha-atingida-durante-protesto.shtml. Accessed 27 April 2014.

20. This series of reports is available at http://apublica.org.br/ditadura.

21. I frame this kind of crime as "citizens' actions" because that is the way in which producers have often referred to crime from favelas' citizens, which otherwise, is different from drug dealers, murderers, and other actors seen as "not part of the community," although they have lived in the same quarter.

22. The image is real and relates to her judgment regarding guerrilla tactics adopted as resistance to the dictatorship. In any case, the point here relates to the use of past images in contemporary political discourses. Particularly during the 2014 election campaign, scholars have seen many genderized elements, content manipulations and serious accusations among candidates, as Jaenisch and Borelli (2011) had seen in 2010, and Dos Santos & Jalalzai (2014) point out regarding the election in analysis.

23. In this case, the producer referred to a story against the hosting of the 2014 World Cup, whose funds could better attend social issues in Brazil, which was a general argument during 2014 demonstrations.

Conclusion

A New Form of Media Power: Inequality at the Center

This book had initially proposed to abandon the term *alternative media* in search of a concept that stemmed directly from the Brazilian media reality. Based on the history of the periphery in Brazil and what producers claimed themselves to be, this work put forward the concept of the *peripheral media*. More than a normative framework of analysis, the peripheral media served to name and understand groups in their contributions to politicizing inequality from the margins of society. Even though no media law changed to democratize public TV and radio during this research, the peripheral media has expanded towards a unique contribution, whether through new forms of engagement with inequality issues or by tackling past views of such issues. Producers have taken individual and collective problems to another level of understanding and publicity by linking apparently unrelated episodes of violence and urban development to the country's old divides. Ultimately, the have built new frames based on stories of ordinary citizens, including *favela* dwellers, which were strategically operated to resonate through the mainstream media.

As a mixed methods research, this work has sought to draw on different ways of understanding this type of content and its producers. I first collected the producers' views by conducting semi-structured interviews, from which I could map their routines, interests, and priorities as reporters of the country's inequality. It became clear that the "coverage of inequality" that I had initially proposed to study was a variety of discourses not only on inequality, but on its consequences and the restrictions that Brazilian society has imposed on a certain group of individuals. Among my findings, I explored many discussions that criticized Brazil's complacency with the lack of full access to the city, the difficulties disadvantaged citizens face when trying to get fair treatment from authorities, and how political debates used to belong to a small elite. The frame analysis, on the other hand, revealed the emergence of fact reporting, as well as the alterations, appropriations, and linkages made out of random content. These are all practical ways of connecting everyday events to historical, broad and complex situations while somehow mirroring their struggle to make sense of many divides.

Both kinds of evidence have offered an unprecedented look into Brazilian producers' daily and unpredictable efforts to create what I call *politicized* discourses in a sense of forging a counterhegemonic meaning. The links found with the country's history and politics show that producers drew on the past silence of the periphery to seize the present's agenda and add more frames to it, give feedback to power, and change their media representations. These linkages have worked to place the disadvantaged in a better position than in the 1970s, for example, reflecting the broader socioeconomic change in the country of the last decades. On the other hand, after this three-year analysis, I perceived that the struggle over a politicized meaning also reflected many of the values that were present in Brazil's alternative press of the 1970s, as its close attachment to popular culture (Festa & Silva, 1986; Kucinski, 1991; Woitowicz, 2009), and yet, there were new possibilities of reversing the persistent trivialization of inequality.

The methods employed in this book have allowed further clarification of the complexity of discourses. Here, it comprised content alteration, the *metaphorization* of the news or placing linkages to other content, or the remix of original content. This multiangled qualitative analysis of discourse, despite the difficulties in capturing it, is aimed at a fresh reminder of the potential stemming from discourse/collective frame analysis. Because I invested in looking at it by assessing the intent behind producers' headlines, I could identify instances that clearly purport to the adjustment of media representations. Derogatory terms such as *favelado* are subtle references to reality that producers have transformed into other slangs, ironies, or simply into provocations so they could show off their talents and skills.

The contribution of this book is therefore to enlarge the knowledge on the coverage of inequality from Brazil's periphery by deepening in their discursive strategies. This vast repertoire on Brazil's own type of intersectional inequality conveys multiple messages that are different from seeing only poverty or scarcity, as history shows. Theoretically speaking, producers have applied both Gramsci's (2011) "war of position" (by refusing to adhere to certain terms and mainstream-produced frames) and "war of movement" (by stressing discursive avenues, appropriating content, and seeking to *occupy* society's understanding of what was going on in the periphery). It was not possible, though, to perceive further deployment of these forms of "politicization" over the context of formal politics (e.g. to reach the Brazilian Congress and to get the buy-in of politicians), as fragmentation, distrust, and lack of understanding of the power dynamics are major drawbacks to which all producers have referred.

In the next sections, I detail and organize the elements that show this new politicization of the periphery, noting its existence as a self-feeding media environment made of different kinds of media outlets, each one with its own contributors, repertoire, and frames. This conclusion chapter sees their extensive coverage of social issues encompassing other media realms, public affairs, and the mainstream journalism. From a passive agent, which has essentially aimed to react, resist, or disrupt the "broader" media environment as "alternative media" (Couldry & Curran, 2003), I propose that we dislocate the focus from disruption into a creative process that integrates to the so-called mainstream, constitutes a fluid form of discourse, appropriates momentum to finally seize the hegemonic discourse. I also contend that producers have operated it without necessarily subscribing to social movement membership (e.g. Downing, 2008) or only by working or hybridizing with the mainstream protocols (Kenix, 2011; Hackett & Gurleyen, 2015). In the last part, I read these developments alongside Mouffe's theory of participatory democracy and agonistic communication. I interpret this new type of media power not on the grounds of transparency, ethics and truth as these values are known, but as a loud and chaotic intervention aimed at disrupting Brazil's flawed consensus on inequality.

ENGAGING WITH THE POLITICIZED PERIPHERY

This research has set out to evaluate if the periphery could develop new forms of "politicization" in the face of decades of representational constraints. I initially defined politicization as the ability "to enhance, stretch, or transform the meaning of known adjectives and categories connected to inequality." In this sense, I conclude that there has been a higher visibility of inequality issues, due to a set of strategies led by media producers based on their use of the Internet. What appeared as the real dilemma for this book was to decide between discourses that seemed to follow a broader politicization of *everything* versus a centered politicization of inequality, as initially hypothesized. After electing a range of aspects to look at and which could give the foundations for this concept of politicization (adjustment of media representations, the diversity of frames, and the feedback to power), the focus on inequality is unequivocally what is at stake for most media producers from the periphery, which becomes even more apparent as I refer to their pieces of repertoire.

As a way of explaining this complex system of framing social issues, I first stress the adjustment of representation. The terms of this "adjustment," taking into account the concepts that Young (2001) discusses, have in the *rolezinhos* a perfect example. Once the CCTV images were made available, producers were quick to establish *another* version of the facts. That adjustment meant that the urge for having young, dark-skinned men removed from shopping centers was no longer acceptable, regardless of the situation in which they are involved. On the other hand, newspaper-published pictures were also key to frame conflicts among social classes, with the *arrastões* (Chapter 2), helping producers stretch facts that were publicly known and relatively accepted.[1] On the "media" aspect of their intervention, there was an "adjustment" in the appropriation of CCTV footage: from a privately owned, non-newsworthy and bulky material of the everyday into a public record of an otherwise natural event.[2] The "deliberative, utilitarian and goal-directed" aim (Benford & Snow, 2000:624) exists as the *intent* to seize this and correlated pictures made from past images, a *new,* continuous and uninterrupted coverage of inequality.

Secondly, I shall discuss the diversity of frames. Radical outlets such as *Coletivo Papo Reto* and *Brasil 247* have broken with the *harmonious* portrait of the community-attached reporter, which used to privilege team work and an image of union, to display the blood, anger and scarcity they found in the *favelas.* This shift complicates the 1970s' community cooperation outlook, where the progressive consciousness of the oppressed was, arguably, at its outset (Freire, 1970), meaning, overall, a different ethics of empathy and solidarity. That point deserves further investigation. However, to what concerns the evidence herein discussed, peripheral media producers have evoked individualism and *personality* via their Facebook texts, for instance. Selfies and private stories challenged the limits between spontaneity and strategic design of oneself. This self-framing, in my view, pertained to closeness, familiarity and also legitimacy, authority and an unprecedented ability to framing reality.

Despite meeting all my expected findings, this broader change in frames and intentions from the periphery does not imply that producers have totally abandoned old partnerships. A long-term agenda of cooperation with NGOs and other third parties still help them at giving feedback to power, for example. This partnership appears with the continuation of the historical process of *educomunicação*, discussed in chapter 3. This proactive side of "grooming" citizens has resisted the decades and shown a critical ability that was not present in the mainstream media "internships." If we compare these actions with the 1990s' *Jornal da Cidadania,* the NGO-linked newspaper that had a direct rapport with the government (Stacciarini, 2007), one realizes that this new face of the periphery is not only *tactical* in a procedural sense of guiding new media producers and teaching them, as past studies suggested (Postill, 2013; Boler, 2008), they seemed to have learned from this NGO reality the ways in which they can increase their possibilities of reaching higher spheres of government and decision-making.

These three different levels of politicization have much varied, depending on the locations and the actors taking part from the periphery. However, not all media production from the periphery serves the same purpose to adjust representation or they propose new frames or speak to the state. What I attest is the higher likelihood that these events start to happen often and multiply among ordinary citizens. As I examined in Chapter 2, movements based on the northeast could strongly reject gentrification as a result of wealthy developers flagrantly profiting from the unawareness of the public and clientelist councils (*Ocupe Estelita*), others in São Paulo innovated by featuring homeless and indigent individuals on the cover of websites (*SP Invisível* blog), and middle-class students paired with the poor on the São Paulo's outskirts to discuss issues such as the budget for culture (*Vai da Pé*). The extent to which this politicization provoked an alignment among producers, despite them being in distinct contexts, appeared one case of discursive practices demonstrating all its power.

On the other hand, there is no 'one-size-fits-all' politicization, as the local context remains essential for creating and reformulating older demands for equality. The remake of the *favelado* to fit into a new class of networked individuals is a telling new *repertoire*. Even though reimagining the *favela* as an accessible and peaceful place, dwellers have made clear the point at which they disagree with mainstream media representations of themselves when showing otherwise, and yet they kept their preference for being named as "*favelados.*" The real break with a Gramscian notion of elite "consensus" has happened in that moment, when producers challenged who is the narrator and who *can* be the real interpreter of inequality. There is a side of *adjustment* on the way the *favela* exists to the outside world, leaving behind the expectation of progress to promote not new facts (sadly, brutal crimes, which are not necessarily new), but new biographical and personalized frames that put more pressure over society, pressure in terms of policy making and pressures of acceptance regardless. This "putting a face" revitalizes the way the community accepts what is an "ordinary" crime and stops the anonymization its victims.

Following a Foucauldian perspective (Foucault, 1982), these small actors were not rejecting or justifying power, but amalgamating with power. I explored the case of the *Belo Monte* dam. Producers have attacked the poor level of transparency in mainstream reports on the project. While I did not confirm any intent of "rivalling" the mainstream media coverage on both distribution and profit side, producers have assumed the latter's mission of "straight talking" with power. Other than that, there is a strong legacy of values that stem from the greater causes of democracy, such as the need for "checks and balances" (Keane, 1991; McQuail, 2010) and the issue of political *clientelism* (Waisbord, 2000; Hallin & Papathanassopoulos, 2002) to which they have shown a deep level of consciousness. Both aspects have grown strong in outlets that started small, such as *Agência Pública*, *SP Invisível*, *Vai da Pé* and, to some extent, *Coletivo Papo Reto,* but which have seen their possibilities increase. The lack of direct ties with power (in the private-realm of influence) has not prevented that they could seriously perceive a degree of accountability in what they did. In 2016, *Agência Pública* took part in the team the journalists to interview the then-President Dilma Rousseff[3] in a crucial moment of her political career. Would that confirm their prominence and perhaps the prominence of other of these groups?

Another point that I would like to stress is how producers have operated outside of the framework of large social organizations, unions, and political bodies (Festa & Silva, 1986; Woitowicz, 2009). What I mean by *outside* is the extent to which their content, angles, and opinions stem from an agenda that has not appeared as aligned with that of these actors. As I have discussed in much of the empirical chapters, what is published is made possible by the appropriation of existing material (from the mainstream media, mostly), in which the discourse and the repertoire includes a range of issues that do not entail a single message. Actually, each producer's strength lies in the brevity of their content, under a self-realization that it is possible to communicate with strength and resonance through small pieces of content that run without sponsors or alignment, with no pretention to complexity or stability in their discourse. In brief, it is to transform the way in which language can point to further aspects of life, most of which relating to a post-materialist view of inequality (e.g. income gaps). I do not assume that this book has covered all these post-materialist ways of engaging with inequality, especially in such a nuanced country as Brazil.

In sum, notwithstanding the lack of alignment and homogeneity in the frames presented here—the "one-sided" view of reality, the "reification" problem, or the "affective amplification" of facts might still belong to this debate as well (Gamson, 1992; Benford, 1997). This frames-as-reflexivity approach was key to reveal the wealth in vocabulary and the core of innovation, but media producers do not aim to "balance" out media coverage. To denaturalize the inequality, they might still follow the current news media priorities, adding to existing conversations. For instance, when they reminded society of the invisible costs and risks of the *favela* pacification programs, in a moment of overall positivity over the economic growth and when external expectations were on the rise. The same role to promote contradiction could be said of the *Belo Monte* dam, which resulted in optimistic views of the thousands of jobs it would create, but which costed a small city and large indigenous communities their land and their peace. The extent to which these dialogues represent another chapter of media democracy in Brazil is something I intend to develop more about, problematizing these findings with past perceptions of alternative media.

The Peripheral Media and the Media Democracy Agenda

I return to one of the earliest topics of this book, which is the position of the alternative media amid the historical media concentration in Brazil. For some authors, this lack of diversity in ownership has been a major factor that limits the development of a more democratic media environment (Amaral & Guimarães, 1994; Albuquerque, 2000; Waisbord, 2000; Abreu, 2006; Porto, 2012). As said, while not intending to discuss the entire media democracy project, there are issues that this research helps to give an updated account. The further participation of the peripheral classes in the media or the diversity of existing media frames, for example, could add up to how one sees the state of these ideas in the context of Brazil. As there is no consensus on which set of elements really constitute "media democracy," as Keane (1991:131), for instance, described the "right of reply," and other authors saw the understanding of political institutions (e.g. Miguel, 2000; Abreu & Lattman-Weltman, 2006). In 2018, researchers have seen a decline in engagement with institutions, as communications become disruptive and populism is on the rise (Bennett & Livingston, 2018). It is in this context that the peripheral media contribution becomes more symbolic and relevant to analyze.

This emphasis on the diversity of frames is not to suggest that other features of a media environment, such as the access to broadcast and efficient public service media, are less important (Hackett & Zao, 2005). As far as these issues of access are still dysfunctional in Brazil, the peripheral media has demonstrated that a great strength of producers' autonomy to "cover" and provide their versions of reality. This step advances the perception that the media has to be a government-supervised media business or subject to "concessions." Producers have, after all, shown themselves aware of democratic procedures and how decisions are taken. But giving new frames to the audience have appeared as a crucial thing to offer in the case of Brazil. Invariably, past studies have seen the small number of frames that the average citizen receives from the mainstream media, which has been seen as a little diverse, if not conservative (Aldé, 2004; Porto, 2007).

The peripheral media ability of generating multiple frames has improved the necessity of issues, but as demonstrated in chapter 5, it improved the proximity of communities with institutional power. Looking back, alternative publishers, journalists and agitators have lived between moments of success and dispersal, high excitation with politicians or total despair. Sodré (1998), for instance, had several movements in which radical journalists of the past have kept their resilience in moments of coups and crisis in the early 20th century, but those were times of profound suspicion from the periphery regarding how things could change.

Festa & Silva (1986) saw the dispersal of many alternative journalists once re-democratization occurred, as they joined political parties or pursued other careers. Pereira (1986), an ex-alternative journalist himself, also argued that the reorganization of the political scenario had weakened the strong alternative press in that decade. In all those movements, the lack of a further ownership of institutions and of how everyday issues *can* be argued about and resolved also stemmed from the poor comprehension of these processes. Furthermore, communities had to comply with rigid partisan interpretations of reality, from one side or the other of the spectrum, which could have delayed a better comprehension of the political environment and how it could improve their lives. In this way, the politicization discussed in this book allowed that a new repertoire, mostly concerning poverty, precariousness and violence, could meet other vocabulary that was restricted to the content seen at the mainstream media level.

In any case, there are many barriers to overcome, either in vocabulary or in the settlement of this new understanding of politics, which appear more important in an increasingly conservative Brazil. While there are linkages that have been importantly established, such as that of violence and the disregard with the periphery by the state, most producers still have to overcome de-politicized interpretations of their being "detached, rebellious, and counterhegemonic" (as in Downing, 2001). The moments in which they mostly connected with a mainstream discourse, as in the case of disappearances and murders by the police, were the moments in which they could record and demonstrate abuse that happened with consent from the main political forces in charge. At the same time, it is not possible to credit all the alliances and collaborators that have given this active, extensive web of producers the chance to improve their discourses, and target audiences from other layers of Brazilian society.

In relation to the past impediments to a better media democracy in Brazil, it is possible to re-think democratization without producers having to topple the "media dynasties" (Sinclair, 2002). The argument of "modernisation" of the press (as in Abreu, 2002) has yet to better consider the modernization of discourse as a key indicator that has been met in the peripheral media. A more

Figure C.1. The peripheral media contributors and main challenges.

efficient and clear discourse from the periphery has meant new capabilities in their "right to reply" without them having to *become* the mainstream media. Hence, the fact that such counterhegemonic discourses are welcome and repeated in this web of contacts gives more reason to believe in a democratic advance, especially being aware of the authoritarian background regarding the alternative media.

The Alternative Media as a Counterhegemonic Discourse

While this book has not vowed to change any definition of alternative media, it proposes a new breadth. In the case of Brazil, it is the local context, history that leads us to find the periphery as an underestimated interlocutor. I note in this section some of the differences from this approach to other well-known studies on the alternative media. For example, Downing's (2001) study of the "radical media" saw "marginalised, popular cultures" which often meant "grassroots," an entity that is less coherent than that of a social movement (Downing, 2008). Other studies have tied up the alternative media to a form of journalism, based on the action of groups that aimed at the professional production, importing mainstream media settings into their routines (Harcup, 2003; Forde, 2011). Taking Downing (2001) and Rodríguez (2001)—as I also discussed the *citizens' media* earlier—both the periphery and cohorts studied by other authors have employed counterhegemonic efforts to get a place in the local media environments. Different from them, I see distinct conceptual formations.

While these authors have seen specific settings within which producers operate the notion of "community" very strongly, even when referring to "anarchic" cultures, the peripheral media have, instead, gathered no targeted public at large. If we want to read the periphery as a "community," we have to skip the sense of a closed, and coherent project or group with which case studies have been formed (as in Rodríguez, 2011; Davis, 2015), and prioritize its side of multi-ethnic, multi-class group that produces content for a likewise diverse public. The peripheral media stands out, in reality, because of its discursive strength and not due to the communal legitimacy. I found that politicizing commemorative dates, creating versions of popular sayings, re-employing politicians' discourses, and challenging assumed truths from the state aimed to re-orientate the audience and not necessarily make them engage among themselves. As a result, this research's data have dwelt far more on the struggle against media stereotypes, and the quest of individualized personality long denied to this vast periphery.

This relationship between producers' personal needs and their media outputs complicates the "alternative" media as with only one purpose, one membership. If the "proletarian" audience has been the "binding" assumption for radical journalists in European societies (e.g. Jameson, 1998), the only "binding assumption" found in this case was the resistance against a trivializing and inferior status that stems from the context of high inequality. In Gramsci (2011), we learn that a way of fighting *cultural*, *political*, and *bourgeois* hegemonies has been one of playing different "antagonisms" on all these fronts. This different, but concomitant way of differing in the media environment suggests that the alternative media, conceptually speaking, appears in this study as an entity that is more abstract and as fluid as its discourse can be.

What I defend here is that these *personal* antagonisms have existed both through constructive approaches, seen in educational efforts (*educomunicação*) or in reactive efforts (being society's *watchdog*). These ambiguous forms of receiving the alternative media discourse, in different moments of one's media experience and seized in moments of crises and controversy, must receive a proper development from the audience studies' perspective. The extent to which this book advances relates to the new ways to build counter-hegemony while one considers this universe as one of the "alternative media," contributing to a more elastic and informal advent than an otherwise cohesive, whether activist or harmonious, idea of community or alternative media. It is on the grounds of this personalized aim to release discourses from the margins that I return to Mouffe's ideas of participatory democracy to reflect on what the centrality of the discourse as a democratic practice.

THE PERIPHERAL MEDIA AS A WORKING MODEL OF PARTICIPATIVE DEMOCRACY

Apart from the new reconsideration of the "alternative media" as a discourse and of its transformative role over Brazil's periphery, I also return to an early discussion on what value the politicization of the discourse has in contemporary society. The peripheral media contention has often created a scenario in which one *has* to agree with the inequality issues that they discussed. But how can this be read within a broader democratic scenario? As a politicized, and yet political contention, how can this allure the average citizen? By engaging with these forms of discourse, we skip what Fenton (2016) argued about going beyond the "veneration of horizontality," having new frames discussed by the periphery indicates that producers felt compelled to assign responsibilities, discuss policy plans, and propose feasible changes to institutions—therefore nailing what "the political" means for a broad, often unaware population. Even though I had no evidence that they are involved with formal politics at this moment, there is an "informal learning," as Mercea (2016:192) pointed out, that leads communities to a "discursive inflexion," in which, I argue, facts appear in permanent flux or uncertainty so that, where once existed indifference, no resistance to a certain angle or catch-phrase is possible.

This significance of this political contention certainly dwells on the inability of the disillusioned to trust or engage with political forces of change. Because institutional deliberation has always appeared elusive for many Brazilians, due to either corruption or the inability to talk "the language of power" (Dagnino, 2004), producers reached for frames that represent them in connection with power. I have witnessed many chaotic interpretations of the facts, which, instead of absorbing polarization and pacifying issues, had as a main goal to provoke reaction and publicity. In other words, their action resonates with what Mouffe (2000) saw as an antithesis of the deliberative solemnity into a loud, contradictory and often simultaneous debate:

> "To be sure, the aim of the theorists who advocate the different versions of 'deliberative democracy' is commendable. Against the interest-based conception of democracy, inspired by economics and skeptical about the virtues of political participation, they want to introduce questions of morality and justice into politics, they are looking for new meanings of traditional democratic notions like autonomy, popular sovereignty, and equality. Their aim is to reformulate

> the classical idea of the public sphere, giving it a central place in the democratic project." (Mouffe, 2000:745)

What is at stake here is not "civic learning" through ICTs or the political participation of those who do not normally engage with politics (Bennett, 2003b). I believe it is at a level before that, precisely the level where Mouffe refers to learning, to acquiring "autonomy, popular sovereignty" (Mouffe, 2000b). At the end of three Workers' Party terms in the presidency, when a political crisis loomed, and the impeachment of ex-president Rousseff was in its early stages, I still saw much strength in producers holding their opinion, fighting for what they believed. Watching the controversial terms of Dilma Rousseff's impeachment, the narrative of a fair country had dissolved thanks to the corruption that has stolen money from social projects. I did not look deeper into the latter discourse neither in further implications from the discourse of corruption; however, by applying this research's results to a broader political history, these facts still resonated within a context of political awakening that has accompanied a more participative periphery. Historically, there has been a clear intervention by alternative media in periods of political and economic crisis, as I pointed out in chapter 1, this turbulent time has attested to the periphery's presence on different media platforms.

Mouffe's call for abandoning the "rational consensus" tells us that a random elaboration of media frames should not be deemed as invalid for the democratic process. Although this "framing it loud" may sound a challenging way of operating in Western settings (Carpentier, 2011), in Brazil, however, the "rational consensus" have often translated into an acceptance of inequality through the myth of "racial, pacific democracy." In short, the "rational" consensus has meant to engage with a kind of politics that has reproduced inequality, so abandoning it has appeared as an obvious path for producers. As discussed in Chapter 3, the "citizen shot by the police" becomes, in the peripheral media, the "black and poor—another one of us dead." The refusal of the rationality behind journalism objectivity (though changing) makes this media production less dependent on the old kind of consensus that saw the cancellation of the constitutional guarantees that have affected a full generation in Brazil (Fleury, 2014).

This counterhegemonic process is one of allowing different voices to assess their own value and distinctiveness, whether from the *favelas* or other poor neighborhoods. This allowance for free debate, following a hierarchy of values of the periphery, also removes concerns that all discourse impositions are authoritarian, as Mouffe's participatory antagonism theory seems to suggest (Carpentier, 2011). As in Atton (2002:18), the antagonism of the alternative media, as a counter-cultural movement, has fulfilled a cycle in the American West Coast; yet in South America, it brought cultural dimensions and other possibilities for citizenship, which were not always popular (Dagnino, 2004, 2010; Carvalho, 2009). On the other hand, any concern that this detachment from professional, moral or linguistic standards could lead to more isolation has found no grounds in this evidence (e.g. Garcêz & Cal, 2012). Otherwise, the display of political sentiments has provided the mainstream society with an inventory of opinions and images, sometimes breaking into the mainstream media repertoire.

It is also important to differentiate this political contention from the actual approximation with the political establishment. The peripheral media's strength emerges from the political and social issues that derive from inequality, politicized as the result of decades lying in the imaginary of an indifferent society. This form of outrage may or may not flourish as a mature civic body. Their creative discourse is still distinct from weaving direct efforts or links with voters or with politicians. This book has aimed to approach a preliminary stage of this political ecology, which is one of removing impediments for a collective reflection by using the periphery as a starting point. As far as this environment has gathered many *favela* media outlets, journalism agencies, and the NGO-funded initiatives as part of the same framework of action, it is yet to convince important players of both media and political establishment of its feasibility and on the merits of its discourse. I highlight next some limitations that prevented other topics from coming up in this book.

BEYOND THE PERIPHERY: LIMITATIONS OF THIS BOOK AND FUTURE RESEARCH

Emerging scholarly research has invested in Brazil's alternative media in an unprecedented scale of engagement and theorization. Custodio (2017), for instance, drew on the political profiles of *favela* media activism, through which he found individualism and structure in the producers' motivations. Waisbord and Segura (2016) saw media movements in Latin America battling law change and further inclusion of the disadvantaged groups. These studies have investigated the agency of small or large groups that have used the media to achieve new milestones in policy, seeking the promotion of communities and native views of society. These studies have also sought to understand different levels of participation within institutional or community boundaries in such dynamics that could act as the foundation for a further engagement with mainstream society. In contrast to these studies, this book has not approached participation or interaction with society at this level of analysis.

Because it sought a more intimate portrait of producers' views, this book has not embraced the *process* of media making nor has it engaged in conceptualizing *participation*. On the one hand, this allowed bringing these outlets into the context of a single *coverage* straight from the periphery, creating a way of researching differences from hegemonic discourse without resorting entirely to mainstream media comparison. On the other hand, there are pros and cons in not engaging with ethnographic research. In my view, because I privileged the views producers offered me in the interviews as data, I was not denying their self-affirmation as journalists, writers, photographers, and self-assigned professions related to the creative industries. Similarly, I did not seek to interpret their activity as—or, to some extent, frame it to—one of *activism*. I do not argue that the above studies classify the alternative media as *activism,* but that is certainly another kind of analysis that is not the focus in this study. Aware of the legacy scholarship that has approached the alternative, community and activist media as products of the same realms (Rodríguez, 2001; Downing, 2001; Barassi, 2015), I found out that this book could contribute more if dedicating space to producers' outputs, rather than drawing on assumptions on the size or periodicity of their organization or any other method they use.

Moreover, this book could not achieve the full grasp of each specific geographic environment's inequality. To generalize what I saw as the "periphery" entails the lack of an exhaustive overview of each location. The same is true to the extensive literature on Brazil's alternative media, as authors have concentrating strategic media locations, such as the *favelas* (also in Bailey et al., 2007; Davis, 2015; Baroni, 2015) or "alternative journalism" (Peruzzo, 2008; Carvalho, 2014) while seeing them within the social movement framework (Gomes & Nascimento, 1998; Gohn, 1999; Fonseca, 2007; Carneiro, 2006; Bailey et al., 2007; Downing, 2008). I, however, adopted a line of inquiry close to Festa and Silva (1986), Kucinski (1991) and Woitowicz (2009), which are studies that compile the alternative media produced in many settings to then appreciate their meaning as a whole. Hence, seeing the periphery as one (but distributed in multiple sites and discourses) allowed me to collect similar positions and therefore I intended to unify the agency of multiple voices. First, because this approach meets an existing perception that many Brazilians have shared about the periphery. On the other hand, that approach misses more details to complement demographic, statistic, and social research that brings about quantitative aspects of each region or location.

Even though Brazil is going through deep changes since the impeachment of President Dilma Rousseff in 2016, with the prospects of a competitive election in 2018, theorizing on top of a single "periphery" can still relate to a sort of reality that has been unchanged for decades and still remains. This book has approached the bottom-line of politicization among disadvantaged citizens, based on the premise that they sense inequality to the extent that it has become one of their political priorities. Yet, future research can explore the fractures within existent, yet fragile commitments on the issue, looking at how communities can also split over some of these issues, which otherwise appeared here on the grounds of the received support and alignment, not of its differences. The strongly committed dwellers, such as those living in the *favelas*, can also suffer from internal conflicts that can reach the media making. Newly created institutions such as *Data Popular*, a research institute tailored to create statistics on low-income families, shows that recent movements as such exist, and qualitative assessments could help to map, and understand where the periphery goes to in the future, which may disclose fresh challenges of media representation.

Ultimately, in the turbulent universe of formal politics, polarisation and fracturing of the political debate must be probed against the rise of the right-wing alternative media groups, as well as against the concept of "alternative media." Through well-accessed outlets such as *O Antagonista* in Brazil or *Breitbart News* in the US, conservative groups have created their own pages, while the mainstream journalism lately seized the debate on "fake news" (McNair, 2017). In this process, the "alternative" brand was likened to the dissemination of untrue stories with no consideration for what could be the legitimacy of new sources legitimacy (Bennett & Livingston, 2018).

In this debate, while I do not believe that right-wing actors should appear as only "racists" or simply as "conservatives" (Girotto Neto, 2014), their emergence justifies new incursions into the alternative media scene. As my focus was consciously directed at social justice, without penetrating and engaging with the deep partisan fractures that existed in Brazil, I am aware that other civic purposes and socioeconomic aspects can also be analyzed through the methodology developed in this book. It could yet help researchers to contrast right-wing alternative media with those that still carry expectations of social justice. Are these other groups also interested in inequality? In what sense? To what extent could the peripheral media share premises with groups of other partisan inclinations? These questions must also be responded to on the grounds of more data on partisan affiliation, which, again, was not the focus of this book. I summarise this chapter and the key discussions advanced in the conclusion.

CONCLUSION

This chapter has listed all the conclusions reached in this book. In the first part, I summarized my departure from a scenario of uncertainty and lack of focus on the alternative media and the periphery, in which this book sought to contribute for understanding the politicization of inequality from these communities, observed by following frame and discourse analyses. Besides pointing to this politicized, consensus-breaking coverage and its nuances, the contribution of this book is to advance knowledge on the peripheral media environment. I saw the periphery promoting several adjustments of representation, increasing the diversity of frames, and providing the right type of feedback to powerholders. I also reflected on implications to past scholarly debates. First, for the debate on media concentration, still much centered at media organizations. Second, for the possibilities of looking at the alternative media as a fluid and highly reproducible discourse. Third, I approximated the ideas in this book to Mouffe's participatory democracy theory, particularly because outlets demonstrated a new front of agonistic contention in Brazil. Future studies could profit from exploring the peripheral as a single location, as well as exploring this concept's dimension according to each individual's ability to forge new realities through new media.

NOTES

1. Young men removed from environments that are deemed as "middle-class" is not new in Brazil as demonstrated by this episode, or by the other case of the *arrastão* discussed in chapter 3 of this book. More context in Penglase (2007), Jaguaribe (2014), Perlman (2010).
2. That language is found in many peripheral outlets, mostly in newspaper *Brasil 247*.
3. Interview available at https://www.animalpolitico.com/2016/06/ellos-no-me-sacaron-yo-sigo-siendo-presidenta-dice-dilma-rousseff/. Accessed 20 September 2017.

Afterword

In this afterword, I would like to reflect on Brazil's changing political environment to the extent that it affects this book's findings and conclusions. I would like to discuss some of these developments to allow more context so as to enhance the understanding on the interviews and content-related research amidst a divided Brazil. My research efforts took place during the final procedures to depose the President Dilma Rousseff. After that, the country would see more of the economic crisis, live the political turmoil that resulted in the President Michel Temer's ascension to power, then the probing of more corruption allegations involving the new President. As Brazil prepares for the 2018 elections, the tragic murder of Marielle Franco, a Rio de Janeiro's Councillor, who was originally from the periphery, has become a crime headlined on newspapers from around the world.

In the face of all these events, I engage with recent scholarly debates that brought up themes that relate to what I call the *peripheral media*. Since this research's start, during the 2013 protests, the contentious and polarizing role of digital media in the latter events appear likened to the same movements that culminated into the Rousseff's impeachment (Santos, 2018). Although this research has not directly drawn on the political crisis, but on the historical marginalization of the periphery, it is not possible to ignore the several "activist" acts that took the streets of Brazil and elsewhere (Harvey, 2012; Maricato et al., 2016). These events have also seized a great deal of research efforts put out by academics, as much of the interest in bottom-up digital contention has flowed into understanding the urgency of the 2013 protests in light of concerns over populism, and the lack of public dialogue (Gerbaudo, 2012; Gohn, 2014; Gomes, 2016; Avritzer, 2017; Santos, 2018).

Meanwhile, the tensions that led to impeach Rousseff and the political polarization that ensued from it have both led to renovated discussion on the centrality of the mainstream media to anti-democratic practices. I visited some of these debates in chapter 5. The issue of media monopoly returns as potential cause of such influence from the mainstream media to the political turmoil, during which the latter was arguably campaigning against the Workers' Party government (Mello, 2017; Vanden, 2017; van Dijk, 2017). The impeachment also appears as "Latin American" elites bearing a "civilizing" mission, having the media as a partner to sustain privileges of their own (Albuquerque, 2017; Bentes, 2018). Social media networks such as Twitter have come up as another polarizing factor by "reaffirming users' beliefs" instead of mediating different opinions (França et al., 2018).

Without downplaying the gravity of these issues in Brazil, it is possible to see much of these debates somehow present in the content of this book. The extent of the unpredictability has none the less caused surprise. Many producers who have spoken to me had no clear idea of the depth of this upcoming crisis, neither did we know of the impeachment result, though we knew about its proceedings. As a result, there was tranquillity enough from the interviewees to criticize Rousseff's policies to culture, which, as discussed in Chapter 5, could not give producers the boost they needed to take the periphery even further. The dissatisfaction with mainstream media portraits has been channelled through the events, such as the *rolezinhos,* in the context that had the "war" against *favelas* led by Rio de Janeiro ex-governor Sergio Cabral being broadcasted on live TV in 2010 with full agreement by the mainstream society. In 2018, Cabral is in jail due to corruption charges.

I would like to ground this book's findings in the context of slow-feeding political participation of disadvantaged, of which the peripheral media is part. Avritzer (2017) argued that what has changed since the crisis has begun is that a new standard of this participation has become more visible and up to a test. Populations with connection to social movements have helped to polarize fields that led to the Rousseff's government de-legitimation, while center-right crowds have been united through another model of participation, differing from the former due to its NGOs membership and voluntarism (as seen in chapter 5). In my perception, inasmuch as the political instability can be disruptive to the Brazilian democracy, it might not be enough to dismantle the hypothesis of an active, politicized peripheral media, even amid a greater *prominence* of conservative groups (Fortes, 2016). In this case, I would not trade this media prominence of a few radical groups of the right for what could be a sustainable move into enabling a higher autonomy of repertoire and political discourse that were clearly demonstrated by the many examples of this book.

On the one hand, the book has started considering a backdrop of marginalization of the periphery on multiple levels to explore evident discourse changes after a decade of political stability. On the other, in the face of the crisis, it is not to argue on the "disappearance" of social inequality on the mediascape (Escosteguy & Coutinho, 2017), but on small advances. For instance, Custódio (2017) unveiled complex ways in which *favela* residents "cope" with everyday constraints, where many actors influence one's involvement with media activism, which lies beyond such external events. Davis (2017) saw citizen journalism taught in a classroom environment in Brazil. These developments help to reinforce the character of improvement also seen in this book, especially after 2010. It is not enough to stress that the Federal Government had innovatively invested in the alternative media which could open the ground for other similar policies that also fund grassroots communications. On top of that, producers have developed a robust repertoire to talk security, better wages, and healthcare, as they demanded the right to circulate in shopping malls and the right to be known through markers that until recently were seen as derogatory.

In 2018, the murder of Marielle Franco, herself a spokeswoman from the periphery, was a tragic episode that revealed a major attempt to wound the periphery's increasing power to communicate. As much as Franco's action and presence had been unparalleled and it will be missed by many dwellers of the periphery, her election and fluency had attested to the prominence of interlocutors like her. Other communicators with similar political expectations have appeared in this book at length. Recent studies have seen how social media come allowing them to chase other possibilities, either browsing careers and compare lifestyles (Spyer, 2017) or spread their "black girlhood" (Gillam, 2017). Likewise, this book has highlighted a burgeoning scene that has given no evidence of its waning. Hence, one of the reasons that this crime has been so shocking for Brazilians and foreigners alike is the encompassing of her social mobility that Franco's media appearances have given, to which this fatality seemed to pose a threat.

In sum, the *Peripheral Media* connects with these key developments of recent Brazil by documenting the extent to which the periphery had joined a broader movement of polarization and dissent, but overall, showed how it has become such a prominent entity. Of course, the crisis-stricken Brazil becomes an obstacle against the promotion of these cases into an upper, strategic level of the political discussion, and this is a problem that blurs the view of how democracy as a whole, as it is hard to predict how it will look like in the future (Kingstone & Power, 2017). In this book, however, one can possibly visualize the periphery transcending many political battlefields, helping to create a language through which inequality is better assessed and understood nationwide. There is still a long journey towards full recognition and normalization of one's status in a society that has cemented inequality through images and pre-conceptions. In spite of the recent turmoil, this book has offered tools to analyze the periphery, which tends to become a stronger layer of Brazilian society, especially after the crisis, hopefully one that can influence the mainstream with its discourse.

Appendix A

Notes on Methods

In this appendix, I lay out the main criteria for this book's research. The primary methods were discourse analysis and frame analysis. The former based on semi-structured interviews conducted with selected media producers and the latter using content from a sample of five outlets. In this appendix, I will first layout the sample criteria. In this part, I discuss how I got to a preliminary number of outlets (50), then to the outlets that based the frame analysis (5), and, finally, I present how I reached to the interviewees (24). In a second part, I debate how I performed the analysis and interpretation of the interview material and the content. In sum, my choice of method responds to gaps in the literature, which constantly focused on ethnographic description, enabling a more precise answer to this book's questions on Brazil's peripheral media and the politicization of inequality.

The main rationale for this research's methods was the need to engage with the repertoire of the periphery. What I mean by *repertoire* is their discourse and their proposals for social change: questioning them and probing their outreach and resonance. The diversity of outlets and interviewees was key to probe the convergence into the same intent. Hence, I had to initially resort to a purposive sampling strategy (Riffe et al., 2014:77; Bryman, 2012:418) and then run the chosen outlets through a *maximum variation* sampling effort. The necessity for the purposive sampling strategy lies in controlling the size of the sample, which had to follow outlets that corresponded to the tradition of the alternative media in Brazil and, at the same time, represented the different landscapes they cover (as in Holanda et al., 2008, for example).

Both Kucinski (1991) and Strelow and Woitowicz (2009) mentioned ex-mainstream journalists, NGOs, and members of civil society as alternative media producers. Publications such as *Movimento* or *Opinião,* or the newspaper *Resistência* (Ferreira, 2009), have all become references for the alternative press due to their agenda in favor of the disadvantaged, but also because of their ability to gather "committed" journalists around the same ideals (Pereira, 1986).

My purposive sampling effort then had to contemplate different kinds of coverage, although that precision would clash with limited resources and time. Lindlof & Taylor (2011) stressed that the purposive sample strategy must follow a few critical cases. I proposed to incorporate multiple locations, social classes, and traditions (e.g. in the *favelas*, urban suburbs, hills, and low-income households). Once I determined that my sample would follow these variables, my *maximum variation* sampling (Lindlof & Taylor, 2011:113) had to incorporate theoretical assumptions of diversity in Brazilian alternative media, and to cover distinct periods (Kucinski, 2008; Woitowicz, 2009) and the emerging mediatized communities (Peruzzo, 2013; Custódio, 2014).

Finally, I found that four types of groups would suit this research's goals, as they are the most cited in the foregoing research. These groups were *independent journalism* groups, *NGO-sponsored* outlets, the so-called *community media* (which refers to locally focused outlets), and *radical, proletarian* newspapers (as per definitions found in Downing, 2001). I could have chosen a *snowballing* strategy by relying on references from producers of media partners or colleagues to find other producers; however, that would have compromised diversity and autonomy. To ensure a fair breadth of coverage, I chose outlets that had been publishing for more than two years.

To find this mix of diverse but systematic media outlets, I resorted to two sources. First, I used the 2015 *Free Media Points* program's project list. This federal government program invited media producers from across Brazil to apply for grants, priming for projects that were especially promoting the voice of minorities and excluded communities to apply. This index, which names projects and their locations, was publicly available on the website of the Ministry of Culture. I was thus able to index projects from all Brazilian regions, which led me to groups from less developed regions, such as the northeast. At the same time, by targeting *subscribed* projects and not *approved* projects, I did not constrain my sample to the universe of grant receivers, nor to the government's choice criteria. To focus on the criteria aforementioned, I had to choose groups independently of their platform or the format of their content, which meant equally including groups with websites or social media pages, as far as they were part of an *online* ecology.

Consistent with the *maximum* variation of this sample, I still had to ensure that projects that had not applied for this grant were also in the scope. I thus selected outlets that stood out for their comprehensive coverage of inequality, enough to raise the attention of other studies (Carvalho, 2014; Davis, 2015; Custódio, 2014b; Cunha et al., 2012). These studies guided me to other possible outlets, showing groups that had achieved certain prominence on social media or had established income sources and production independence. By picking half of the sample from the universe of grant applicants and the other half from recent literature, I reached a significant variation within the same scope (coverage of inequality), allowing me to add robustness to the claim of a broader contribution from the alternative media, not only from one or two outlets. This mixed sampling strategy may potentially inform future studies, as no literature has pinpointed the criteria one should follow to reach a comprehensive sample body of *alternative* media outlets in Brazil. Past focus has been on groups belonging to the same historical context but disregarding discursive or ideological differences (e.g. Festa & Silva, 1986).

I finally reached a sample of 50 media outlets, from which I picked six for my frame analysis (three from the government's list and three from the literature). The outlets which were not included in the frame analysis, or those from which I have picked up no names for the interviews, were nonetheless helpful for enriching this research. These remaining outlets offered this research further examples of topics or points that may coincide with both frame and discourse analyses in the discussion, despite this research has not engaged with these outlets further than this. My intention was to show that, if different outlets can follow the same frames and standards, then it is possible to analyze the coverage of inequality under different conditions and from a set of distinct contexts and platforms (Rubin & Babbie, 2009:150).

Regarding the size of this sample, there is no consensus on an ideal number when studying alternative media. Authors often worked with one or two cases when trying to perform an inventory of Brazilian alternative media (Festa & Silva, 1986; Peruzzo, 2008; Kucinski, 1991; Woitowicz, 2009; Primo, 2009). Recent compilations of alternative media case studies show scholars dwelling on a set of three or four outlets (Atton, 2015). At the same time, the *Free Media Points* program listed more than five hundred media projects that had subscribed to the scheme from across Brazil. As Bryman (2012:418) argued, the sample size of qualitative studies should satisfy criteria including saturation and heterogeneity. In qualitative studies, sample size should reflect the conceptual basis followed and the significance of the data (Lindlof & Taylor, 2011:116). In this book, it meant having a good grasp of discourses produced in the periphery, even though this periphery could exist in different conditions. Therefore, choosing six outlets that could—each one—stand for these variations of the periphery seemed reasonable for this research.

Likewise, being a Portuguese-language reader allowed me to read and analyze 120 randomly chosen articles for the frame analysis (20 per outlet) from articles published both on websites, social media, and online forum spaces during 2013, 2014, and 2015. A similar number of articles was examined in other cognate studies that conducted a media frame analysis (Redden, 2014). However, the assumption in this study was that the chosen articles capture different aspects of inequality in their coverage and reflect a diverse authorship.

The rationale for choosing six outlets to perform a frame analysis considers the possibility of analyzing in-depth the repetitions and emphases on the outlets. Still considering the same preliminary list, I thus chose five outlets of distinct groups of professional or non-professional producers that could represent the "periphery" or those that covered the demands from the periphery. At the same time, although this sampling is illustrative of the alternative media scene in Brazil, I do not assume that these outlets are an exhaustive sample of all kinds of outlets or of all possible formats they may assume within their media ecology. Therefore, the sampled ones were to more likely correspond to the image of the periphery that stems from the state, the media, and the mainstream society. Therefore, their scope and location are aspects that are more important to look at than their "presence" on Facebook or Twitter. While I do not aim to stress the meaning of "outlet," a more generic notion of *content* is enough to ground this research on basic notions of intent and authorship.

The first outlet analyzed was the *Agência Pública*, a journalism agency which is a constant reference for scholars and professional journalists in Brazil (Carvalho, 2014). This agency offered much coverage of the marginalized in Brazil, receiving multiple awards for its coverage. Then I chose the *Viva Favela* website, whose coverage has aimed to offer a more positive portrait of Rio de Janeiro's *favelas*, assembling different models of textual or pictorial contribution (Davis, 2015). *Rio on Watch* is a portal written in English and Portuguese, featuring opinion pieces and commentary from both foreign and Brazilian writers; it also focuses on improving the media coverage of the *favelas*. The other outlet covering the *favelas*, but from the perspective of the periphery (which includes other communities and the Rio's outskirts), is the *Coletivo Papo Reto*. As not all Brazilian suburbs are necessarily considered *favelas,* I chose *Mídia Periférica* as a blog based on the outskirts of Salvador, in the state of Bahia. Of similar profile, I chose the magazine *Vai da Pé*, which represents the outskirts of São Paulo. The final choice for the frame analysis was the newspaper *Brasil 247*, as this online outlet brought a political/partisan perspective.

Another part of this effort lies in my wish to use a few mainstream media outlets to discuss the extent to which these peripheral media outlets can offer what I understand here as the *counterhegemonic* coverage. That choice appears consonant to the literature on media frames, which is as focused on the mainstream media as it is on social movement media (Tarrow, 1992); comparing mainstream and alternative media can also be seen in other studies on media and poverty (e.g. Redden, 2014). Thus, I selected the biggest mainstream media outlets in Brazil, as this could offer a glance into the so-called *dominant* narrative to which producers have often reacted. I chose the outlets that have featured in other studies on the Brazilian media (Fox & Waisbord, 1997; Waisbord, 2000), namely *G1* (Internet portal owned by Globo organizations) and *Folha de S.Paulo*. As this does not intend to be a study on the mainstream media, I limit my search of both organizations' websites to events or facts covered at the peripheral media level, which is the core of this research. I now analyze the criteria that this research applies to the interviews with media producers.

ON THE INTERVIEWEES

From a total of 50 producers that I contacted who were working for the above outlets, 24 responded. They were based in different Brazilian states. From them, 21 were interviewed in this research. By disclosing who were the producers interviewed in this research, I can project some of the limitations of gender, for instance, that still persist in the alternative media realm, only 33% of the interviewees were women. Though not conclusive to attest that there is a gender imbalance in the whole media environment, we can look at it carefully that these data can refer to a sector that is more progressive and forward-looking with regards to inequality and the issues that affect the disadvantaged, but it can still reflect broader socioeconomic, gender, and racial unbalances. Here, for instance, I point to the smaller number of women, but there might exist other imbalances which were not possible to check with proper depth. In any case, all interview scripts and procedures were approved by the author's university ethical committee.

Regarding the diversity of interviewee's locations, I have targeted producers who have mirrored key states in Brazilian territory. Even though most of them were based in São Paulo or Rio de Janeiro, many of them were originally from other smaller states. This wide representation could potentially cover the totality of the living conditions in the country, from the impoverished North and Northeast to the wealthier South and Southeast. By inviting producers from the biggest states and from distant locations, this research could unveil the different, but complementary challenges that inequality poses to the whole country.

At the same time, the size of the cohort that accepted to take part in this research (and probably of those who compose the alternative media in Brazil in general) poses constraints in that respect, as not *all* profiles were available so as to do justice to a diverse country such as Brazil. Selected interviewees thus represented a cohort which is consonant with the set criteria and mirror groups covered in other studies (Kucinski, 1991; Rodríguez, 2001; Downing, 2001; Atton, 2015). For instance, most producers were slightly younger, with 57.4% at the 20–30 years old range, 36.2% at 30–40 years old, and 6.4% at 40–50. When producers described themselves, they were clear on the number of platforms they adopted, their routines of publication. There is a preference for using the Internet as the standard platform, but a reasonable number has added another format to their online media presence, with many citing radio, video, exhibitions, conferences, and print as alternatives to reach other populations. This presence was not at first related to any expectation of generating income but one of increasing publicity and mobilization.

Although producers have not provided evidence of their funding, I have informally inquired and checked independently what information was disclosed on their websites or available according to Brazilian funding body. I found that overall funding sources were much fragmented. I concluded that a significant number of them were sourcing their media projects from voluntary work (55.6%) and skill sharing, but still with a small fraction admittedly having received public grants (2.8%), as others mentioned social movements (2.8%), individual donations, and other types of grants from NGOs, for example (16.7%). While only 2.8% chose not to disclose their source, it was not possible to know what other support those on a voluntary basis could potentially have.

Interviews followed a flexible theoretical script, which included questions on the periphery, media democracy in Brazil, on the past coverage of inequality, and about alternative media networking, following the model of a semi-structured interview (Bryman, 2012:471; Seidman, 2015). I departed from the points indicated in the introduction, especially when approaching the so-called periphery in terms of their opinions with their media representations. On the profile of these media producers, I balanced it according to past studies. For instance, Festa and Silva (1986) mentioned alternative journalists and social movement members as actors carrying strong political and partisan values. Kucinski (1991) spoke to professional journalists, activists, and grassroots organizations that were part of the same pool of pro-democracy producers. Woitowicz (2009) featured alternative journalists, social movement leaders, and academics. Peruzzo (2008) mentioned activists and community leaders as important mentors for the alternative media. I compared these profiles with my script, although I remained open to other profiles that could happen to author digital media outlets.

Reaching out to producers from remote areas was particularly challenging, even via online video conference (Skype), but all interactions have respected ethical concerns such as privacy, identity checking, and informed consent[1] (King & Horrocks, 2010:101–02). Nevertheless, I did not name media producers when quoting them directly, for various reasons. This identification could harm them due to the political implications of their positions, whether it be when they are applying for funds amid a politically changing scene in Brazil or when they are publishing and engaging with audiences. Identification could potentially harm quoted individuals and potentially the third parties mentioned. Having discussed the main lines of this study's interviews, I now qualify the criteria for the analysis of the content and interviews next.

ANALYZING FRAMES

This research's use of media *frames* has not engaged with investigating the manipulative power of the mass media's hidden agendas (Entman, 2004, 2007) or the process whereby social movements build frames (Benford, 1997). Instead, I returned to Goffman's (1974) view of framing as the "organisation of experience," extending it to see how producers organize their interpretations of reality through their outlets. *Frame* here stems from choosing image and language to cover inequality, as I study the complexity of these constructions as viewpoints or simply as "dissent" (Messaris & Abraham, 2001; Cooper, 2010). I applied Gitlin's view (1980:7–10) that framing may work as a *selection* of important facts "based on tacit theories." These "tacit theories" have guided this study to verify how they inform this organization of experience—how this intent to frame the issue of inequality leads to the interpretation of facts and opinions. Yet, how producers come including news content from the mass media, and based on that, structuring their discourses around a single agency (Benson et al., 2012). Therefore, the frame is the mechanism through which I find what these agendas are, and which allow the study the implications for the coverage of inequality in Brazil, whether presented as a politicized topic or based on the old charity frame. The possibility of finding this intent to politicize the periphery—which is what I see as advancement is the reason why I have not chosen content analysis, for instance.

Another reason for using frames is to make use of the documental work that has already revealed the past alternative press's strong drive for social justice (Festa & Silva, 1986). With regard to how some past media outlets were leaning towards Marxist left-wing partisanship (Pereira, 1986), frames could ease a new interpretation of the new data against this old historical development. By organizing this analysis around specific frames, this book could depart from this broad impression of a "socially conscious" alternative media, moving towards more specific frames or intents that may update producers' role in modern Brazil. Likewise, I do not assume that frames are always exact or make assumptions about their fairness (based on past ethics or according to the ethics of contemporary mainstream journalism, as in Atton & Hamilton, 2008), but at least this method can attest to producers' culture and habits (Reese, 2010). As discussed in Chapter 1, the more politicized the frames appear, the more this book could defend a contribution from the alternative media to an enhanced discourse on inequality. I dwell more on this by explaining the link of this frame analysis to the following discourse analysis.

In terms of finding frames in the content of the outlets analyzed, I considered what Van Gorp (2010:85) defined as "shared notions of symbolic significance, such as stereotypes, values, archetypes, myths, and narratives." In addition, I also saw what Tarrow (1992) mentioned as existing "group opportunities" in discursive patterns, as they can motivate a change in behavior and in society. Moreover, Goffman (1974:65) argued that framing involves a process of "alteration," in which one creates a new order of values to reframe "what is going on." For this work, I worked with ideas, group opportunities, and discursive opportunities (alterations, metaphors) to arrive at what Benford and Snow (2000) saw as *political opportunity*. I see this concept in how producers could somehow succeed in attracting mainstream media attention, such as during parliamentary debates, enabling overall community or society awareness.

Because this research has adopted this approach of seeing frames as tools to identify reflexivity and repertoire. I am aware of the limitations regarding the subjectivity of this method (Opp, 2009), so I refrained from seeing frames as part of the publicity obtained through the mainstream media narrative only, as well as a rigid form of media construction. For instance, Tarrow (1992) mentioned the case of the Israeli-Palestinian conflict as a case for *given* frames, which have become globally known in the media. Otherwise, in Benford and Snow (2000:624), we learn that frames should follow "strategic processes" or those that are "deliberative, utilitarian, and goal directed." Gamson and Modigliani (1989) suggested capturing catchphrases, keywords, and metaphors to confirm how semantics can lead to frames, as discussed in the above section. I followed a triple conceptualization of this frame analysis that could establish a direct relationship with political opportunities. In sum, I considered the reframing of news and commentary, the use of discursive opportunities (e.g. hyperboles, catchphrases, or metaphors), and the investment in alterations of content through "remixing" (i.e. old content used with new purposes).

I also looked at frame analysis when applied to news stories (D'Angelo & Kuypers, 2010). For example, whenever the mainstream media have featured socially-sensitive issues on Brazilian TV—e.g. "a new soap opera staged in *favelas*"[2]—alternative producers could, in this way, capture momentum by *appropriating* that agenda to provide a more realistic outlook of what it really feels like "living in the *favela*." Alternative media producers could *alter* celebratory accounts, from diverting their purpose of feeding tourism and commoditization to *transforming* such narratives by telling about the harsh treatment of its black dwellers or reporting on the uncollected litter, for example. Producers would have used the soap opera as a starting point to lobby for public policies and to bargain for an equivalence of public services offered in that community. Here, the analysis of this frame has indicated the use of the *telenovela* as *political opportunity* to politicize the inequality surrounding the *favelas*, which might be hidden from the wider public who watch the program.

FRAMING POLITICIZATION OR CHARITY

One of the ways I had to perceive differences in the discourse of the contemporary periphery lied in investigating if there was any new "politicization" in their discourse. The origins of this frame are in the radical and alternative press that thrived during the dictatorship (Sodré, 1998; Barbosa, 2007), but which could revive in contemporaneity from the periphery. For example, to frame issues that mainstream society has yet to understand as "rights" (Fischer, 2008). Through *politicization*, producers catch a subject and reverse its coverage towards the debate on inequality. It can also be *politicized* to *help* individuals, but in a way of guaranteeing a broader, higher-level change, as opposed to only provoke compassion and charity. The new labor laws for house cleaners is another example: instead of siding with the bosses, the producers talked about the inequality that exists in this profession.

A second frame (charity) dwells on how the alternative media could present softer examples where inequality does not appear challenged as an issue. What Brazilians have called "solidarity campaigns" keeps much of this commotion around poverty, but less attention paid to inequality. For example, in the 1990s, massive tele-charity campaigns were boosted by Globo TV, in which TV programs asked for donations to schools and hospitals aimed at helping disadvantaged children (Stacciarini, 2007; Lattman-Weltman, 2007). Their lack of emphasis on public policies led scholars to dismiss it as *voluntarism* (Gomes, 2008). The final aim of this frame analysis was then to decide whether "politicization" has more prominence over the "charity" frame. This is not to argue that the "charity" discourse must be depoliticized. Brazil's experience with *mutirões*, community-organized groups that perform public service duties (Boschi, 1987) such as cleaning sewages and food distribution, shows that the charity discourse could be also political. The meaning of charity also differs from the potential connotations of "solidarity" in a European sense (Stjerno, 2009).

However, the prevalence of *politicization* can be decisive to show a new inclination for politics from the periphery. In Kucinski's (1991) documental book, *Journalists and Revolutionaries*, all the success of changing public conversation during dictatorial times is owed to the use of a robust, proactive, pro-minorities and therefore *politicized* discourse. Festa and Silva's (1986) reference to *popular and alternative communication* likens a moment of harmony and reciprocity, the opposite to what I call *politicization,* to the inevitable demise of the alternative media producers in Brazil in the late 1980s. That said, looking for politicization in this research is a way of seeing the revitalization of the first tradition of dialoguing with power, to sound off demands and set changes in a constitutional framework.

Having set the concepts for each of the frames, which are the rationale and criteria to interpret the frame analysis, the process of operationalizing it was designed to minimize the complexity of selecting content and recording each of the decisions by both coders. Once 20 articles from each sampled outlet were selected, the articles' headlines and hyperlinks to the original story were pasted into an Excel spreadsheet, which served as the main guide to both coder 1 and coder 2. In this document, coders could click on the hyperlinks, read the full article or story, then use the columns indicated to record agreement or disagreement with each of the other frames. Coders followed the decision matrix based on which they reflect on the extent that producers are politicizing inequality or promoting *charity.* The decisions and the original content will support further interpretation and collection of repertoire. To reduce these imprecisions and to shed light on the reasons behind these frames, I complement this research's inquiry with data from the interviews, on which I performed a discourse analysis.

PERFORMING INTERVIEWS AND DISCOURSE ANALYSIS

The notion of coverage as *repertoire* draws on Potter & Wetherell's (1999) idea of investigating taxonomies, languages, and terms to which groups refer when they aim for social change. By choosing a semi-structured interview template (Potter & Whetherell, 1999; Seidman, 2015), I could create theoretically informed questions (Weingraf, 2001), particularly using the past of the alternative media in Brazil, and then adopting a more flexible approach in which unexpected revelations and other details of their involvement could pop up. The decision to conduct interviews also derives from my wish, as a researcher, to reduce hierarchies between me and my interviewees. I could thus agree with them in moments when I could capture their thoughts, not excerpting any pressure in their everyday lives that could either constrain or magnify their daily reporting (Seidman, 2015).

At first, I questioned the producers' mission and the value of their outlets. I compared the past mobilization of the alternative media around the inequality agenda with these producers' present coverage. I also remained attentive to the fluid goals, tensions, and differences between the online production and what producers really achieve with face-to-face interactions with their subjects, collaborators, and sponsors (Angeluci & Huang, 2015). Secondly, I included questions about their actual role as media producers, questioning what influences their practice had over their agenda on social issues, and the degree to which stories had stemmed from them or from other actors, such as social movement leaders (Rauch, 2007). Third, I brought up questions that stemmed directly from the early repertoire of the alternative press in Brazil, especially regarding their critical relationship with Brazilian democratic institutions and their understanding and denouncing inequality (as in Woitowicz, 2009).

While I did not assume that every interview had to cover all these three areas, the data generated in the interviews were meant to supply the material for a discourse analysis. The central point for this analysis was to cover existing attempts to politicize inequality, based on producers' language and repertoires. Looking at past literature (Kucinski, 1991) and with recent literature on alternative media worldwide (e.g. Atton, 2015), little is known about what media producers have to say outside an activist purpose. How could a new mapping of a native repertoire represent a change towards recognizing, interpreting, and finally, politicizing inequality? The analysis of this repertoire, as expressed in interviews, was supplemented with cross-references to the content found on websites, blogs or social media platforms.

The analysis and interpretation of this discourse could identify "change" as it manifests through innovative perspectives (i.e. introducing concepts or readings that are not commonly available in Brazil's press) or through the way in which producers work on new linkages (e.g. inequality and crime, inequality and citizenship). Still, I looked at how producers have taken their understanding to new directions or in line with the background offered in the introduction. In this way, this discourse analysis could hint at a historically orientated engagement of these producers with their reality or, instead, at a new engagement that leads or creates new agendas. To remove any trace of subjectivity from this analytical effort, I split the arguments shared among producers from those that differ from each other. By grouping the parts in which producers agree or disagree separately, I could create different branches of a same argument, which have been based on so-called corpus of "linguistic evidence" (Potter & Wetherell, 1999:156).

Following Potter and Wetherell (1991), I saw as an advantage in the possibility to engage with reflexive patterns as they appeared in the interviews. By focusing on "repertoire," I remained aligned with this research's strategy of studying the discourse of the peripheral media, meaning the display of contradictions or emphases that are important for understanding the dialogue with the dominant narrative of the mainstream. In terms of the presentation of the results, I chose to italicize terms and expressions that evidenced new language standards, which, to a greater or lesser extent, can confirm the politicization of inequality that I had hypothesized in the beginning. Because I literally quoted producers' discourse, I also had to perform quick literature reviews so that I could interpret empirical evidence, checking it against the theoretical background. This reflexivity has also opened space for new intersections between inequality, poverty, and racism, which I tend to analyze as long as it connected to the central research question.

This interplay between empirical, theoretical, and reflexive perceptions is necessary in mixed method studies, which are based on laying out distinct technological and social realities (Hesse-Biber *et al.*, 2015). That mix is also useful to avoid the sensation that the analysis is grounded on "views from nowhere" or that mixed methods carry too much "positivism" (Giddings, 2006). Often, this content brings up *new* images of this subject (1), revealing their politics of naming and framing of inequality (2) that may or may not represent an advance of the approach to social issues seen in the past (3). Yet, to systematize these new images in these three different ways, I had to resort to a few generalizations, as for instance, by referring to "media producers" as a single group, the same for "mainstream media," even if I am aware of the multiple differences between these individuals and organizations.

The collected repertoires in these three moments have been interpreted on the grounds of: 1) their relationship with one of three areas that guide the analysis on "politicization," namely: adjustments of representation, the diversity of frames, and the ability to give feedback to power; 2) the rich ecology of social engagement that forms the history of alternative and mainstream media in Brazil (Abreu, 2002; Porto, 2007); 3) acknowledging the specific settings of Brazil's contemporary politics (Castro et al., 2014), which differs a lot from the repressive governments of the 1970s and 1980s (Fleury, 2014), so producers' responses have shed light on how the periphery of a modernized Brazil is aware and responds to new struggles, but also reminds society of old trivialized inequalities (Reis, 1999; Henriques, 2000).

Furthermore, part of the interviews happened in a climate of intense political polarization that marked the 2014 presidential elections in Brazil, followed by a political and economic crisis in 2015, but before the trial and impeachment of ex-president Dilma Rousseff in 2016. Therefore, some producers have been understandably cautious in replying to my requests. However, producers with whom I spoke opened up about different aspects of their media production, among other aspects relating to their agenda on social issues, human rights, and overall inequality. I have translated the selected parts to include in this book, aiming to ensure accuracy, but I have left in the original language the terms that could reflect key concepts or those whose meaning would be lost if translated into English. I discuss next the validity and reliability of both analyses conducted in this research.

VALIDITY AND INTERCODER RELIABILITY

I employed another Portuguese-speaking coder to review a sample of the articles and interview transcriptions in Portuguese, as well as to double-check the frames assigned to the former. The calculation of reliability indices can show how often the two coders agreed on the classification of each item (Riffe et al., 2013:114). Moreover, the calculation of the percentage of agreement can make the analysis more robust (Lombard et al., 2002:594). However, even if different coders come to disagree, there might still exist a discovery and a significance of each frame identified. Therefore, disagreeing does not mean invalidating the premises of this research. In any case, it was important to check perceptions, as notions of politicization and solidarity may vary from one person to another. Following similar procedures of past studies that also employed frame analysis (e.g. Redden, 2014), 10% (or 12 articles) have been proportionally extracted from the main sample (Riffe et al., 2013:108). Cohen's (1968) *kappa* was applied to both frames, as they presented the same index below. Despite the many controversies regarding this index, including the chance of coincidence between coders (Lombard, 2002; Neuendorf, 2002), the low complexity of this frame and the small number of articles posed a reduced risk.

As displayed above, results have shown that, while not all proposed frames are recurrent in the sample, there is a low level of disagreement between the coders. For Cohen's *kappa*, an index of at least 0.7 is an adequate level of reliability (Riffe et al., 2013:125), even though indices of 0.7 tend to show enough consistency for exploratory research (Lombard et al., 2002:593). In this research, this part of validation scored at 0.81, which has met expectations. In the next section, I discuss some limitations of this book's methods.

LIMITATIONS OF THE METHOD

Over and above the limitations discussed thus far in this chapter, the focus on discourse and on framing entails other limitations that should be addressed in future research. First, I do not follow the "categorisation" of alternative media practices as it has appeared in other studies (Atton & Hamilton, 2008; Forde, 2001). In brief, I skipped popular terms, such as "alternative journalism," "activist" or "radical" media (Downing, 2001). I engaged with a new taxonomy that could address Brazil's complex history between alternative media and power, which still poses a dilemma on how to engage with these previous taxonomies and their own complexities. From these two possibilities, I decided to privilege the former, as only a brief borrowing from the extensive vocabulary on the alternative media would otherwise appear anecdotic. This same choice and rationale applies to other political taxonomies such as "radical," "neoliberal," but which do not compromise the understanding of "politicization" in this research as a phenomenon distinct from these assumptions

A second limitation emerges from not investing in ethnographic methods. As far as ethnographies have much contributed to the knowledge on alternative media, this research could add more if it could capture other sides of peripheral media production. If we look at recent studies regarding the alternative media in Brazil that cover the disadvantaged (Custodio, 2017; Davis, 2015), we see a constant turn to a descriptive ethnography. As a method, ethnographies attend well to the purpose of looking at alternative media if one aims to look at organizational and format-based inquiries that involve small groups of media producers (e.g. Atton & Wikenden, 2005). By contrast, this research has set out to analyze how a wider "coverage" leads to a counterhegemonic discourse from the periphery, through frames and new expressions. The chosen interview method is more suited to advancing the knowledge of media producers, but not details of their process, behaviors or practices, which may vary from region to region and from platform to platform. On the one hand, this decision has helped this research to explore the depths of the counter-hegemony of an under-represented discourse; on the other, this approach limits our visibility of specific actions or procedures or of producers' association as a group.

Finally, as an epistemological contribution, this book draws on an effort to interpret phenomena and offer subtle meanings that lie under the assumption of the "periphery" in Brazil. Because it invests in *stressing* the characteristics, motivations, and reactions from Brazil's periphery in relation to inequality, this work cannot offer more precise guidance or more basic data about "who are the producers," "where are they expected to be," or "how many projects are expected to come up in the next decade," which could add on to knowledge, as it could fulfil a demographic or socioeconomic research gap. The same absence still exists in relation to their sources of income and their budget, for example. One can find this idea of a "guide" to the alternative media scene in South and Central America in a few publications (Vinelli, 2010; Atton, 2015). To alleviate the absence of these data, I will open my research data to the point it does not compromise interviewee's privacy and to the degree that it clarifies the profile of media producers according to information that I collected (their age, location, and production methods). This is a body of knowledge that may be valuable for future research. However, it only faithfully reflects the research design employed in this analysis and it is not meant to be an exhaustive map of this field.

NOTES

1. The interviewed received full approval from City, University of London's Ethical Committee.
2. The popularization of favelas in soap operas had in the very successful "Avenida Brasil" (2012) its peak. Most of this upbeat representation appeared broadcasted on Globo TV's programs, although it is still not a unanimity (La Pastina et al., 2014).

Appendix B

Sampled Outlets and Description

Number	*Title*	*Platform*	*Brief description*
1	100 Ko	Internet	Blog covering the everyday life in *favelas* of Rio de Janeiro.
2	A Voz da Periferia	Internet, printed sheets	Blog with comments on social issues from Fortaleza, Ceará.
3	Agencia Pública	Internet	Journalism agency focused on inequality, human rights. It is based in São Paulo and operates with a staff of journalists.
4	Alma Preta	Internet	Group of producers focused on covering the racialized consequences of inequality.
5	Aparecidos Políticos	Internet, print, interventions	Art and media group focused on protesting against the remains of the Brazilian military dictatorship, they are based in Ceará.
6	Bahia 1798	Internet	Group based in Bahia covering the struggle of Afro-Brazilians for equality.
7	Blogueiras negras	Internet	Feminist blog focused on covering racialized inequality in Brazil, dedicating part of its coverage to social activism.
8	Brasil 247	Internet	Radical online newspaper covering Brazil's politics.
9	Casa Preta	Internet	Collective aimed at covering stories that approach the poverty associated with the Afro-Brazilian community.

(continued)

Number	*Title*	*Platform*	*Brief description*
10	CCJ Recife	Internet, conferences	NGO-linked group aimed at *educomunicação* for young people, based in Recife.
11	Coletivo Camaradas	Internet	Collective acting in the city of Crato, Ceará.
12	Coletivo Nigéria	Internet, video	Multimedia group based in the city of Fortaleza, Ceará.
13	Coletivo Papo Reto	Internet	Collective based in Rio de Janeiro aimed at covering human rights, inequality, especially focused on Rio de Janeiro.
14	Coletivo Rever	Internet	Started out as a collaborative group, this collective put out a magazine focused on human rights and inequality in the state of Sergipe.
15	Desabafo Social	Internet, conferences	Collective based in Bahia, Alagoas and Sergipe aiming for the defence of human rights and media democracy.
16	DNA Urbano/ ES	Internet, exhibitions, conferences	Mix of hip-hop, skate, and graffiti collective publishing content on the periphery of Vitoria, Espirito Santo.
17	Enecos Piauí	Internet	University-based collective advocating for media democracy and inequality of representation
18	Favela News Recife	Internet, video	Collective linked to the Shine a Light foundation, aimed at training disadvantaged young people in Recife. The group is based in both Recife and Florianópolis.
19	Favelados pelo Mundo	Internet	Facebook-based publication focusing on *favelados* and their trips around the world.
20	Força Tururu	Internet	Collective based in Paulista, Pernambuco. They are focused on public service issues in disadvantaged communities of the northeast.
21	Gatomídia	Internet, video	Youtube-based group aimed at the young people from *favelas.*
22	Imagem Comunitaria	Internet, TV	Nonprofit organization based in Belo Horizonte aimed at providing consultancy to grassroots communications. Their partnership is overall focused on television.

Number	*Title*	*Platform*	*Brief description*
23	Imersão Latina	Internet, exhibitions, conferences	Activist collective that runs a blog on the inequality affecting the indigenous people in Brazil and Latin America.
24	Instituto Amazonico de Educação e Comunicação Popular (IACEP)	Internet, radio, conferences, interventions	Amazon-focused group with the aim of developing communications in that region.
25	Internet Sem Fronteiras Institute	Internet	Nonprofit institution focused on digital divide and training people to produce their own communications.
26	Jornalistas Livres	Internet	A collective of media activists, journalists, and media producers based in São Paulo. It is anchored on Facebook, website, and social media.
27	Juventude Sem Terra	Internet, print	The group derived from the Landless Rural Workers, but here focusing on its young membership.
28	Mídia Ninja	Internet	Group of activists and media producers focused on covering inequality, human rights, and "progresssive causes."
29	Mídia Periférica	Internet	Mix of blog and radio show covering the outskirts of Salvador, Bahia.
30	Nina Campinas	Internet, exhibitions	Collective aimed at boosting feminist-oriented reports on inequality and human rights.
31	Nonada—Jornalismo Travessia	Internet, radio	Journalism group from Porto Alegre aimed at raising consciousness on social issues.
32	Observatorio de Direitos	Internet	Representing an activism group, the Observatorio de Direitos focuses on disadvantaged populations of Rio de Janeiro but also is aimed at covering Brazil's affairs regarding human rights and inequality.
33	Outras palavras	Internet	Blog of news and commentary based in São Paulo.
34	Periferia Digital	Internet	Social media pages focused on inequality issues of the city of Fortaleza, Ceará.

(continued)

Number	Title	Platform	Brief description
35	Polo Jequitinhonha	Internet, TV	Group formed at the University of the Jequitinhonha Vale, which is focused on boosting grassroots communications.
36	Portal Viva Favela	Internet, TV	Website aimed at covering positive developments in Rio de Janeiro's *favelas*.
37	Rede Join	Internet, conferences	Network of "young Internet activists" based in the city of Agudos.
38	Rede Mocoronga	Internet, radio	Collective of media producers focused on North Brazil, especially disadvantaged populations around the Amazon river.
39	Redes da Maré	Internet	Group based in Maré *Favela,* newtowking among activists, NGO contributors, and dwellers.
40	Renajoc	Internet, TV, interventions	Network of yong media producers acting in North Brazil.
41	Revista Afirmativa	Internet	Magazine aimed at seeking equality for minorities in Brazil.
42	Revista Capitolina	Internet	Feminist magazine covering the gender-related aspects of inequality.
43	Revista Gambiarra	Internet, conferences	Magazine formed by one journalist and a publicist who team up to cover socially-sensitive stories in Vitoria da Conquista, BA.
44	Revista NNA	Internet	Facebook-based magazine, later incorporated into the Jornalistas Livres network.
45	Rio on Watch	Internet	Portal focused on news and commentary on Rio de Janeiro's *favelas,* it is organized by an interdisciplinary team, originally writing in English.
46	SP Invisivel	Internet	Started as an Instagram account aimed at portraying the homeless population in São Paulo. It later emerged into a magazine and website.
47	Vai da Pé	Internet, print	Magazine founded by ex-university colleagues in São Paulo. It covers the periphery of the City, focusing on political and cultural activism, such as the hip-hop scene and pro-citizenship demonstrations.

Number	*Title*	*Platform*	*Brief description*
48	Viração	Internet, print, audiovisual	A set of magazines, websites, and foundations aimed at training young people so they can produce content on the periphery.
49	Voz da Baixada	Internet, print	Collective publishing a newspaper in the Baixada Fluminense, Rio de Janeiro.
50	Voz das Comunidades	Internet	Originally a blog founded by Rene Silva, a dweller of Alemão *Favela,* in Rio de Janeiro. It mainly covers issues of poverty and inequality affecting other communities.

Bibliography

Abers, R. (2000). Inventing local democracy: grassroots politics in Brazil. Lynne Rienner Publishers.

Abramovay, M. (1999). Gangues, galeras, chegados e rappers: juventude, violência e cidadania nas cidades da periferia de Brasília. Editora Garamond.

Abreu, A. A. (2006). A democratização no Brasil: Atores e contextos. Rio de Janeiro, RJ, Brasil: FGV Editora.

———. (2002). A modernização da imprensa (1970–2000). Zahar.

———. Lattman-Weltman (2006) "Uma institutição ausente nos estudos de transição." In: Abreu, A (2006). A Democratização no Brasil. Rio de Janeiro: Editora FGV.

Adghirini, Z. L.; Pereira, F. H. (2006). Perfil profissional no ciberjornalismo: o blog como espaço de autoria e identidade na web. Anais do IV SBPJOR, Porto Alegre.

Adghirni, Z.L. (2008). Blogs: A invasão dos profanos do mundo digital na esfera sagrada do jornalismo, in Proceedings of the Sixth Congress of The Brazilian Society of Journalism Researchers (SBPJor), São Paulo: SBPJOR.

Aguiar, S. (1998). Informação exemplar. Jornal da Cidadania, Rio de Janeiro, 02.

Albernaz, A. (2002). The Internet in Brazil: from digital divide to democracy. New York. Available at http://www2.gtz.de/dokumente/bib/gtz2009–0424en-cairo-informal-areas.pdf. Accessed 26 Jun 2016.

Albuquerque, A. (2000). Um outro "Quarto Poder": imprensa e compromisso político no Brasil. Revista Contracampo, (04).

———. (2017). Protecting democracy or conspiring against it? Media and politics in Latin America: A glimpse from Brazil. Journalism, 1464884917738376.

Aldé, A. (2004). A construção da política: democracia, cidadania e meios de comunicação de massa. FGV Editora.

Aldridge, M., & Evetts, J. (2003). Rethinking the concept of professionalism: the case of journalism. The British journal of sociology, 54(4), 547–64.

Allan, S. (2013). Citizen witnessing: Revisioning journalism in times of crisis. John Wiley & Sons.

Almeida, P. D. (2007). Defensive Mobilization: Popular Movements against Economic Adjustment Policies in Latin America. Latin American Perspectives, 34(3), 123–39.

Alvermann, D. E., Moon, J. S., Hagwood, M. C., & Hagood, M. C. (2018). Popular culture in the classroom: Teaching and researching critical media literacy. Routledge.

Alves, L. R. (1986) "Comunicação e Cultura Popular: No meio do redemoinho." In: Festa, R.; Silva, C. E. L. Comunicação Popular e Alternativa no Brasil. São Paulo: Paulinas.

Alves, M. H. M. (1984). Grassroots organizations, trade unions, and the church: A challenge to the controlled abertura in Brazil. Latin American Perspectives, 73–102.

Alves, M., & Evanson, P. (2011). Living in the crossfire: Favela residents, drug dealers, and police violence in Rio de Janeiro. Temple University Press.

Amaral, M. F. (2005). Sensacionalismo, um conceito errante. Intexto, (13), 103–16.

Amaral, R (2002) "Modernization to prevent change." In: Fox, E.; Waisbord (Eds.) (2002). Latin politics, global media. Austin: University of Texas.

———. Guimarães, C. (1994). "Media monopoly in Brazil." Journal of communication (0021–9916), 44 (4), p. 26.

Amoroso, M., Brum, M., & Gonçalves, R. S. (2014). Police, participation et accès aux droits dans des favelas de Rio de Janeiro: l'expérience des Unités de police de pacification (UPP). L'Ordinaire des Amériques, (216).

Amparo Alves, J. (2014). Narratives of violence: The white imagination, and the making of black masculinity in City of God. CS, (13), 313–37.

Anderson, H. (2015). "Prisoners' Radio." In: Atton, C. 2015. The Routledge Companion to Alternative and Community Media. London: Routledge.

Androvandi, A. (2010). A favela no horário nobre da TV aberta brasileira: uma análise da novela" Duas Caras." Dissertation. PUCRS

Angeluci, A. C., & Huang, G. (2015, 09). Rethinking media displacement: The tensions between mobile media and face-to-face interaction. Rev. Famecos (Online) Revista FAMECOS, 22(4), 173. doi:10.15448/1980–3729.2015.4.21005.

Antunes, B. A. F. (2014). Crítica de mídia feminista na Web: uma análise sobre os blogs Cem Homens, Escreva Lola Escreva e Blogueiras Feministas.

Araújo, P. C. (2002). Eu não sou cachorro, não: música popular cafona e ditadura militar. Record.

Arias, E. D. (2009). Drugs and democracy in Rio de Janeiro: trafficking, social networks, and public security. University of North Carolina Press.

Atton, C. (ed) (2015). The Routledge Companion to Alternative and Community Media. London: Routledge.

———. (2013). An alternative Internet: Radical media, politics and creativity. Cambridge: Cambridge University Press.

———. (2002). Alternative media. Sage.

———. (2002b). News cultures and new social movements: Radical journalism and the mainstream media. *Journalism Studies*, *3*(4), 491–505.

——— & Hamilton, J F (2008) Alternative journalism. Sage.

——— & Wickenden, E. (2005). Sourcing routines and representation in alternative journalism: A case study approach. Journalism Studies, 6(3), 347–59.

Aufderheide, P. (1993). Latin American grassroots video: Beyond television. Public Culture, 5(3), 579.

Avritzer, L. (2000). Public deliberation at the local level: participatory budgeting in Brazil. In Experiments in Deliberative Democracy Conference, Madison, WI.

———. (2017). The impeachment of Dilma Rousseff: introduction. Critical Policy Studies, 11(3), 349–51.

Azevedo, F. A. (2006). Mídia e democracia no Brasil: relações entre o sistema de mídia e o sistema político. Opinião Pública, 12(1), 88–113.

Bailey, O. G.; Cammaerts, B.; Carpentier, N. (2007). Understanding alternative media. McGraw-Hill International.

———. (2009). Citizen journalism and child rights in Brazil. In: Allan, S; Thorsen, E., eds., Citizen journalism: global perspectives. New York: Peter Lang.

Baiocchi, G. (2003). Radicals in Power: The Workers' Party and Experiments in Urban Democracy in Brazil. Zed Books.

Baker, C. E. (2007). Media concentration and democracy: why ownership matters. Cambridge: Cambridge University Press.

Barassi, V. (2015). Activism on the web: Everyday struggles against digital capitalism. London: Routledge.

Barbosa, A. (2010). "Da ideologia editorial aos critérios de noticiabilidade: Processo de construção de veículo de imprensa alternativa digital para a América Latina popular." Ciberlegenda, 1(23), 73–83.

Barbosa, M. (2007). História cultural da imprensa Brasil-1900–2000. Mauad Editora Ltda.

Bardoel, J.; Deuze, M. (2001). Network Journalism: converging competences of old and new media professionals. Australian Journalism Review, 23(2), 91–103.

Baroni, A. (2015). The Favelas Through the Lenses of Photographers: Photojournalism from community and mainstream media organizations. Journalism Practice, (ahead-of-print), 1–17.

———. (2012) Participatory Content Creation and Collective Intelligence in Rio de Janeiro's Favelas. International Journal of Technology, Knowledge & Society, 8(3).

Barros, R. P. D., Henriques, R., & Mendonça, R. (2001). A estabilidade inaceitável: desigualdade e pobreza no Brasil.

Bastos, M. T., da Cunha Recuero, R., & da Silva Zago, G. (2014). Taking tweets to the streets: A spatial analysis of the Vinegar Protests in Brazil. First Monday, 19(3).

Beaton, M. E., & Washington, H. B. (2015). Slurs and the indexical field: the pejoration and reclaiming of favelado 'slum-dweller.' Language Sciences, 52, 12–21.

Becker, M. L. (2009). Inclusão digital e cidadania: as possibilidades e as ilusões da" solução" tecnológica. Editora UEPG.

———. (2009b). Mídia Alternativa: antiempresarial, antiindustrial, anticapitalista. Recortes da Mídia Alternativa: histórias & memórias da comunicação no Brasil. Ponta Grossa: Editora UEPG.

Belfort, M. (2013) "Favelado, afinal o que é isso"? 04.10.2013. Redes da Maré. Available at http://redesdamare.org.br/blog/noticias/artigo-favelado-afinal-o-que-e-isso/. Accessed 10 Jul 2016.
Benford, R. D. (1997). An insider's critique of the social movement framing perspective. Sociological inquiry, 67(4), 409–30.
——— & Snow, D. A. (2000). Framing processes and social movements: An overview and assessment. *Annual review of sociology*, 611–39.
Bennett, W. (2003). New media power. In: Couldry, N; Curran, J. (2003). Contesting media power. Rowman & Littlefield.
———. (2003b). Civic learning in changing democracies. In: Dahlgren, P. (2013) Young citizens and new media. Routledge.
——— & Livingston, S. (2018). The disinformation order: Disruptive communication and the decline of democratic institutions. European Journal of Communication, 33(2), 122–39.
Benson, R; Blach-Ørsten, M.; Powers, M.; Willig, I., & Zambrano, S. V. (2012). Media systems online and off: Comparing the form of news in the United States, Denmark, and France. Journal of Communication, 62(1), 21–38.
Bentes, I. (2009). Redes colaborativas e precariado produtivo. Periferia, 1(1), 53–62.
Bentes, I. (2018). The impeachment was a fascist and conservative turn against culture. Journal of Latin American Cultural Studies, 27(1), 43–61.
Bertol, R. (2003). Como os sem-terra se inventaram pela mídia: a novidade social nos anos 90. Revista Estudos Históricos, 1(31), 3–23.
Birman, P.; Lehmann, D. (1999). Religion and the Media in a Battle for Ideological Hegemony: The Universal Church of the Kingdom of God and TV Globo in Brazil. Bulletin of Latin American Research, 18(2), 145–64.
Blasco, M.; Krause Hansen, H. (2006). Cosmopolitan aspirations: New media, citizenship education and youth in Latin America. Citizenship Studies,10(4), 469–88.
Boal, A. (2000). Theater of the Oppressed. Pluto Press.
Boler M (2008) Digital Media and Democracy: Tactics in Hard Times, Cambridge, MA: MIT Press.
Boschi, R. R. (1987). A arte da associação: política de base e democracia no Brasil (Vol. 4). Iuperj.
———. Diniz, E. (1991). O corporativismo na construção do espaço público. Corporativismo e desigualdade: a construção do espaço público no Brasil. Rio de Janeiro: IUPERJ/Rio Fundo.
Brandão, B., & Conceição, W. D. S. (2017). O crack, o corpo e a rua. Analisando trajetos e andanças na cidade. Ponto Urbe. Revista do núcleo de antropologia urbana da USP, (20).
Branford, S.; Kucinski, B. (1995). Brazil, carnival of the oppressed: Lula and the Brazilian Workers' Party. Latin America Bureau.
Bryman, A. (2012). Social research methods. Oxford University Press.
Bugs, G. (2014). ICTs Encouraging Changes in the Citizen's Relationship with Government and Urban Space: Brazilian Examples. The Journal of Community Informatics, 10(3).

Butler, U. M.; Princeswal, M. (2010). Cultures of participation: young people's engagement in the public sphere in Brazil. Community development journal.

Cabral, A. (1996). Rompendo fronteiras: a comunicação das ONGs no Brasil. Paulinas.

Caldeira, T. P. R. (2000). City of walls: crime, segregation, and citizenship in São Paulo. University of California Press.

———. (2012). Imprinting and moving around: New visibilities and configurations of public space in São Paulo. Public Culture, 24(2 67), 385–419.

Cardoso, R. (1978). Sociedade e poder: as representações dos favelados de São Paulo. Ensaios de Opinião, 2(4), 38–44.

Carneiro, L. L. V. (2006). O ideário político do MST: marxismo e nacionalismo. Universidade Estadual do Ceará. Fortaleza.

Carpenter, S. (2010, 02). A study of content diversity in online citizen journalism and online newspaper articles. New Media & Society, 12(7), 1064–84. doi:10.1177/1461444809348772.

Carpentier, N. (2011). Media and participation: A site of ideological-democratic struggle. Intellect Books.

Carvajal, M., García-Avilés, J. A., & González, J. L. (2012). Crowdfunding and non-profit media: The emergence of new models for public interest journalism. Journalism Practice, 6(5–6), 638–47.

Carvalho, J. M. D (1999). Cidadania no Brasil. São Paulo: Civilização Brasileira.

Carvalho, G. O. (2000). The politics of indigenous land rights Brazil. Bulletin of Latin American Research, 19(4), 461–78.

Carvalho, G. (2014). Jornalismo alternativo na era digital: análise de reportagens da Agência Pública. *Revista Alterjor*, *10*(2), 126–42.

Castells, M. (2007). Communication, power and counter-power in the network society. International journal of communication, 1(1), 29.

———. (2013). Networks of outrage and hope: Social movements in the Internet age. John Wiley & Sons.

———. Hall, P., & Jennings, L. (1995). Technopoles of the World. Futurist, 29(1), 58.

Castro, F. D., Koonings, K., & Wiesebron, M. (2014). Brazil under the workers' party: Continuity and change from Lula to Dilma.

Castro, J. C. L (2015). Mídia hegemônica, blogs progressistas e disputa de enquadramento. Work presented at Anais do XXVIII Congresso Brasileiro de Ciências da Comunicação. Available at http://portalintercom.org.br/anais/nacional2015/resumos/R10–3254–1.pdf at 20/03/2015.

Chagas, C. (2007) "Você tem fome de quê? O discurso paternalista de Lula da propaganda eleitoral de 2006." UBI. Available at http://www.bocc.ubi.pt/pag/chagas-catia-discurso-paternalista-de-lula.pdf. Accessed 20 June 2015.

Champangnatte, D. M. O. (2015) "TV Globo e Globo Filmes: práticas econômicas e relações com o Estado a partir de perspectivas da indústria cultural e hegemonia." *Sociedade e Cultura* 18, no. 1. 153–64.

Chauí, M. (1993). Conformismo e resistência: aspectos da cultura popular no Brasil. Brasiliense.

Christofoletti, R.; Laux, A. P. (2006). Em busca da credibilidade: monitoramento de cinco blogs brasileiros. Communicare, 6(2).
Cogo, D. (2004). Mídias, identidades culturais e cidadania: sobre cenários e políticas de visibilidade midiática dos movimentos sociais. Vozes cidadãs–Aspectos teóricos e análises de experiências de comunicação popular e sindical na América Latina. São Paulo, 1, 41–56.
Cohen, J. (1968) Weighted kappa: Nominal scale agreement provision for scaled disagreement or partial credit. Psychological bulletin, 70(4), 213.
Comedia (1984) The alternative press: The development of underdevelopment. Media, Culture & Society, 6(2), 95–102. doi:10.1177/016344378400600202.
Conde, M., & Jazeel, T. (2013). Kicking off in Brazil: manifesting democracy. Journal of Latin American Cultural Studies, 22(4), 437–50.
Cooper, S. T. (2010) "The oppositional frame of bloggers." In: D'Angelo, P.; Kuypers, J. A. (Eds.). (2010). Doing news framing analysis: Empirical and theoretical perspectives. Routledge.
Correia, J. C. (2012). Online Journalism and Civic Life. In: The Handbook of Global Online Journalism, 101.
Costa, N. R. (2009). A proteção social no Brasil: universalismo e focalização nos governos FHC e Lula. Ciência & saúde coletiva, 14(3), 693–706.
Couldry, N. (2002). The place of media power: Pilgrims and witnesses of the media age. Psychology Press.
———. (2010). Why voice matters: Culture and politics after neoliberalism. Sage Publications.
——— & Curran, J. (Eds.). (2003). Contesting media power: Alternative media in a networked world. Rowman & Littlefield Publishers.
Cummings, J. (2015). Confronting favela chic: the gentrification of informal settlements in Rio de Janeiro, Brazil. Global gentrifications: Uneven development and displacement, 81–99.
Cunha, F. B., Tsuda, F. C. T., Assis Pereira, G. M., & de Camargo, R. B. (2012). Interferência de rádios piratas na comunicação e navegação do transporte aéreo. Conexão SIPAER, 3(2), 152–64.
Curran, J. (2002). Media and power. Psychology Press.
———. Seaton, J. (2009). Power without responsibility: press, broadcasting and the internet in Britain. Routledge. Part 1.
———. Fenton, N., & Freedman, D. (2016). Misunderstanding the internet. Routledge.
Custódio, L. (2014). Types of favela media activism. Favelas@ LSE.
———. Valuing dialogue and respect in research. Media Development, 4, 9–12.
———. (2017) Favela media activism. Counterpublics for Human Rights in Brazil. Lexington Books.
D'Angelo, P; Kuypers, J. A. (Eds.). (2010). Doing news framing analysis: Empirical and theoretical perspectives. Routledge.
D'Araujo, M. C. (1999). As instituições brasileiras da Era Vargas. São Paulo: FGV.
D'incao e Mello, M. C. (1976). O" Bóia-Fria": acumulação e miséria. Ed. Vozes.

Dagnino, E. (2004). Sociedade civil, participação e cidadania: de que estamos falando. Políticas de ciudadanía y sociedad civil en tiempos de globalización. Caracas: FACES, Universidad Central de Venezuela, 95–110.

———. (1998). Culture, citizenship, and democracy: changing discourses and practices of the Latin American left. Cultures of politics, politics of cultures: Revisioning Latin American social movements, 33–63.

———. (1994). Os movimentos sociais e a emergência de uma nova noção de cidadania. Anos, 90, 103–115.

Dahlgren, P. (2006). Doing citizenship: The cultural origins of civic agency in the public sphere. European journal of cultural studies, 9(3), 267–86.

———. (2013). The political web: Media, participation and alternative democracy. Basingstoke: Palgrave Macmillan.

Dantas, A. (2014). A mídia e o golpe militar. Estudos Avançados, 28(80), 59–74.

Davis, S. (2015). Citizens' Media in the Favelas: Finding a Place for Community–Based Digital Media Production in Social Change Processes. Communication Theory, 25(2), 230–43.

———. (2017). Citizen Health Journalism: Negotiating between political engagement and professional identity in a media training program for healthcare workers. Journalism Practice, 11(2–3), 319–35.

Dean, J. (2010). Blog theory: Feedback and capture in the circuits of drive. Polity.

DeFrancisco, V. (1997). Gender, power and practice: or, putting your money (and your research) where your mouth is. Gender and Discourse. London: Sage, 37–56.

Del Grossi, M.; Graziano da Silva, J.; Takagi, M. (2001). Evolução da pobreza no Brasil–1995/99. Campinas, Instituto de Economia, Texto para Discussão, (104).

Deuze, M. (2006). Ethnic media, community media and participatory culture. Journalism, 7(3), 262–80.

———. (2003) The web and its journalisms: considering the consequences of different types of newsmedia online. New media & society, 5(2), 203–30.

De Souza, M. L. (2006). Social movements as 'critical urban planning' agents. *City*, *10*(3), 327–42.

Didoné, I. M.; Menezes, J. E. D. O. (1995). Comunicação e política: a ação conjunta das ONGs. Paulinas.

Dos Santos, P. G., & Jalalzai, F. (2014). The Mother of Brazil: Gender Roles, Campaign Strategy, and the Election of Brazil's First Female President. Women in Politics and Media Perspectives from Nations in Transition, 167–80.

Downey, J. & Fenton, N. (2003). New Media, Counter Publicity and the Public Sphere. New Media & Society, 5(2), 185–202.

Downing, J. D. (2015). "Conceptualising social movement media: A fresh metaphor? In: Atton, C. (2015). The Routledge Companion to Alternative and Community Media. London: Routledge.

———. (2011). Encyclopedia of social movement media. SAGE.

———. (2008). Social movement theories and alternative media: An evaluation and critique. Communication, Culture & Critique, 1(1), 40–50.

———. (2001). Radical media. Sage.

Earl, J., & Kimport, K. (2011, 03). Digitally Enabled Social Change. MIT Press. doi:10.7551/mitpress/9780262015103.001.0001.

Entman, R. M. (2007). "Framing bias: Media in the distribution of power." Journal of communication (0021–9916), 57 (1), p. 163.

———. (2004). Projections of power: Framing news, public opinion, and US foreign policy. University of Chicago Press.

Escosteguy, A. C., & Coutinho, L. L. (2017). The Rise of The Working Poor within the Brazilian Mediascape: The Mythology of Social Inequality's Disappearance. In Brazil: Media from the Country of the Future (pp. 37–51). Emerald Publishing Limited.

Felix, C. B. (2009) Territórios proibidos: mídia e subjetividade na favela da Maré. Anais do XIV Congresso de Ciências da Comunicação da Região Sudeste.

Fenton, N. (2016). Digital Political Radical. London: Wiley & Sons.

———. & Barassi, V. (2011, 07). Alternative Media and Social Networking Sites: The Politics of Individuation and Political Participation. The Communication Review, 14(3), 179–196. doi:10.1080/10714421.2011.597245.

Ferreira, D. M. M. (2006). Não pense, veja: o espetáculo da linguagem no palco do Fome Zero. Annablume.

Ferreira, P R (2009) "Jornal Resistência." In: Woitowicz, K. J. (2009). Recortes da Mídia Alternativa: Histórias da comunicação no Brasil. Ponta Grossa: UEPG

Festa, R. G.; Silva, C. E. L. (1986). Comunicação popular e alternativa no Brasil. São Paulo: Paulinas.

Fico, C. (1999). Ibase: usina de idéias e cidadania. Garamond.

Figueiredo, C. (2013). Entre sem bater. Leya.

Fischer, B. M. (2008). A poverty of rights: citizenship and inequality in twentieth-century Rio de Janeiro. Stanford University Press.

Fischer, S., & Nascimento, G. C. (2016). Avenida Brasil: estratégias narrativas e efeitos estéticos. Revista Interin, 16(2), 116–30.

Fleury, S. (2014). Building Democracy in an Emerging Society. Brazil Emerging: Inequality and Emancipation, 11. In: Pieterse, J. N.; Cardoso, A. (2014). Brazil emerging: Inequality and emancipation. Basingstoke: Palgrave Macmillan.

———. (2012). Militarization of the social field as integrative strategy: the case of Santa Marta's Police Unit for Pacification. Sociologias, 14(30), 194–222.

Fonseca, F. (2003). O conservadorismo patronal da grande imprensa brasileira. *Opinião Pública*, *9*(2), 73–92.

Fonseca, I. C. D. (2007). Estratégias de Comunicação do MST para se inserir na Esfera Pública. Inovcom, 1(2), Pág-02.

Fonseca, M. F., & Woitowicz, K. J. Mídia alternativa e direitos das mulheres: A pauta do trabalho doméstico na imprensa feminista nos anos 1970 no Brasil.

Ford, T. V., & Gil, G. (2001). Radical Internet use, Radical media: Rebellious communication and social movements, 201–34.

Forde, S. (2011) Challenging the News: The Journalism of Alternative and Community Media. Houndmills, Basingstoke, Hampshire: Palgrave Macmillan.

Fortes, A. (2016). Brazil's Neoconservative Offensive: How right-wing forces coopted and redirected popular discontent in Brazil to oust democratically elected president Dilma Rousseff. NACLA Report on the Americas, 48(3), 217–20.

Foucault, M. (1982). "The subject and power." In: Dreyfus, H. L., & Rabinow, P. (2014). Michel Foucault: Beyond structuralism and hermeneutics. University of Chicago Press.

Fox, E. (1988) Media and politics in Latin America: The struggle for democracy. London: Sage.

———. Waisbord, S. R. (2002). Latin politics, global media. Austin: University of Texas Press.

França, F. O., Goya, D., & Penteado, C. C. (2018). Analysis of the Twitter Interactions during the Impeachment of Brazilian President. In Proceedings of the 51st Hawaii International Conference on System Sciences.

Fraser, N. (1992) "Habermas and the public sphere." In: Fraser, N., & Calhoun, C. (1992). Habermas and the public sphere.

———. (2009). Social justice in the age of identity politics. Geographic thought: A praxis perspective, 72–91.

Freire, P. (1970). Pedagogy of the Oppressed, trans. Myra Bergman Ramos. New York: Continuum.

Freire-Medeiros, B. (2011). 'I went to the City of God': Gringos, guns and the touristic favela. Journal of Latin American Cultural Studies, 20(1), 21–34.

———. Name, L. (2013). Flying for the very first time: Mobilities, social class and environmental concerns in a Rio de Janeiro Favela. Mobilities, 8(2), 167–84.

Freitas, G. B. (2010). A cultura na (da) periferia e a periferia na (da) mídia. Políticas culturais em revista, 2(2).

Freitas, R. O. (2007). A periferia da periferia: mídias alternativas e cultura de minorias em ambientes não-metropolitanos. Cadernos de Ciências Humanas-Especiaria, 10(17), 191–212.

———. Espírito Santo, C. S. (2015). A voz que vem da periferia: o jovem e suas narrativas percebidas na publicização de imagens e postagens nas redes sociais. Pontos de Interrogação—Revista de Crítica Cultural, 4(1), 11–38.

Fuchs, C. (2010). Alternative media as critical media. European journal of social theory, 13(2), 173–92.

———. (2016). Critical Theory of Communication. University of Westminster Press.

Galeano, E. A. V. (2013). Evidências da manutenção das desigualdades econômicas entre as regiões do Brasil no período de 1985 a 2008. Inclusão Social, 6(1).

Gallego, A. H. S. M.; Galindo, D. (2008). Criança Esperança: exemplo do marketing de causas sociais, articulado pelas relações públicas.

Gamson, W. A. (1992). Talking politics. Cambridge University Press.

———. (1995). Constructing social protest. Social movements and culture, 4, 85–106.

———. Meyer, D. S. (1996). *Framing political opportunity*. In: McAdam, D.; McCarthy, J.; Zald, M. (1996) Comparative Perspectives in Social Movements. Cambridge: Cambridge University Press.

——— & Modigliani, A. (1989). Media discourse and public opinion on nuclear power: A constructionist approach. American journal of sociology, 95(1), 1–37.

———. Wolfsfeld, G. (1993). Movements and media as interacting systems. The Annals of the American Academy of Political and Social Science, 114–25.
Garavello, M. D. P. E. (2009). Os blogs e o jornalismo de texto: a campanha para eleição presidencial de 2006 no Brasil (Doctoral dissertation, Universidade de São Paulo).
Gay, R. (2010). Popular organization and democracy in Rio de Janeiro: a tale of two favelas. Temple University Press.
Garcêz, R. L.; Cal, D. G. R. (2012). Deslizes morais na cena midiática: reprodução da intolerância ou oportunidade para novas gramáticas morais? *Compôs*.
Gerbaudo, P. (2012). Tweets and the streets: Social media and contemporary activism.
Giddings, L. S. (2006). Mixed-methods research: Positivism dressed in drag?. Journal of research in nursing, 11(3), 195–203.
Gilens, M. (1996). "Race coding" and white opposition to welfare. American Political Science Review, 90(03), 593–604.
Girotto Neto, A. (2014). A "voz das ruas" e a rearticulação da ideologia conservadora.
Gitlin, T. (1980). The whole world is watching: Mass media in the making & unmaking of the new left. University of California Press.
———. (2013). Occupy's predicament: the moment and the prospects for the movement. The British Journal of Sociology, 64(1), 3–25.
Giumbelli, E. (1994). Faces e dimensões da campanha contra a fome: cronologia, temas, Fundo Inter-religioso. Nucleo de Pesquisa.
Goffman, E. (1974). Frame analysis: An essay on the organization of experience. Harvard University Press.
Gohn, M. D. G. M. (1985). A força da periferia: a luta das mulheres por creches em São Paulo. Vozes.
———. (1999). MST e Mídia. Cadernos do CEAS, 179, 11–29.
———. (2014). Movimentos sociais e redes de mobilizações civis no Brasil contemporâneo. Vozes.
Gomes, A. A. F. (2008). A midiatização do social: Globo e Criança Esperança tematizando a realidade brasileira. Editora E-papers.
Gomes, W. (2016). "Nós somos a rede social!." O protesto político entre as ruas e as redes. In: Mendonça, R. F., Pereira, M. A., Filgueiras, F. Democracia Digital. Publucidade, instituições e confronto político. Belo Horizonte : Editora UFMG.
Gomes, A., & Nascimento, F. (1998). Política, MST e o Rei do Gado. Recife: INTERCOM.
Goncalves, A. A. (2014). Conflicting Frames: the dispute over the meaning of rolezinhos in Brazilian media (Doctoral dissertation, Massachusetts Institute of Technology).
Gondim, L. M. (1981). A manipulação do estigma de favelado na política habitacional do Rio de Janeiro. Revista de Ciências Sociais, 12/12, (1/2) 27–44. Fortaleza. Available at http://repositorio.ufc.br/bitstream/riufc/9716/1/1982_art_lmgondim.pdf. Accessed 10 July 2016.
Goode, L. (2009, 11). Social news, citizen journalism and democracy. New Media & Society, 11(8), 1287–1305. doi:10.1177/1461444809341393.

Graham, S. (2011). Cities under siege: The new military urbanism. Verso Books.
Gramsci, A. (2011). Prison Notebooks. Volume 2. Columbia University Press.
Granja, P. (2015). UPP: o novo dono da favela (Cadê o Amarildo?). Rio de Janeiro: Revan/ICC.
Grijó, W. P. (2014). De Voyeur a Protagonista: Nova classe média e telenovelas no Brasil. Estudos em Comunicação, 17, 191–212.
Grohmann, R. (2014). A midiatização da nova classe média: identidades discursivas na revista IstoÉ Dinheiro. Rumores, 8(16), 146–65.
Guattari, F., & Rolnik, S. (2008). Molecular Revolution in Brazil, trans. by Karel Clapshow and Brian Holmes. Cambridge, Mass and London: MIT Press.
Guazina, L. S. (2013). Jornalismo que tem lado: o caso dos blogueiros brasileiros" progressistas." Brazilian Journalism Research, 9(2), 68–87.
Guidry, J. A. (2003). The struggle to be seen: Social movements and the public sphere in Brazil. International Journal of Politics, Culture, and Society,16(4), 493–524.
Gillam, R. (2017). Representing Black Girlhood in Brazil: Culture and Strategies of Empowerment. Communication, Culture & Critique, 10(4), 609–25.
Gusmão, R. (2000). A ideologia da solidariedade. Revista Serviço Social e Sociedade, (62), 93–112.
Habermas, J. (1991). The structural transformation of the public sphere: An inquiry into a category of bourgeois society. MIT Press.
———. (1992). Further reflections on the public sphere. Habermas and the public sphere, 428.
Haas, T. (2004). Research note: Alternative media, public journalism and the pursuit of democratization. Journalism Studies, 5(1), 115–21.
Hackett, R. A.; Gurleyen, P. (2015) "Beyond binaries? Alternative media and objective journalism." In: Atton, C. (ed) (2015). The Routledge Companion to Alternative and Community Media. London: Routledge.
———. Carroll, W. K. (2006). Democratic media activism through the lens of social movement theory. Media, Culture & Society, 28(1), 83–104.
———. Zao, Y (2005). Media globalization, media democratization: Challenges, issues, and paradoxes. Democratizing global media: One world, many struggles, 1–33.
Hall, A. (2006). From Fome Zero to Bolsa Família: social policies and poverty alleviation under Lula. Journal of Latin American Studies, 38(04), 689–709.
Hall, S. (1982). The rediscovery of ideology: Return of the repressed in media studies. Cultural theory and popular culture: A reader, 111–41.
Hallin, D. C., & Papathanassopoulos, S. (2002). Political clientelism and the media: southern Europe and Latin America in comparative perspective. Media, culture & society, 24(2), 175–95.
Hamilton, J. (2000) "Alternative Media: Conceptual Difficulties, Critical Possibilities." Journal of Communication Inquiry 24.4: 357–78. Print.
———. (2015). "What's Left? Towards an historicised critique of alternative and community media." In: Atton, C. (2015). The Routledge Companion to Alternative and Community Media. London: Routledge.

Hammond, J. L. (2004). The MST and the media: competing images of the Brazilian Landless Farmworkers' Movement. Latin American Politics and Society, 46(4), 61–90.

Harcup, T. (2011). "Alternative journalism as active citizenship." Journalism (London, England) (1464–8849), 12 (1), p. 15.

———. (2005). "I'm doing this to change the world: Journalism in alternative and mainstream media." Journalism studies (London, England) (1461–670X), 6 (3), p. 361.

———. (2003) "'The Unspoken—Said': The Journalism of Alternative Media." Journalism 4.3 (2003): 356–76.

Hartmann, C., & da Silveira, A. C. M. Midiatização da periferia: a mudança do discurso jornalístico na revista Veja.

Harvey, D. (2012). Rebel cities. London: Verson.

———. Maricato, E., Davis, M., Braga, R., Žižek, S., Iasi, M. L.; Peschanski, J. A. (2015). Cidades Rebeldes: Passe livre e as manifestações que tomaram as ruas do Brasil. Boitempo Editorial.

Henriques, R. (2000). Desnaturalizar a desigualdade e erradicar a pobreza: por um novo acordo social no Brasil. Desigualdade e pobreza no Brasil. Rio de Janeiro: IPEA, 1–20.

Herrmann, E., & McChesney, R. W. (2001). *Global media: The new missionaries of global capitalism*. A&C Black.

Hesse-Biber, S. N.; Rodriguez, D.; Frost, N. A. (2015) A qualitatively-drive approach to multimethod and mixed-method research. In: Hesse-Biber, S. N.; Johnson, B. (2015). The Oxford Hanbook of Multimethod and Mixed-Method Research Inquiry.

Hintz, A. (2011). From Media Niche to Policy Spotlight: Mapping Community-Media Policy Change in Latin America. Canadian Journal of Communication, 36(1).

Hobbs, R. (1998). The seven great debates in the media literacy movement. Journal of communication, 48(1), 16–32.

Hochstetler, K. (2000). Democratizing pressures from below? Social movements in the new Brazilian democracy. Democratic Brazil: Actors, institutions, and processes, 167–84.

Holanda, A.; Quadros, C.; Silva, J. A. B., & Palacios, M. (2008). Metodologias de pesquisa em jornalismo participativo no Brasil. Brazilian Journalism Research, 1(1).

Holmes, T. (2016). Reframing the Favela, Remapping the City: Territorial Embeddedness and (Trans) Locality in 'Framing Content' on Brazilian Favela Blogs. Journal of Latin American Cultural Studies, 25(2), 297–319.

Holston, J. (2014). "Come to the Street!": Urban Protest, Brazil 2013. Anthropological Quarterly, 87(3), 887–900.

———. (2009). Dangerous spaces of citizenship: gang talk, rights talk and rule of law in Brazil. Planning theory, 8(1), 12–31.

———. (2009b). Insurgent citizenship in an era of global urban peripheries. *City & Society*, *21*(2), 245–67.

Horst, H. A. (2011). Free, social, and inclusive: Appropriation and resistance of new media technologies in Brazil. International Journal of Communications, 5.

Huggins, M. K. (2000). Urban violence and police privatization in Brazil: Blended invisibility. Social Justice, 27(2 (80), 113–34.

Huguet, C., & Szabó de Carvalho, I. (2008). Violence in the Brazilian Favelas and the Role of the Police. New directions for youth development, 2008(119), 93–109.

Ivanova, A.; Mardones, T. (2014). The phenomenon of Teletón in Chile: A linguistic perspective. Universum, 2(29).

Jaenisch, M. B; Borelli, V. (2011). Dilma Rousseff e José Serra em Carta Capital e Veja: uma análise dos enquadramentos dos (pré) candidatos à presidência em 2010. Estudos em Jornalismo e Mídia, 8(1), 128–45.

Jaguaribe, B. (2014). Rio de Janeiro: Urban Life Through the Eyes of the City. Routledge.

———. (2014b). "Realismo Melodramático: O Rio de Janeiro nas telenovelas Melodramatic Realism." XXIII Encontro Anual do Compôs. Available at http://compos.org.br/encontro2014/anais/Docs/GT13_IMAGEM_E_IMAGINARIOS_MIDIATICOS/beatrizjaguaribecompos2014_2251.pdf. Accessed 10 July 2016.

———. (2004). Favelas and the aesthetics of realism: representations in film and literature. Journal of Latin American Cultural Studies, 13(3), 327–42.

——— & Hetherington, K. (2004). Favela tours: indistinct and mapless representations of the real in Rio de Janeiro.

Jameson, F. (1988). On Negt and Kluge. October, 46, 151–77.

Jankowski, N. W. (2003). Community media research: A quest for theoretically-grounded models. Javnost, 10(1), 5–14.

Jarrín, A. (2010). Cosmetic Citizenship: Beauty, Affect and Inequality in Southeastern Brazil (Doctoral dissertation, Duke University).

Kamel, A. (2004). Combater a pobreza, esquecer as cores. *O Globo*, *14*(11).

Keane, J. (1991). The media and democracy. Cambridge: Polity Press.

Kellner, D., & Share, J. (2005). Toward critical media literacy: Core concepts, debates, organizations, and policy. Discourse: studies in the cultural politics of education, 26(3), 369–86.

Kenix, L. J. (2015). Commercialism and the Deconstruction of Alternative and Mainstream Media. The Routledge Companion to Alternative and Community Media.

———. (2013). A converging image? Commercialism and the visual identity of alternative and mainstream news websites. Journalism Studies,14(6), 835–56.

———. (2008). Framing science: Climate change in the mainstream and alternative news of New Zealand. Political Science, 60(1), 117–32.

Kidd, D. (2014). Social justice media: the case of Occupy. Mediaciones: Revista Académica de Comunicación.

King, N., & Horrocks, C. (2010). Interviews in qualitative research. Sage.

Kingstone, P. R.; Power, T. J. (Eds.). (2000). Democratic Brazil: Actors, institutions, and processes. University of Pittsburgh Press.

Kingstone, P. R., & Power, T. J. (2017). A Fourth Decade of Brazilian Democracy. Available at https://www.upress.pitt.edu/htmlSourceFiles/pdfs/9780822964919exr.pdf. Accessed 02 Jan 2018.

Kitzberger, P. (2010). The media activism of Latin America's leftist governments: Does ideology matter?. Giga Papers. (151).
———. (2013). The media politics of Latin America's leftist governments. Journal of Politics in Latin America, 4(3), 123–39.
Klein, E. C. (2009) "Do muro à letra impressa: Resistência à ditadura e fundação do alternativo Informação em Ijuí/RS." In: In: Woitowicz, K J (2009) Recortes da Mídia Alternativa: Histórias da comunicação no Brasil. Ponta Grossa: UEPG.
Konder, L. (1983). Barão de Itararé (Vol. 37). São Paulo: Brasiliense.
Kramer, E. W. (2005). Spectacle and the staging of power in Brazilian Neo-Pentecostalism. Latin American Perspectives, 32(1), 95–120.
Kucinski, B. (1991). Jornalistas e revolucionários: Nos tempos da imprensa alternativa. São Paulo, SP: Página Aberta.
La Pastina, A. C., Straubhaar, J. D., & Sifuentes, L. (2014). Why Do I Feel I Don't Belong to the Brazil on TV? Popular Communication, 12(2), 104–16.
Lacerda, D. S. (2015). Rio de Janeiro and the divided state: Analysing the political discourse on favelas. Discourse & Society, 26(1), 74–94.
Larkins, E. M. R. (2015). The spectacular favela: violence in modern Brazil (Vol. 32). University of California Press.
Lattman-Weltman, F. (2007). Cidadania e audiência no telejornalismo comunitário da Rede Globo. Direitos e cidadania: justiça, poder e mídia. Rio de Janeiro: FGV, 193–213.
Leite, L. C. M. (2001). Civilização e exclusão: visões do Brasil em Erico Veríssimo, Euclides da Cunha, Claude Lévi-Strauss e Darcy Ribeiro.
Leite, C. S. (2006). Ecos do Carandiru: Estudo Comparativo de quatro narrativas do Massacre (Doctoral dissertation, UFRJ).
Leu, L. (2004). "The Press and the Spectacle of Violence in Contemporary Rio de Janeiro." Journal of Latin American Cultural Studies 13 (3): 343–55.
Levine, R. M. (1998). Father of the Poor?: Vargas and his Era. Cambridge University Press.
Levy, H. (2017) Reporting the 2014 World Cup: Football First and Social Issues Last. *Sport in Society*, 20(5-6), 572–82.
Lievrouw, L. (2011). Alternative and activist new media. London: Polity.
Lima, A. B. (2006). Os sentidos na mídia: o MST em dois jornais diários.Psicologia & Sociedade, 18(3), 97–103.
Lima, L. C. (2000). Euclides da Cunha: contrastes e confrontos do Brasil. Petrobras.
Lima, V. A. (1996). "Os mídia e o cenário de representação da política." Lua Nova 38: 239–71.
——— & Motter, P. (1996). Novas tecnologias de comunicações, neoliberalismo e democracia. Comunicação & Política, 3(1), 12–19.
Lindlof, T. R., & Taylor, B. C. (2011). Sensemaking: qualitative data analysis and interpretation. Qualitative communication research methods, 3, 241–81.
Livingstone, S. (2004). Media literacy and the challenge of new information and communication technologies. The Communication Review, 7(1), 3–14.
———. Van der Graaf, S. (2004). Media literacy. John Wiley & Sons, Ltd.

Loader, B. D., Vromen, A., & Xenos, M. A. (2014). The networked young citizen: social media, political participation and civic engagement. Information, Communication & Society, 17(2), 143–50.

———. Mercea, D. (Eds.). (2012). Social media and democracy: Innovations in participatory politics. Routledge.

Lock, M.; Baldissera, R. (2012). Conversações políticas online e seus efeitos na opinião pública. Contemporanea-Revista de Comunicação e Cultura, 10(3), 686–704.

Lombard, M., Snyder–Duch, J., & Bracken, C. C. (2002). Content analysis in mass communication: Assessment and reporting of intercoder reliability. Human communication research, 28(4), 587–604.

Lugo-Ocando, J. (2008). The media in Latin America. McGraw-Hill/Open University Press.

MacBride, S., & Abel, E. (1984). Many voices, one world: Communication and society, today and tomorrow: The MacBride report (Vol. 372). Unesco.

Mainwaring, S. (1987). The Catholic church and politics in Brazil, 1916–1985. Stanford University Press.

———. (1987b). Urban popular movements, identity, and democratization in Brazil. Comparative Political Studies, 20(2), 131–59.

Maricato, E.; Harvey, D.; Rolnik, R.; Braga, R.; David, M.; Vainer, C. (2013). Cidades rebeldes: passe livre e as manifestações que tomaram as ruas do Brasil. São Paulo: Boitempo: Carta Maior.

Marinho, J. R. (2006). Rádio como exercício de cidadania. CBN, a rádio que toca notícia: a história da rede e as principais coberturas, estilo e linguagem do all news, jornalismo político, econômico e esportivo, a construção da marca, o modelo de negócios. Rio de Janeiro: Editora Senac Rio.

Marques, A. (2008). O Programa Bolsa-Família na mídia e na fala das beneficiárias: o lugar ocupado pelo Estado na configuração dialógica dos espaços de debate público. Revista ECO-Pós, 11(1).

Marques, E.; Bichir, R. (2001). Investimentos públicos, infra-estrutura urbana e produção da periferia em São Paulo. *Revista Espaço e Debates*, *42*.

Marques, F. P. J. A. ; Bailey, O. (2012). Brazilian News Blogs and Mainstream News Organizations: Tensions, Symbiosis, or Independency? The Handbook of Global Online Journalism, 393–411.

Marques de Melo, J. (1999). Luiz Beltrão: pioneiro dos Estudos de folk-comunicação no Brasil. Revista Latina de Comunicación Social, 21.

Martín-Barbero, J. (1998). De los medios a las mediaciones: comunicación, cultura y hegemonía. Convenio Andrés Bello.

———. (2006). Jóvenes: comunicación e identidad. Pensar Iberoamérica: revista de cultura, (10), 1.

———. (2008). Diversidad cultural y convergencia digital. IC Revista Científica de Información y Comunicación, 5, 12–25.

Martins, R. (2015). Mídia comunitária e novas construções periféricas sociais no Brasil. Novos Olhares, 4(1), 21–36.

Matos, C. (2008). Journalism and political democracy in Brazil. Lexington Books.

Mattelart, A.; Piemme, J. M. (1980). "New means of communication: new questions for the Left." Media, culture & society (0163–4437), 2 (4), p. 321.
Mattelart, M., & Mattelart, A. (1990). The carnival of images: Brazilian television fiction. Greenwood Publishing Group.
Mattos Rocha, L. (2013). Young favela dwellers and audiovisual production: representations and self-representations. Global Movements, National Grievances, 526.
Mattos, S. (1984). Advertising and Government Influences: The Case of Brazilian Television. Communication Research, 11(2), 203–20.
Mauro, R. (2014). Aspectos da midiatização do consumo e do sentido de classe social na telenovela: a representação da nova classe C (Doctoral dissertation, Universidade de São Paulo).
Mazzetti, H. (2009). "Mídia alternativa para além da contra-informação." In: Strelow, A. D. A. G; Woitowicz, K. J. (2009). Recortes da mídia alternativa: histórias e memórias da comunicação no Brasil. Editora UEPG.
McNair, B. (2017). Fake news: Falsehood, fabrication and fantasy in journalism. Routledge.
McQuail, D. (2010). McQuail's mass communication theory. Sage Publications.
Medina, C. (1982). Profissão jornalista: responsabilidade social. Forense-Universitária.
Medrado, A. (2007). Community media: important but imperfect. A case study of a community television station in a Brazilian favela. Media technologies and democracy in an enlarged Europe, 123.
Melo, J. M. (2008). Mídia e cultura popular: história, taxonomia e metodologia da folkcomunicação. Paulus.
Mello, A. S. (2017). Media and Public Opinion: Case Study Comparison of the Mensalão and Petrolão Corruption Scandals in Brazil (Doctoral dissertation, University of Oregon).
Mendonça, M. L. M. (2013). Mídia e trabalho doméstico: quando a lei expõe desigualdades. Revista Eptic Online, 15(3), 87–100.
Mendonça, K. S. D. (2015). Entre o mito da retomada do território e a política de silêncio: uma análise do discurso do RJTV sobre a" Pacificação" da Rocinha. Comunicação & Inovação, 16(31), 43–58.
Mendonça, R. F., & Ercan, S. A. (2015). Deliberation and protest: strange bedfellows? Revealing the deliberative potential of 2013 protests in Turkey and Brazil. Policy Studies, 36(3), 267–82.
Mercea, D. (2016). Civic participation in contentious politics. London: Palgrave Macmillan.
Mercer, C. (2002). NGOs, civil society and democratization: a critical review of the literature. Progress in development studies, 2(1), 5–22.
Messaris, P., & Abraham, L. (2001). The role of images in framing news stories. Framing public life: Perspectives on media and our understanding of the social world, 215–26.
Miguel, L. F. (2000). Retrato de uma ausência: a mídia nos relatos da história política do Brasil. Revista Brasileira de História, 20(39), 191–199.
Milioni, D. L. (2009). Probing the online counterpublic sphere: The case of indymedia athens. Media, Culture & Society, 31(3), 409–31.

Mitchell, M. J.; Wood, C. H. (1999). Ironies of citizenship: skin color, police brutality, and the challenge to democracy in Brazil. Social Forces, 77(3), 1001–20.

Monclaire, S.; Magalhães, M. I. S.; Barros Filho, C., Impelizieri, F. (1991). A Constituição desejada: SAIC: as 72.719 sugestões enviadas pelos cidadãos brasileiros à Assembléia Nacional Constituinte (Vol. 1). Centro Gráfico do Senado Federal.

Montoro, T. S. (2002). La violencia como noticia: un análisis de los telediarios de mayor audiencia en Brasil. Universitat Autònoma de Barcelona.

Morais, M. J. (2013). Por dentro do Fora do Eixo: Uma das maiores redes de coletivos culturais do país. Biblioteca Latino-Americana de Cultura e Comunicação, 1(1).

Moreira, D. G. (2009). Coproduções na Rede Globo: protagonismo da periferia, sob a ótica da elite. Fronteiras-estudos midiáticos, 11(3), 211–18.

Morel, M. (1986). Jornalismo popular nas favelas cariocas. RioArte.

Mouffe, C. (2000). The Democratic Paradox. London: Verso.

———. (2000b). Deliberative democracy or agonistic pluralism? Social Research, 66(3), 745–58.

Mutiwba, D. (2015). "Between aspiration and reality: A study of contemporary third-sector media production." In: Atton, C. (2015). Companion of Alternative and Community media. Routledge.

Napolitano, M. (2002). Cultura e poder no Brasil contemporâneo (1977–1984). Juruá Editora.

Nascimento, E. P. D. (2012). É tudo nosso! Produção cultural na periferia paulistana (Doctoral dissertation, Universidade de São Paulo).

Nascimento, M., Cunha, F., & Vicente, L. M. (2008). A desqualificação da família pobre como prática de criminalização da pobreza.

Navarro, Z. (1994). Democracy, citizenship and representation: rural social movements in southern Brazil, 1978–1990. Bulletin of Latin American Research, 13(2), 129–54.

Nemer, D. (2015). Online favela: The use of social media by the marginalized in Brazil. Information Technology for Development, 1–16.

Neuendorf, K. A. (2012). The content analysis guidebook. Sage.

Neri, M. (2008) "The new middle class" or "A nova classe média." Revista Conjuntura Econômica, 62(9), 48–51.

Nunes, M. V. (2004). O rádio no horário eleitoral de 2002: a sedução sonora como estratégia de marketing. Work presented at the IV Encontro dos Núcleos de Pesquisa da Intercom.

O'Dougherty, M. (1998). Auto-retratos da classe média: hierarquias de "cultura" e consumo em São Paulo. Dados, 41(2), 411–44.

Oliveira, C. T. F. (2007). Escuta Sonora: Recepção e cultura popular nas ondas das rádios comunitárias. Editora E-papers.

Oliveira, D. (2011). Jornalismo alternativo: Um potencial para a radicalização da democracia. Signo y Pensamiento, 30, 52–63.

Oliven, R. G. (2013). Taking to the Streets of Brazil. Cultural Anthropology. Durham, NC, USA. (20 dec. 2013),[2].

Opp, K. D. (2009). Theories of political protest and social movements: A multidisciplinary introduction, critique, and synbook. Routledge.

Osorio, R. G. (2013). Classe, raça e acesso ao ensino superior no Brasil. Cadernos de Pesquisa, 39(138), 867–80.

Pardue, D. (2004). "Writing in the Margins": Brazilian Hip–Hop as an Educational Project. Anthropology & Education Quarterly, 35(4), 411–32.

Paiva, R.; Custodio, L.; Sodre, M. (2015). "Brazil: Patrimonialism and media democratization." In: Nordenstreng, K.; Thussu, D. K. (2015). Mapping BRICS Media. London: Routledge. p. 119–24

Pedrozo, S. (2013). New media use in Brazil: Digital inclusion or digital divide? Online Journal of Communication and Media Technologies, 3(1), 144.

Penglase, R. B. (2014). *Living with insecurity in a Brazilian favela: urban violence and daily life*. Rutgers University Press.

———. (2007). Barbarians on the beach: Media narratives of violence in Rio de Janeiro, Brazil. Crime, Media, Culture, 3(3), 305–25.

Pereira Filho, F. J. B. (2004). Caros Amigos e o resgate da imprensa alternativa no Brasil (Vol. 267). Annablume.

Pereira, R. (1986). "Viva a imprensa alternativa." In: Festa, C.; Silva, C. E. (1986) Comunicação popular e alternativa no Brasil. São Paulo: Paulinas, 53–79, 1986.

Pereira, A. B. (2005). De rolê pela cidade: os pixadores em São Paulo (Doctoral dissertation, Universidade de São Paulo).

Perlman, J. (2010). Favela: Four decades of living on the edge in Rio de Janeiro. Oxford University Press.

Peruzzo, C. M. K. (2013). Movimentos sociais, redes virtuais e mídia alternativa no junho em que "o gigante acordou"? MATRIZes, 7(2), 73–93.

———. (2008). Conceitos de comunicação popular, alternativa e comunitária revisitados. Reelaborações no setor. Palabra Clave, 11(2).

Pickard, V. W. (2006, 05). United yet autonomous: Indymedia and the struggle to sustain a radical democratic network. Media, Culture & Society, 28(3), 315–36. doi:10.1177/0163443706061685.

Pinheiro-Machado, R., & Scalco, L. M. (2014). Rolezinhos: Marcas, consumo e segregação no Brasil. Revista Estudos Culturais, 1(1).

Pino, J. C. (1997). Sources on the history of favelas in Rio de Janeiro. Latin American Research Review, 32(3), 111–22.

Pinto, C. R. J. (2005). A sociedade civil e a luta contra a fome no Brasil (1993–2003). Sociedade e estado, 20(1), 195–228.

Pinto, O. L. V. (2013). Os protestos no Brasil, ou Sobre como a passagem de ônibus revelou contradições. Badiou Studies, 2(1), 156–59.

Pires, J. L. (2004). Minhas verdades: Histórias e pensamento de um negro favelado. [S.L.].

Platon, S; Deuze, M. (2003). Indymedia Journalism A Radical Way of Making, Selecting and Sharing News? Journalism, 4(3), 336–55.

Porto, M. (1998). Novas tecnologias e política no Brasil: a globalização em uma sociedade periférica e desigual. In XXI Congress of the Latin American Studies Association, Chicago, Sept.

———. (2007). "Frame Diversity and Citizen Competence: Towards a Critical Approach to News Quality." Critical studies in media communication (1529–5036), 24 (4), p. 303.

———. (2012). Media power and democratization in Brazil: TV Globo and the dilemmas of political accountability. Routledge.

Potter, J.; Wetherell, M. (1999). Discourse and Social Psychology: Beyond attitudes and behaviour. London: Sage.

Pretto, N. D. L., & Assis, A. (2008). Cultura digital e educação: redes já. Além das redes de colaboração: internet, diversidade cultural e tecnologias do poder. Salvador: EDUFBA, 75–83.

———. & Bailey, O. G. (2011). Digital culture in Brazil: Building peeracy?. International Journal of Media & Cultural Politics, 6(3), 265–81.

Primo, A. (2009). A busca por fama na web: reputação e narcisismo na grande mídia, em blogs e no Twitter. Intercom.

———. (2011, 12). Blogs and their genres: Statistical evaluation of 50 blogs in Portuguese. Matrizes, 4(1), 129. doi:10.11606/issn.1982–8160.v4i1p129–147.

Purdy, S. (2005). "Inequality." In Globalization: Encyclopedia of trade, labor, and politics. Santa Barbara, CA: ABC-CLIO.

Rahman, F. (2014). *We are not all Malala.* Wired Citizenship: Youth Learning and Activism in the Middle East, 153.

Ramos, D. O. (2015). Iniciativas de Jornalismo Independente no Brasil e Argentina. Revista Extraprensa, 9(1), 114–23.

Rauch, J. (2007). Activists as interpretive communities: Rituals of consumption and interaction in an alternative media audience. Media, Culture & Society, 29(6), 994–1013.

———. (2015). Exploring the Alternative–Mainstream Dialectic: What "Alternative Media" Means to a Hybrid Audience. Communication, Culture & Critique, 8(1), 124–43.

Redden, J. (2014). The mediation of poverty: The news, new media, and politics. Lanham: Lexington Books.

Reese, S. D. (2010). Finding frames in a web of culture. (2010). Doing News Framing Analysis: Empirical and Theoretical Perspectives, 17–42.

Rêgo, C. (2014). Centering the Margins: The Modern Favela in the Brazilian Telenovela.

———. La Pastina, A. C. (2007). Brazil and the globalization of telenovelas (pp. 99–115). D. K. Thussu (Ed.). New York: Routledge.

Reis, E. P. (1999). Elite perceptions of poverty: Brazil. IDS Bulletin, 30(2), 127–38.

———. (2000, 02). Percepções da elite sobre pobreza e desigualdade. Rev. Bras. Ci. Soc. Revista Brasileira De Ciências Sociais, 15(42), 143–52. doi:10.1590/s0102–69092000000100010.

———. Moore, M. (2005). Elite perceptions of poverty and inequality. Zed Books.

———. Schwartzman, S. (2002). Pobreza e Exclusão Social: Aspectos Sociopolíticos. Versão Preliminar, World Bank.

Requejo-Alemán, J. L.; Lugo-Ocando, J. (2014). Assessing the Sustainability of Latin American Investigative Non-profit Journalism. Journalism Studies, 15(5), 522–32.

Rheingold, H. (2003). The virtual community: Homesteading on the electronic frontier. MIT Press.

Riaño, P. (Ed.). (1994). Women in grassroots communication: Furthering social change (Vol. 16). Sage Publications.

Riffe, D.; Lacy, S.; Fico, F. (2014). Analyzing Media Messages 3rd Edition: Using Quantitative Content Analysis in Research. Routledge.

Robinson, L.; Schulz, J.; Williams, A. (2017) Brazil: Media from the country of future. Emerald Group Publishing.

Rocha, M. I. B. D. (2006). A discussão política sobre aborto no Brasil: uma síntese. Revista Brasileira de Estudos de População, 23(2), 369–74.

Rodríguez, C. (1994). The rise and fall of popular correspondents in revolutionary 'Nicaragua.'

———. (2001). Fissures in the mediascape: An international study of citizens' media. Hampton Press (NJ).

———. (2001b). Sociedad civil y medios ciudadanos: arquitectos de paz para el nuevo milenio. Revista de Estudios Sociales, 73–82.

———. (2011). Citizens' media against armed conflict: Disrupting violence in Colombia. Unversity of Minnesota Press—1982–1990. In meeting of the Association for Education in Journalism and Mass Communication, Kansas City, MO.

———. Kidd, D.; Barker-Plummer, B. (2005). Media democracy from the ground up: mapping communication practices in the counter public sphere. Report to the Social Science Research Council. New York.

———. Ferron, B.; Shamas, K. (2014). Four challenges in the field of alternative, radical and citizens' media research. Media, Culture & Society, 36(2), 150–66.

Rohlinger, D. A., Kail, B., Taylor, M., & Conn, S. (2012). Outside the mainstream: Social movement organization media coverage in mainstream and partisan news outlets. In Media, Movements, and Political Change (pp. 51–80). Emerald Group Publishing Limited.

Rolnik, S.; Guattari, F. (2008) Molecular Revolution in Brazil. Semiotexte.

Rosas-Moreno, T. C., & Straubhaar, J. D. (2015). When the marginalized enter the national spotlight: The framing of Brazilian favelas and favelados. Global Media and Communication, 1742766515574114.

Rubin, A.; Babbie, E. R. (2009). Essential Research Methods for Social Work. London: Cengage Learning.

Russell-Wood, A. J. R. (1998). The Making of Brazil: Portuguese Roots, 1500–1822. Journal of Latin American Studies, 30(01), 181–215.

Salata, A. (2016). Defining the Middle Class Boundaries in a Changing Society: Is There a New Middle Class in Brazil? In Third ISA Forum of Sociology (July 10–14, 2016). Isaconf.

Sanglard, G. (2003). Filantropia e assistencialismo no Brasil. Independent.

Santoro, L. F. (1989). A imagem nas mãos: o vídeo popular no Brasil. Summus Editorial.

Santos, B. D. S., & de Sousa Santos, B. (2006). The rise of the global left: The world social forum and beyond (No. Sirsi) i9781842778012.

Santos, N. (2018). The Brazilian Protest Wave and Digital Media: Issues and Consequences of the "Jornadas de Junho" and Dilma Rousseff's Impeachment Process. In Networks, Movements and Technopolitics in Latin America (pp. 113–31). Palgrave Macmillan, Cham.

Sassen, S. (2008). Territory, authority, rights: From medieval to global assemblages. Princeton University Press.

Scalon, C., & Salata, A. (2012). Uma nova classe média no Brasil da última década?: o debate a partir da perspectiva sociológica. Sociedade e Estado,27(2), 387–407.

Schneider, B. R. (1992). Politics Within the State: Elite Bureaucrats and Industrial Policy in Authoritarian Brazil. University of Pittsburgh.

Schudson, M. & Anderson, C. (2009). Objectivity, professionalism, and truth seeking in journalism. The handbook of journalism studies, 88–101.

Segre, R. (2009). Formal-Informal Connections in the Favelas of Rio de Janeiro: The Favela-Bairro Programme. Rethinking the Informal City: Critical Perspectives from Latin America, 11, 163.

Seidman, I. (2015). Interviewing as qualitative research. New York: Teachers' College Press.

Sen, A. (1999). Development as freedom. Oxford University Press.

Serbin, K. P. (2002). Perfis cruzados: Trajetórias e militância política no Brasil do século XX. Rio de Janeiro: Imago. Available at http://www.espacoacademico.com.br/093/93serbin.htm. Accessed 11 July 2016.

Shahin, S., Zheng, P., Sturm, H. A., & Fadnis, D. (2016). Protesting the Paradigm: A Comparative Study of News Coverage of Protests in Brazil, China, and India. *The International Journal of Press/Politics*, 1940161216631114.

Silva, M. O. (2011). Pobreza, desigualdade e políticas públicas: caracterizando e problematizando a realidade brasileira. Revista Katálysis,13(2), 155–63.

Silveira, S. A. D.; Machado, M. B., & Savazoni, R. T. (2013). Backward march: The turnaround in public cultural policy in Brazil. Media, Culture & Society, 35(5), 549–64.

Sinclair, J. (2002) "Mexico and Brazil: The aging dinasties." In: Fox, E.; Waisbord (Eds.). (2002). Latin politics, global media. Austin: University of Texas.

Snow, D. A., Rochford, E. B., Worden, S. K., & Benford, R. D. (1986, 08). Frame Alignment Processes, Micromobilization, and Movement Participation. American Sociological Review, 51(4), 464. doi:10.2307/2095581.

Spitulnik, D. (2017). Alternative small media and communicative spaces. In *Media and democracy in Africa* (pp. 177–205). Routledge.

Soares, K. G. (2016). "Globo, Eu não sou tuas negas": Uma análise da comunicação contra-hegemônica em rede no movimento de boicote a minissérie Sexo e as Negas. Revista da Associação Brasileira de Pesquisadores/as Negros/as (ABPN), 8(20), 86–102.

Sodré, N. W. (1998) História da Imprensa no Brasil. (p.306–15). São Paulo: Maua.

Soihet, R. (1997). Mulheres pobres e violência no Brasil urbano. História das mulheres no Brasil, 3, 362–400.

Soreanu, R. (2015). What can a face do? What can an arm do? The Brazilian uprising and a new aesthetic of protest.

Souza, D. D. C. A. (2007). Pichação Carioca: etnografia e uma proposta de entendimento. UFRJ. Available at http://comunidadesegura.org.br/files/pichacao%20carioca.pdf .Accessed 02 Jan 2015.

Souza, F. N.; Dalberto, L. C. (2013) Patroas vs empregadas: O conflito de classes retratado nas novelas. Logos. 20 (1).

Souza, J., & Sinder, V. (Eds.). (2005). Imagining Brazil. Lexington Books.

Souza, J.; Barbosa, J. L. (2005). Favela: alegria e dor na cidade (Vol. 3). Senac.

Spink, M. J. P., & Spink, P. (2006). Práticas cotidianos e a naturalização da desigualdade: uma semana de notícias nos jornais. Cortez.

Spyer, J. (2017). Social Media in Emergent Brazil: How the Internet Affects Social Mobility (Vol. 11). UCL Press.

Stacciarini, J. H. R. (2002) Pluralidade, publicização e multiplicação do fazer político: A Ação da Cidadania contra a Fome, a Miséria e Pela Vida no Território Brasileiro (1992–1997). Phd Book. Universidade Estadual Paulista.

Stjerno, S. (2009). Solidarity in Europe: The history of an idea. Cambridge: Cambridge University Press.

Straubhaar, J. D. (1991). Beyond media imperialism: Assymetrical interdependence and cultural proximity. Critical Studies in Mass Communication, 8(1), 39–59. http://doi.org/10.1080/15295039109366779.

———. (1984). Estimating the Impact of Imported versus National Television Programming in Brazil. Studies in Mass Communication and Technology. Norwood, NJ: Ablex.

Strelow, A. D., & Woitowicz, K. J. (2009). "Takes on the Alternative Media: Stories and memories of Communication in Brazil." Recortes da mídia alternativa: Histórias & memórias da comunicação no Brasil. Ponta Grossa, Paraná: Editora UEPG.

Stroud, S. (2013). The defence of tradition in Brazilian popular music: politics, culture and the creation of música popular brasileira. Ashgate Publishing, Ltd.

Sweet, C. (2013). "Brazil Woke Up Stronger?: Power, Protest And Politics In 2013." Revista De Ciencia Política (Santiago) Rev. Cienc. Polít. (Santiago) 34.1 (2014): 59–78. Print.

Targino, M. D. G. (2015). Jornalismo de Fonte Aberta e seu Enfrentamento às Teorias do Jornalismo: O caso do centro de mídia independente Brasil.

Tarrow, S. (1992). Mentalities, political cultures, and collective action frames. Frontiers in social movement theory, 174–202.

Telles, E. (1992). Residential segregation by skin color in Brazil. American Sociological Review, 186–97.

———. (2015). Demography of Race in Brazil. The International Handbook of the Demography of Race and Ethnicity (pp. 151–67). Springer Netherlands.

Telles, V. (2004). Desigualdade: mas qual a medida?. Hexapolis: desigualdades e rupturas sociais em metrópoles contemporâneas: São Paulo, Antananarivo, 71.

Thussu, D. K. (Ed.). (2006). Media on the move: global flow and contra-flow. Routledge.

Tilly, C. (2001). Relational origins of inequality. Anthropological Theory, 1(3), 355–72.

——— & Tarrow, S. G. (2007). Contentious politics. Boulder, CO: Paradigm.

Trigueiro, O. M. (2005). A espetacularização das culturas populares ou produtos culturais folkmidiáticos. Seminário Nacional de Políticas Públicas para Culturas Populares. Brasília.

Turino, C. (2013). O desmonte do programa CULTURA VIVA e dos Pontos de Cultura sob o governo Dilma. Revista Murro em Ponta de Faca, (7), 5–6.

Unicef. (2003). Annual report 2003. UNICEF.

Valladares, L. D. P. (1978). Passa-se uma casa: análise do programa de remoção de favelas do Rio de Janeiro. Zaha

———. (2000). A gênese da favela carioca. A produção anterior às ciências sociais. Red Revista Brasileira de Ciên

———. (2005). A invenção da favela: do mito de origem a favela. com. Rio de Janeiro: FGV.

Van Dijk, T. A. (1996). Power and thc news media. Political communication in action, 9–36.

———. (Ed.). (1997). Discourse as social interaction (Vol. 2). Sage.

———. (2017). How Globo media manipulated the impeachment of Brazilian President Dilma Rousseff. Discourse & Communication, 11(2), 199–229.

Vanden, H. E. (2017). Cycles of protest and social movements in Brazil: The MST, the 2013 protests, and the 2016 movements around impeachment. In The New Global Politics (pp. 60–74). Routledge.

Van Gorp, B. (2010). Strategies to take subjectivity out of framing analysis. Doing news framing analysis: Empirical and theoretical perspectives, 84–109.

Vargas, J. H. C. (2014). Black Disidentification: The 2013 Protests, Rolezinhos, and Racial Antagonism in Post-Lula Brazil. Critical Sociology, 0896920514551208.

Veneu, M. G. (1990). O flâneur e a vertigem: metrópole e subjetividade na obra de João do Rio. Revista Estudos Históricos, 3(6), 229–43.

Vianna, H. (1990). Funk e cultura popular carioca. Revista Estudos Históricos, 3(6), 244–53.

Vicino, T. J., & Fahlberg, A. (2017). The politics of contested urban space: The 2013 protest movement in Brazil. *Journal of Urban Affairs*, *39*(7), 1001–16.

Vieira, T. A. S. (2014). Mídia ninja entre a tecnologia, a política e a prática profissional. Razón y palabra, (85), 21–11.

Vieira, S. M., Fernandez, M., & Mesquita, N. C. (2018). Representatives and the Represented: Political Parties, Participation, and the Brazilian Protests in 2013. In Civil Society and Political Representation in Latin America (2010–2015) (pp. 33–54). Springer, Cham.

Villareal, M. G. (2015). Does ideology matter for mass media democratization in Latin America? Peace Monitor. Available at http://www.monitor.upeace.org/innerpg.cfm?id_article=1090.

Vinelli, N (2010). "Alternative media heritage in Latin America." In: Downing, J. D. (Ed.). (2010). Encyclopedia of social movement media. Sage Publications.

Wacquant, L. (2003). Toward a dictatorship over the poor? Notes on the penalization of poverty in Brazil. *Punishment & Society*, *5*(2), 197–205.

———. (2008). The militarization of urban marginality: Lessons from the Brazilian metropolis. *International Political Sociology*, *2*(1), 56–74.

Wainberg, J. A. (2015). O valor do" egocard": afetividade e violência simbólica na rede Fora do Eixo. Revista FAMECOS-Mídia, Cultura e Tecnologia, 22(1).

Waisbord, S. (2000). Watchdog journalism in South America: News, accountability, and democracy. New York: Columbia University Press.

———. (1997). The Narrative of Exposés in South American Journalism Telling the Story of Collorgate in Brazil. International Communication Gazette, 59(3), 189–203.

———. Segura, M. S. (2016). Media movements: civil society and media policy reform in Latin America. Zed Books.

Waltz, M. (2005). Alternative and activist media. Edinburgh University Press.

Wampler, B., & Avritzer, L. (2004). Participatory publics: civil society and new institutions in democratic Brazil. Comparative politics, 291–312.

Weller, W. (2000). A construção de identidades através do Hip Hop: Uma análise comparativa entre rappers negros em São Paulo e rappers turcos-alemães em Berlim. University of Brasília. Available at http://repositorio.unb.br/handle/10482/7371. Accessed 02 June 2014.

Wengraf, T. (2001). Qualitative research interviewing: Biographic narrative and semi-structured methods. Sage.

White, Y. M. (2014). Being Dark-Skinned and Poor in Brazil: The Intersectionality of Skin Color, Income, and Gender (Doctoral dissertation, Vanderbilt University).

Wilkin, P. (2008). Global communication and political culture in the semi-periphery: the rise of the Globo corporation. Review of International Studies, 34(S1), 93–113.

Williams, R. (1962, 2013). "The Existing Alternatives in Communications." Monthly Review Mon. Rev. 65.3: 92. Print.

Winters, M. S., & Weitz-Shapiro, R. (2014). Partisan protesters and nonpartisan protests in Brazil. *Journal of Politics in Latin America*, *6*(1), 137–50.

Woitowicz, K. J. (2009) Recortes da Mídia Alternativa: Histórias da comunicação no Brasil. Ponta Grossa: UEPG

———. (2014). A resistência das mulheres na ditadura militar brasileira: imprensa feminista e práticas de ativismo. Estudos em Jornalismo e Mídia, 11(1), 104–17.

Wolfe, J. (1994). "Father of the Poor" or "Mother of the Rich"?: Getúlio Vargas, Industrial Workers, and Constructions of Class, Gender, and Populism in Sao Paulo, 1930–1954. Radical History Review, 1994(58), 81–111.

Wood, C. H., Carvalho, J. A. M (1988). The demography of inequality in Brazil. Cambridge: Cambridge University Press.

Young, I. (2002). Inclusion and Democracy. Oxford: Oxford University Press.

Yúdice, G. (2003). The expediency of culture: Uses of culture in the global era. Duke University Press.

Zayani, M. (2014). Networked publics and digital contention: The politics of everyday life in Tunisia. Oxford.

Index

About the Author

Helton Levy is a journalist and a media researcher based in London, UK. He has worked in Brazil for nearly a decade reporting on politics, social movements, and inequality.

www.ingramcontent.com/pod-product-compliance
Lightning Source LLC
LaVergne TN
LVHW060008290926
849146LV00003B/50